INTERNATIONAL EXPRESS

INTERMEDIATE
Student's Book

Keith Harding & Liz Taylor

OXFORD
UNIVERSITY PRESS

OXFORD
UNIVERSITY PRESS

Great Clarendon Street, Oxford OX2 6DP

Oxford University Press is a department of the University of Oxford.
It furthers the University's objective of excellence in research, scholarship,
and education by publishing worldwide in

Oxford New York

Auckland Cape Town Dar es Salaam Hong Kong Karachi
Kuala Lumpur Madrid Melbourne Mexico City Nairobi
New Delhi Shanghai Taipei Toronto

With offices in

Argentina Austria Brazil Chile Czech Republic France Greece
Guatemala Hungary Italy Japan Poland Portugal Singapore
South Korea Switzerland Thailand Turkey Ukraine Vietnam

OXFORD and OXFORD ENGLISH are registered trade marks of
Oxford University Press in the UK and in certain other countries

© Oxford University Press 2005

The moral rights of the author have been asserted

Database right Oxford University Press (maker)

First published 2005

2009 2008 2007 2006 2005
10 9 8 7 6 5 4 3 2 1

ISBN-13: 978 0 19 457483 9
ISBN-10: 0 19 457483 0

Printed in China

ACKNOWLEDGEMENTS

*The authors and publisher are grateful to those who have given permission to reproduce the following
extracts and adaptations of copyright material*: p 17 Fictitious interview with Julie Pankhurst,
Friends Reunited. Reproduced by permission of Friends Reunited. pp 22–3 Fictitious
interview with Martin Leach, CEO Maserati. Reproduced by kind permission. p 29 Attitude
Toward Difficulty of Languages by Liddy Gerchman, A.B Mount Holyoke College, class of
2002. Reproduced by kind permission of Liddy Gerchman. p 54 Information about Ford
Company (NZ) Ltd from www.sparc.org.nz. Reproduced by permission of SPARC. p 58
Fictitious interview with Chris Stewart. Reproduced by kind permission of Chris Stewart.
p 65 'Grown-up gap year: The Banker', *The Sunday Times*, 11 August 2002. Reproduced by
permission of NI Syndication. p 74 'Indians learn to be Brad and Britney' from BBC NEWS
at www.bbcnews.co.uk Reproduced by permission. p 78 Information about WaterAid
from www.wateraid.org and WaterAid Ethiopia, Country Strategy, November 2002.
Reproduced by permission of WaterAid. p 83 Information from Lloyds TSB Direct Access
leaflet. Reproduced by permission. pp 84–5 'Barcelona and Sydney: the hosts who got the
most' © Emma Daly and David Fickling, *The Guardian*, 8 December 2002. Reproduced by
permission of Emma Daly and David Fickling. p 85 'Sydney's Eco Friendly Olympics' by
Patrick Barkham, *The Guardian*, as shown on www.simplyfamily.com. Reproduced by kind
permission of Patrick Barkham. p 97 'Voyeurism arrives on the high street' as shown on
www.bangladeshinfo.com. Reproduced by permission of Bangladeshinfo.com Limited.
p 101 Fictitious interview with Lennart Dahlgren, IKEA. Reproduced by kind permission.
p 104 'Dealing with staff morale' from BBC NEWS at www.bbcnews.co.uk Reproduced by
permission. p 107 'Interview jitters and how to avoid them' by Roger Eglin, *The Sunday
Times*, 29 September 2004. Reproduced by permission of NI Syndication. p 110 Case study 3
adapted from *Riding the Waves of Culture* by Fons Trompenaars and Charles Hampden-Turner
(Nicholas Brealey Publishing, London, 1997) p 64. Reproduced by permission of Nicholas
Brealey Publishing, London. p 114 Extract from OHLT: *Intercultural Business Communication*
© Cornelson Verlag, Berlin, 2004. Reproduced by permission. p 114 Extracts from OALD
7e. Reproduced by permission. p 116 Interview with Leah Pattison taken from Midweek
BBC Radio 4, 24 March 2004. Reproduced by kind permission of the trustees of Leah
Pattison and the BBC. p 127 'Zap! Go to the top of the class' by Alan Travis, 24 March 2001
© Guardian Newspapers Ltd. Reproduced by permission of Guardian News Services
Limited. p 127 'Computer games stunt teen brains' by Tracey McVeigh, 19 August 2001 ©
The Observer. Reproduced by permission of Guardian News Services Limited.

Sources: pp 12–13 www.allaboutbranding.com; p 120 Extract from 'Don't trust computers
with e-votes, warns expert', *The Guardian*, 17 October 2002.

Although every effort has been made to trace and contact copyright holders before
publication, this has not been possible in some cases. We apologize for any apparent
infringement of copyright and if notified, the publisher will be pleased to rectify any
errors or omissions at the earliest opportunity.

Illustrations by: Geoff Waterhose/Just For Laffs pp 53, 112; Henning Löchlein pp 57, 127;
Francis Blake p 83; Peter Bull p 125; Willie Ryan p 94.

Commissioned photography by: James King Holmes pp 9, 14, 15, 24, 34, 44 (woman in
kitchen), 56, 66, 86, 98, 128, 129.

*The publisher would also like to thank the following for permission to reproduce the following
photographs*: Action Plus p 84 (1992 Olympics/Peter Tarry); Agora p 19 (interior of Agora
office building); Alamy Images pp 12 (carnival in Rio/Robert Harding Picture Library,
woman on beach/mediacolor's, advertising posters in Milan/Robert Mullan), 13 (Scottish
castle on lake/Jon Arnold Images), 23 (engine/Transtock Inc.), 26 (sign on Welsh beach/
Photofusion Picture Library), 32 (Chinese text/Doug Steley), 52 (modern building and canal
boat/GP Bowater), 64 (young people on river boat/Jamie Marshall), 72 (signs in San Francisco/
Robert Harding Picture Library), 84 (stadium construction/Paul Doyle), 88 (signing a cheque/
Eyebyte), 96 (homeless person sleeping in street/David Hoffman Photo Library),
96 (children in slum home/The Photolibrary Wales), 103 (young man/Hugh Sitton),
108 (sherry barrels/David Sanger, fresh olives/Peter Bowater, olive grove/Peter Bowater),
120 (depressed man in office/Photofusion Picture Library); Anthony Blake Photo Library p
41 (sushi plate/Maximilian Stock, antipasto plate/Martin Brigdale); Beatwax p 17 (Friends
Reunited logo, Julie Pankhurst); Bridgeman Art Library p 32 ('Wonders of the Creation and
the Curiosities of Existence' by Zakairy, Rosetta Stone); Cephas Picture Library p 44
(Spanish tapas/ Stockfood); Chris Stewart p 58 (Chris Stewart in Andalucía/Miguel Ruiz de
Almodovar Sel); Corbis pp 12 (Mt Cook, New Zealand/BSPI), 12 (two Japanese girls with
mobile phones/ BSPI), 26 (traffic signs painted on street/Randy Faris), 32
(hieroglyphs/Gianni Dagli Orti), 36 (night shopping scene in Tokyo/Bob Kirst), 36 (Japanese
women with shopping bags in street/Gideon Mandel), 49 (man talking to group in
lobby/Ronnen Eshel), 54 (woman jogging up stairs/Jim Cummins), 54 (man stretching on
office floor/Rob Lewine), 60 (man and woman in Vancouver/Dan Lamont), 64 (Prince Harry
plants tree in Chile/Kieran Doherty/Reuters), 70 (Moscone Convention Centre/Roger
Ressmeyer), 72 (San Francisco cable car/Jan Butchofsky-Houser), 72 (San Francisco street at
night/ML Sinibaldi), 74 (office centre in India/Sherwin Crasto/Reuters), 85 (Stadium
Australia/Dallas and John Heaton), 96 (Bombay, India/Viviane Moos), 100 (Russians
queuing for McDonald's in Moscow/Peter Turnley), 120 (dead fish on beach/Pilar
Plivares/Reuters); DK Images pp 26 (bilingual airport sign/Alan Williams), 30 (group of
people in business meeting/Steve Bartholomew), 126 (TV studio/Matthew Ward);
eBookers.com p 16 (Dinesh Dhamija, eBookers logo); Desert Resort Mandawa p 48 (court
at the resort); Getty Images pp 36 (women in department store/David Sacks/Image Bank),
41 (baked potato/Marc Berenson/FoodPix), 55 (man exercising/Paolo Curto/Image Bank), 58
(young teacher/Wendy Ashton/Stone), 62 (businesswoman on phone/Bruce Ayres/Stone,
woman throwing rubbish/Barry Yee/Image Bank, businesswoman with ream of paper/Alex
Freund/Image Bank, young man leaping in the air/ImageBank), 64 (women crossing a
mountain stream/Photographer's Choice), 71 (man looking at parking signs/Jack
Louth/Stone), 84 (security checking stadium/AFP), 88 (woman jogging in Paris/ImageBank),
90 (power crisis, woman making a speech/Stone+), 93 (young businesswoman
smiling/ImageBank), 104 (team bonding/ ImageBank), 110 (international businessmen
laughing/Romily Lockyer/ImageBank, Japanese and Western businessmen playing
golf/Larry Dale Gordon/ImageBank), 111 (Japanese couple greeting Western couple/Larry
Dale Gordon/Image Bank), 120 (e-voting trial/AFP), 124 (skyscraper, graph and financial
data/Photographer's Choice, two diplomats wearing interpreter headsets/Stone+), 126
(Will Smith greets fans/AFP, girl showing Gameboy Advance and Atari TouchMe, Michael
Maze and Finn Tugwel at Olympic medal ceremony/AFP); Grazia Neri pp 22–3 (engineers,
Martin Leach, CEO of Maserati/Guglielino de Michel); Ikea p 101 (Lennart Dahlren); John
Wright p 116 (Leah Pattison in India); Lonely Planet Images p 42 (tourists at market at
Plaka/Jon Davison), 71 (parking sign in San Francisco/Glenn Beanland); Magnum Photos p
100 (Moscow at night/Gueorgui Pinkhassov); Misión del Sol p 48 (swimming pool at Misión
del Sol hotel); OUP pp 16 (man and woman on beach/Photodisc), 35 (taking notes in
meeting/Photodisc), 65 (smiling woman/ImageSource), 93 (smiling man/ImageSource), 108
(olive oil bottles/Photodisc); Panos Pictures pp 42 (shop selling electrical goods in
Vietnam/Patrick Brown), 78 (feet on cracked earth/Crispin Hughes); PhotoLibrary.com pp
26 (newspapers/Christopher Irion), 27 (business meeting), 90 (father and son
shouting/ImageSource); Photonica pp 46 (smiling woman in kitchen), 65 (smiling man),
113 (man sitting at computer in despair); Piercy Conner Ltd p 96 (plan of the Microflat);
Powerstock pp 55 (man doing t'ai chi/Pixtal), 106 (chef in a kitchen/SuperStock);
Punchstock pp 26 (keyboard with Chinese and Roman characters/Corbis), 26 (Tombuctou
sign/Corbis), 41 (basket with croissants/Photodisc), 65 (nurse/Photodisc), 68
(workers/Photodisc), 73 (San Francisco aerial view/Digital Vision), 76 (businesswoman at
podium/Comstock), 93 (man with hands crossed/Thinkstock), 103 (young
woman/Photodisc), 111 (international businesspeople in a warehouse/image 100), 115
(Asian businessman/Digital Vision), 123 (microphones/Stockbyte), 130 (man at
podium/Comstock); Rex Features p 97 (Warren Bevis in his microflat at Selfridges/Nils
Jorgensen); Rosetta Project pp 32 (Rosetta Disk/Rolfe Horn/The Long Now Foundation),
33 (Rosetta motif background); St. Luke's p 19 (St Luke's logo); Travmedia p 48 (hotel room
at Coogee Beach Hotel); Water Aid p 78 (logo); Zefa Visual Media UK Ltd p 106
(businesswoman/ Masterfile), 110 (businessmen/Masterfile).

*The author and publisher would also like to thank the many teachers and institutions who provided so
much advice and assistance in the development of this new edition of International Express, in
particular*: Sarah Bickerdike; Tracy Byrne; Marta Ferkovic and Lana Varšek of Contego,
Zagreb; Claire Giffen; Alison Gourd Juillan; Alastair Lane; Philippa Skillman; the staff and
students of St Giles College, Highgate.

Special thanks are due to: Neil Wood.

Welcome

to International Express
Intermediate New Edition

Introduction

There are twelve units and three review units in this book. Each unit has four main parts: Language focus, Wordpower, Skills focus, and Focus on functions. The unit begins with an 'agenda'. This gives you the language contents of each unit.

Language focus

First, you learn new grammar, or revise grammar you studied before. You listen to a dialogue or read a text which presents the grammar in a real-life situation. Then you study examples of the grammar to understand how to use it correctly. You think about how the grammar works and you complete the rules.

Practice

You use the grammar in different practice situations: sometimes in speaking activities, sometimes in writing exercises. The exercises help you to learn the new language and use it with confidence. You do some of the practice activities with another student or in a group.

Wordpower

In the second part of the unit you learn new vocabulary. You also learn ways to organize and remember useful words and phrases.

Skills focus

In the third part of each unit you improve your listening, speaking, and reading skills. You listen to interviews or read longer texts and you discuss topics in pairs or groups. You also practise writing.

Focus on functions

In the last part of each unit you learn the phrases you need for socializing with people at work or outside work. You also learn the phrases you need for telephoning in English.

Pronunciation

These exercises help you with pronunciation problems. You listen to examples and practise the correct pronunciation.

Review units

There are three review units. You choose what to revise and complete the review exercises. You can use the Pocket Book for the areas that you need to review again.

Pocket Book

In a pocket at the back of the *International Express* Student's Book there is a separate reference book with useful language from the Student's Book. You can use the Pocket Book in your lessons and take it with you when you travel. It has a Grammar section, with grammar tables and summaries for each unit; a Focus on functions section, with a summary of all the phrases for socializing and telephoning; and other useful information and reference material.

Listening scripts and Answer key

The scripts of all the listening material and the answers to the exercises are at the back of the Student's Book. You can study these after the lesson.

Workbook

There is an *International Express* Workbook which has extra exercises on grammar, vocabulary, and social English. It has a Student's Cassette or CD with more pronunciation and social English exercises for further practice.

Good luck with learning English.

We hope you enjoy using *International Express*!

Contents

	Language focus	Wordpower	Skills focus	Focus on functions
7 Bridging the culture gap				
p.68	• Modal verbs: *must/mustn't/needn't, have to/need to* • Pronunciation: contractions	• City descriptions file • British English and American English	• International outsourcing	• Giving talks and presentations
8 On a global scale				
p.78	• Arrangements and intentions: Present Continuous, *be going to* + infinitive, *will* + infinitive	• Money and finance file • Collocations	• Hosting a major event	• Types of business communication • Texting • Pronunciation: sentence stress
Review Unit B p.88				
9 What if ... ?				
p.90	• Time clauses • Expressing probability • 1st and 2nd Conditionals	• Phrasal verbs file • Dictionary skills (2) • Pronunciation: stress in phrasal verbs	• Urban living	• Writing emails
10 Transitions				
p.100	• Present Perfect Simple and Present Perfect Continuous • Time phrases	• Job descriptions file • Collocations • Word-building • Pronunciation: word stress	• Getting your ideal job	• Describing a process • Interviewing techniques
11 Critical incidents				
p.110	• 3rd Conditional • *should have (done)/ shouldn't have (done)* • Pronunciation: weak forms, sentence stress	• Culture file • Confusing words • Dictionary skills (3)	• A tough choice	• Business correspondence
12 Hard news, soft news				
p.120	• Reporting spoken language: statements, questions, orders, and requests	• Politics and current affairs file • Collocations	• News and views	• Social responses • Common expressions • Saying goodbye • Pronunciation: showing degrees of enthusiasm
Review Unit C p.130				
Listening script p.132				
Answer key p.143				

UNIT 1
An international project

▼ **AGENDA**

▷ Tense review
▷ Present Simple and Present Continuous
▷ Action and state verbs
▷ Personal information file. Learning vocabulary
▷ National branding
▷ Introductions and greetings. Welcoming a visitor

Language focus ❶ Read the home page of the company website and the email.

1 What is NMP?
2 What services does NMP offer?
3 What project are Piet and Rosa working on now?
4 Who is Eric Carlin?

NETWORK
MULTIMEDIA
PRODUCTIONS

NMP is an independent multimedia production company which has won several media awards. It is owned and run by Piet van Els and Rosa Lanson.

NMP specializes in the travel and cultural sector, providing:

■ home
■ site plan
■ company history
■ staff
■ FAQ

Video – from training and marketing videos to programmes for international television audiences

Web design, consultancy, and management – to help your company get the most out of the Internet

Media presentations – everything you need for a successful conference, seminar, or product launch

Management training – videos and e-learning products on a variety of subjects

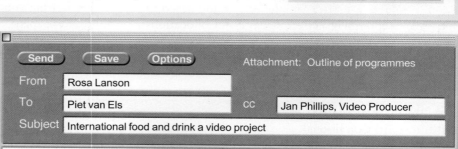

Send	Save	Options		Attachment: Outline of programmes
From	Rosa Lanson			
To	Piet van Els	cc	Jan Phillips, Video Producer	
Subject	International food and drink a video project			

Piet

Here are a few more details on the International Food and Drink project. The project will consist of ten programmes, each focusing on the food and drink of a different country. At the moment, we want to look at Spain, Italy, France, India, China, Japan, Lebanon, Thailand, Mexico, and the USA. The programmes will include interviews with well-known chefs in each country. There will be information on the food and drink in each country, and some typical recipes.

As you know, the chef Eric Carlin has agreed to be our new presenter and interviewer. He's very interested in the food of different countries and fortunately he loves travelling, because the project will involve a lot of travel.

I've arranged for Eric to meet us for lunch on Monday to discuss some preliminary ideas. I hope that's OK with you.

Rosa

2 🎧 **1.1** Eric Carlin is meeting Piet van Els for lunch. Listen to part of their conversation and answer the questions.

1 When did Piet and Rosa set up the company?
2 How long have they known each other?
3 What are their different responsibilities at NMP?
4 What do the new managers do?
5 Do Piet and Rosa's jobs involve a lot of travelling?

3 **Grammar quiz**

Read the following sentences from the conversation in **2**. Answer the questions below.

a Rosa and I set up the company fifteen years ago.
b We've known each other since we were at university.
c We've been NMP for two years.
d Paul, our new Financial Manager, deals with the financial aspects.
e We both travel a lot.
f At the moment Rosa's travelling even more than usual.

1 In which sentence(s) is the speaker talking about
 • the past?
 • the present?
 • a time from the past to the present?

2 Match the verbs with the tense: Present Simple, Present Continuous, Past Simple, or Present Perfect Simple.

Present Simple and Present Continuous

Match the sentences in A with the categories in B.

A
1 We usually **meet** at least once a day.
2 She's **leaving** the office now.
3 You're **meeting** her this afternoon.
4 She **knows** the market very well.
5 She's **working** on two big launches at the moment.
6 He **deals** with all the financial aspects of the business.

B
a an action happening at the moment of speaking
b a regular or habitual activity
c a temporary activity happening around now, but perhaps not at the moment of speaking
d a future arrangement
e a long-term activity
f a long-term state

 Pocket Book p. 11

Action and state verbs

Read the examples and complete the rules. Write *simple* or *continuous*.

Action verbs
● Louise **works** on promotions. She's **working** on two big launches at the moment.
● Rosa and Piet **travel** a lot. At present, Rosa is **travelling** even more than usual.
● Piet often **has** business lunches. He's **having** lunch with Eric at the moment.

State verbs
● Rosa **understands** what the customers **want**. Rosa ~~is understanding~~ what the customers ~~are wanting~~.
● She **knows** the market very well. She's ~~knowing~~ the market very well.
● Louise **has** a lot of work at the moment. Louise ~~is having~~ a lot of work at the moment.

● Verbs which express an action or activity, e.g. *bring, arrive, manage, travel, work*, are used in both simple and _____ tenses. They are called **action verbs**.
● Verbs which express a state, e.g. *understand, believe, know, want, be, like*, are not normally used in _____ tenses. They are called **state verbs**.
● Some verbs, e.g. *have, see, look, taste, think*, are used in both _____ and _____ tenses. They express either an action or a state.

 Pocket Book p. 2

Practice

1 Complete the sentences. Use the Present Simple or Present Continuous form of the verb in brackets.

1 I _____ to work by train this week – my car's broken down. (travel)

2 He's Swedish. He _____ from a town just outside Stockholm. (come)

3 They _____ German, but they _____ actually French. (look)/(be)

4 This wine _____ awful. Let's speak to the waiter. (taste)

5 Sorry, I _____ a film on Friday. How about Saturday? (see)

6 I _____ a word of Japanese – it's so embarrassing! (not understand)

7 She _____ of changing cities because she _____ happy here. (think)/(not be)

8 Why _____ the sauce? Is it too spicy? (you, taste)

9 He _____ eight weeks' holiday a year. Lucky thing! (have)

10 I _____ his point, but I don't agree. (see)

11 _____ for the newspaper? I _____ it's in the kitchen. (you, look)/(think)

12 I _____ abroad quite a lot. Almost every month, in fact. (travel)

13 I'm afraid they _____ a meeting. Can I take a message? (have)

14 _____ lunch to work on Fridays too? (you, bring)

2 Read the answers Eric Carlin gave in an interview with Louise, the Promotions Manager for NMP. What questions do you think Louise asked?

Example 1 *Where were you born?*

1 I was born in Cornwall, in a small seaside town, but my parents moved to London when I was four.

2 Yes, I grew up in London and went to school there.

3 I went to college to study for a diploma in Cookery, Catering, and Hospitality Management. I'd been interested in cookery since I was fourteen. My mother went out to work then and I had to cook for my younger brother and sister.

4 After the course, I started working as a chef in London. I worked at two restaurants, the Hilton and the Buckingham, where I was Head Chef.

5 After the Buckingham, I went to France and then to Italy. Partly to learn more about cooking and partly to learn the language.

6 I speak English, French, and Italian. I really enjoy speaking other languages – although I'm not so good at writing.

7 I've had my own restaurant since 1999. It's hard work, but I love it.

8 Apart from cookery, I enjoy playing tennis in the summer and skiing in winter.

9 Yes, I do. My ambition is to open my own cookery school.

3 🎧 **1.2** Listen to the interview. Write Louise's actual questions.

1 *Where were you born?*

2 _____

3 _____

4 _____

5 _____

6 _____

7 _____

8 _____

9 _____

4 Work in pairs. Interview your partner to find out about his/her background, studies, past and present work, interests, and future plans. Then tell the class about your partner.

5 Work in groups. Read the questions and discuss your ideas.

1 Eric Carlin speaks three languages and enjoys learning other languages. How many languages do you speak? Do you enjoy learning other languages?

2 What makes a good language learner?

3 How can you become a better language learner?

Personal information file. Learning vocabulary

1 Read the suggestions for learning vocabulary.

1 Which suggestions do you agree with?
2 Which methods do you already use?
3 Which new suggestions would you like to try?
4 Which other methods of your own do you use?

- When you read something in English, don't stop to look up every new word in the dictionary. Try to guess the meaning of a new word before you look it up in a dictionary.
- Don't learn every new word you meet. Learn the words that are most useful to you and your situation.
- With a problem word, or a word with no easy translation, write it in your notebook in an English sentence which shows the meaning.
- Test yourself regularly by covering the translation of English words in your notebook.
- Use both English–English and bilingual dictionaries.
- Try to put words into topic groups when you write them down. For example, words connected with travel, entertainment, work, etc.
- Carry your notebook round with you and try to learn 5–10 new words a day. (It helps if the notebook is small and portable!)
- Use a new word as soon as you can. This is always the final step in learning vocabulary.

2 You have two minutes. Learn the words in the box. Then cover the box and write the words you remember.

3 Work in pairs. Compare the words you managed to write down. Did your partner remember any words which you forgot?

Organizing vocabulary

1 Divide the words in the box into four topic groups and give each group a heading. Add two more words to each group.

2 Work in pairs. Choose six of the words and use them to give information about yourself to your partner.

3 Complete the following groups with suitable words. Compare groups with a partner.

	an offer		*project*	
to make	*a mistake*		*general*	manager
	_____		_____	
	_____			

home		*book*
frame	work	*place*
_____		_____

4 Complete the word family table.

Verb	Noun (thing)	Adjective	Noun (person)
employ	_____	_____	employer/employee
_____	negotiation	negotiable	_____
operate	_____	operational	_____
_____	tour/tourism	_____	tourist

Word box:

centre
surfing
subject
flat
full-time
exercise
degree
garden
colleagues
course
salary
college
commute
holiday
suburbs
evening class

A

home	college
public	TV
working	gap
dress	family
health	

B

club	pet
programme	hours
year	code
cooking	friends
transport	

5 Combine the words in boxes A and B to make compound nouns. More than one combination may be possible.

Example *public transport*

6 Work in pairs. Ask each other questions using the compound nouns in **5**.

Example *Do you go to work by public transport?*

Recording vocabulary

1 What information is important to record when you learn a new word?

Example *correct spelling*

2 Look at the 'word frame' for *specialize*. Which of these items are used?

1 correct spelling
2 part of speech (noun, verb, adjective, adverb, etc.)
3 pronunciation and stress
4 use in a sentence
5 a definition in English
6 a translation
7 grammatical information, e.g. preposition used with word
8 similar or related words, e.g. *specialist*

Word frame: *specialize*

Word (and stress)	● ● ● *specialize (to specialize in something)*
Sentence/context	*NMP specializes in the travel and cultural sector.*
Definition	*(Verb) = to give most of your attention to one subject or product*
Word family (and stress)	● ● ● ● ● *(noun) = speciality (the thing)* ● ● ● *(noun) = specialist (the person)*
Grammar	*Verb + in + noun/gerund* *He specializes in giving financial advice.*
Translation	

3 Choose two of the words below, and write a similar word frame for each. Use a dictionary to help you.

to apply	keen	to manage	responsible

Reviewing vocabulary

Answer the questions and then exchange ideas with a partner.

1 How important is it for you to review vocabulary?
2 How often do you do it?
3 Which methods do you find work best?

Asking for help with vocabulary

1 Match the situations in A with an appropriate question in B.

A
1 You don't understand the meaning of a word.
2 You didn't hear what the teacher said.
3 You want to translate a word in your language into English.
4 You don't know how to spell a word.
5 You want to borrow your partner's dictionary.
6 The teacher is speaking too quickly.

B
a Sorry, can you repeat that?
b What's the English for … ?
c Can you speak a little slower?
d What does … mean?
e How do you spell it?
f Can I borrow your dictionary?

2 Write alternative questions for the situations in A above.

Skills focus

National branding

1 Work in groups.

1 What is a 'brand'? Can you think of any well-known brands? Can countries be brands?
2 Look at the pictures. Which countries do you associate with them? Is the image of each country positive, negative, or neutral?
3 What adjectives would you use to describe each country in the pictures and its people?

2 Work in pairs. Look at the list of countries. Which of the adjectives in A and which of the nouns in B do you associate with them?

	A	B
Brazil	fun-loving	carnival
Germany	practical	technology
Italy	traditional	football
Ireland	adventurous	Guinness
Jamaica	stylish	the outdoor life
Japan	high-tech	heritage
New Zealand	authentic	efficiency
Scotland	fashion-conscious	reggae music
Singapore	rational	engineering
Switzerland	relaxed	precision

3 Compare your answers with other students. Discuss your reasons.

4 Read the article *Selling your country – national branding* to check your answers to **2**. Then answer the questions.

1 What difficulties can a country have as a result of national branding?
2 Which countries have been successful at national branding?
3 How did Scotland actually 'sell itself' and promote its brand?

Selling your country – national branding

Most countries have an image. If someone says 'Jamaica', you think of beaches, reggae music, and people with a relaxed approach to life. If they say 'Brazil', you might think of carnival or football, and people who love to have fun. Other images probably come to mind when you think of Italy, Germany, or New Zealand. Ask different people what their image of these places is and you'll probably find they have a similar picture. Italians are seen as stylish and fashion-conscious, Germans as practical and rational, and New Zealanders as adventurous and loving the outdoor life.

These images are often the result of stereotypes, but they are also used in a positive way as a 'national brand', just like company brands such as Coca-Cola, Swatch, or Gucci. Several countries have realised that emphasizing this image or brand can be used to promote trade, tourism, and investment.

A national brand is generally a positive thing, but sometimes a country becomes trapped by its image – technology brands from Japan, heritage brands from Britain, engineering brands from Germany, efficiency and precision from

5 Work in pairs or groups. Think of a country – not your own and not one mentioned in the article. Make lists of

1 the adjectives you associate with it.
2 the products and services you associate with it.

6 Use your lists to interview other students and find out if they have the same image of the country.

7 Think about your own country. What associations do people of other nationalities have about your country and its people?

1 Are they true? Are they positive?
2 How would you 'brand' your country?
3 How is the brand different from neighbouring countries?

8 Work in groups.

1 What problems and misunderstandings can you have when you meet or work with people from other countries and cultures?

   Examples *language difficulties, different ways of greeting*

2 What problems can you have the first time you visit another country?

   Example *not knowing the system of ordering and paying in a bar or café*

3 Suggest what you can do to avoid or overcome these kinds of problems.

9 Make a list of cultural tips for foreign visitors to your country. Include some of the topics below and add topics of your own.

- Introductions and greetings
- Queuing
- Ordering and paying in cafés, bars, and restaurants
- Using public transport
- Invitations
- Tipping
- Eye contact and gestures

Switzerland, and so on. This can make it difficult for people to accept 'non-typical' brands. For example, Italy's brand image as a fashion and style producer made it difficult for Olivetti, a computer manufacturer, to create a successful export business.

As with companies and products, there is also the problem of competition. How do you choose between 'Malaysia, Truly Asia' and 'Amazing Thailand'? In Singapore, for example, you can see TV adverts for the high-tech hub of Asia, trying to attract foreign professionals who usually make their home in Hong Kong, Japan, or South Korea.

But there have been many successes in national branding. Countries such as New Zealand, Ireland, and Spain have all developed successful brands, not just for tourism but for other products and exports as well. In every major city in the world there is sure to be a Lord of the Rings fan who is drinking Guinness in an Irish pub, watching Real Madrid on TV!

Scotland is another country which has actively and successfully launched its brand. In 1994 the economic development agency created a special project called 'Scotland the Brand'. They defined the positive image of Scotland as one of quality, tradition, and authenticity. They held marketing events and promotions, and recruited companies who were able to promote this brand. The result was an immediate 200% rise in food, drink, and cultural exports. The success is continuing today.

The Scottish success showed that even small countries – perhaps especially small countries – can benefit from selling themselves with their national brand.

Introductions and greetings. Welcoming a visitor

Introductions and greetings

1 🎧 **1.3** Eric arrives at NMP to meet Piet. Listen to the conversation.

1 What does Piet say when he greets Eric?
2 How does Piet introduce Eric to Claire?
3 What do Eric and Claire say when they are introduced?

2 Work in pairs. Write what you would say in the following situations.

1 You are at a conference. Introduce yourself to the person sitting next to you.
2 You are meeting a visitor you have never met before in a hotel lobby. You see someone you think might be your visitor. Speak to her.
3 Introduce a person visiting your organization to a colleague.
4 You arrive at a new company. Introduce yourself to the receptionist.
5 Introduce two friends of yours at a party.

3 Read the introductions below. Match them with the situations in **2** above.

a Signor Butani, I'd like to introduce you to a colleague of mine, Michelle Johns.
b Good morning. My name is Giles Truro. I have an appointment at 10.30.
c Can I introduce myself? I'm Javier Corzon from Global Auto, Madrid.
d Excuse me. Is your name Karen Miles?
e I don't think you know each other, do you? Julia, this is Claude.

4 Write F (formal), N (neutral), or I (informal) next to each of the introductions in **3**.

5 Match the phrases in A with appropriate responses in B.

A	B
1 How's work?	a Pleased to meet you, too.
2 How are you?	b Not too bad thanks. A bit busy.
3 Pleased to meet you.	c How do you do.
4 I haven't seen you for ages!	d Yes, that's right.
5 How are things going?	e Very well, thanks. And you?
6 How do you do.	f It's good to see you again, too.
7 Nice to see you again!	g No, I've been away a lot recently.
8 You must be Marco.	h Everything's going fine, thanks. What about you?

6 Which of the phrases in **5** would you use

a when you meet someone for the first time?
b when you meet someone you already know?

7 Walk around the class. Practise introducing yourself and others, and greeting people.

Welcoming a visitor

1 Work in pairs. List four topics which people often talk about when they meet professionally for the first time. Write a question on each topic to ask a visitor.

2 Piet van Els is welcoming Bob Wyatt, a visitor from Toronto, Canada. Read the conversation.

1 What topics do they talk about?
2 What questions do you think they asked?

Piet So, did you have any problems finding us?

Mr W No, none at all. I walked here. My hotel is only a few minutes away.

Piet Oh really? Which _____ [1]?

Mr W I'm staying at the Garrick. It's in King Street. Do you know it?

Piet I know the name. What _____ [2]?

Mr W Oh, it's very pleasant. I always stay there when I come to London.

Piet How often _____ [3]?

Mr W Four or five times a year. What about you? _____ [4]?

Piet Yes, I do quite a lot of travelling – mostly in Europe, but I go to Canada and the States as well – about two or three times a year.

Mr W Canada? That's interesting. _____ [5]?

Piet No, I've never been to Toronto, but I had a wonderful holiday on Vancouver Island not long ago.

3 🎧 **1.4** Listen to the conversation. Write the questions.

4 Read later extracts from the conversation between Piet and Mr Wyatt. What questions do you think they asked?

1 **Piet** _____?
   Mr W Just three days. I'm flying back the day after tomorrow.
2 **Piet** _____?
   Mr W I've been with Star TV for four years now.
3 **Mr W** _____?
   Piet Yes, it is. We do get good weather in London sometimes!
4 **Piet** _____?
   Mr W I went to New Zealand with my wife and our two daughters.
5 **Piet** _____?
   Mr W Yes, I play ice-hockey in winter and I do some sailing in summer.

5 🎧 **1.5** Listen to the extracts from the conversation. Write the questions.

6 Study conversations **1.4** and **1.5** between Piet and Mr Wyatt.

1 Who asks questions? The host (Piet) only, or both the host and the visitor?
2 Do they give *Yes* or *No* answers only?
3 How do they show interest in what the other person is saying?

7 Role-play. Work in pairs.

Student A You are Piet van Els or Rosa Lanson.

Student B You work for a multimedia company in your country. It's your first visit to NMP.

1 Student A welcomes Student B to NMP. Speak for three minutes.
2 Change roles.

How good were you at building a conversation? How could you improve?

 Pocket Book p. 27

UNIT 2
New companies

▼ **AGENDA**

▷ **Past Simple and Present Perfect Simple review**

▷ *used to* + infinitive

▷ **Subject and object questions**

▷ **Work file. Dictionary skills (1)**

▷ **Company and job profile**

▷ **Answering the phone. Making and changing appointments**

Language focus

1 How do you use the Internet? Have you ever bought anything online? Which websites did you use? What name do we give to companies that do business over the Internet?

2 Read about ebookers, a successful dot com company. How is it different from more traditional travel agencies?

ebookers.com

ebookers.com is the largest online travel agency in Europe. It specializes in selling discounted flights, but also offers a complete range of travel products: hotels, car hire, package holidays, and travel insurance.

Dinesh Dhamija is the Chief Executive Officer (CEO). He set up ebookers.com after nearly twenty years in the travel agency business. Dinesh was born in Australia and grew up in India, Afghanistan, what was then Czechoslovakia, and the Netherlands, so international travel is in his blood. He and his wife Tani, who used to be a flight attendant, opened a travel agency in 1980. This early experience of the industry helped him when the internet revolution arrived.

As Dinesh says, 'Before the Internet, we used to run a traditional high street travel agency and we built up good contacts with airlines and hotel groups. This was very useful later on. But the real secret of successful online booking in the travel business is the ability to offer big discounts.'

Dinesh was quick to see the potential of the Internet and opened an online department of his travel agency in 1996. He founded ebookers.com three years later. Using his many contacts, and with a lot of hard work, he was able to negotiate discounts of up to 65% on standard prices and fares. He has signed special contracts with 120 airlines and over 20,000 hotels. ebookers.com now operates in eleven European countries and employs a total of 900 staff.

Travel is now the largest internet consumer sector in Europe – it accounts for 30% of all 'e-commerce'. ebookers.com do 70% of their business online and 30% over the phone. According to Dinesh, 'People want to travel, but fortunately for us they don't want to travel further than their computer to arrange it!'

3 Find a word or phrase in the text that means:

1 holidays where everything (travel, accommodation, etc.) is included in the price
2 reductions in price
3 the possibility for something to happen
4 to talk to someone in order to decide or agree about something
5 written legal agreements
6 the people who work for an organization

4 Look at the information about another dot com company, Friends Reunited. What service do you think the company offers?

Friends Reunited

Home | Dating | Family tree | Extras

Welcome to Friends Reunited

Find friends from
school ⬍ | Go

Click to sign in

Search by name

Message boards

Help

The website to find old friends, get back in touch, and organize reunions.

Free to search

Friend reunited lets you find old friends and read what people you've lost touch with are doing now. It's free to search and see entries for the 11 million members.

Register here FREE

5 🎧 **2.1** Listen to part of an interview with Julie Pankhurst, one of the founders of Friends Reunited, and tick T (true) or F (false).

	T	F
1 Julie Pankhurst got the idea for Friends Reunited when she was on leave from work.	☐	☐
2 Julie and her husband did not have any internet skills.	☐	☐
3 The Friends Reunited service is free to online members.	☐	☐
4 The business has developed very quickly.	☐	☐
5 Friends Reunited only operates in the UK.	☐	☐
6 The service now includes workplaces as well as schools and universities.	☐	☐

6 **Grammar quiz**

1 Match the sentences in A with the categories in B.

A
1 He and his wife opened a travel agency in 1980.
2 He has signed special contracts with 120 airlines.
3 We didn't want to make it difficult.
4 Friends Reunited has been one of the most successful dot com companies.

B
a a past state
b a past action
c a state that began in the past and continues to the present
d an action which happened in a period from the past to the present

2 Match the verbs in A with the tense: Past Simple or Present Perfect Simple.

 Pocket Book pp. 9, 12

used to + infinitive

1 Read the examples and complete the rule.
  • His wife **used to be** a flight attendant.
  • At school we **used to play** games and **have** fun.

  • Use *used to* + _____ to describe past habits, routines, and states that are now finished.

2 Find another example of *used to* in the ebookers.com article.
3 What is the negative form of *used to*?
4 What is the question form?

5 Match the sentences in A with the categories in B.
A
1 I usually drive to work.
2 I used to drive to work.
3 I am used to driving to work.

B
a an activity which I do regularly, and which is no longer new or difficult
b a present habit or routine
c a past habit or routine

 Pocket Book p. 16

Subject and object questions

1 Read the examples. What is the difference in the verb form in subject and object questions?

Subject questions

- **Somebody** built up good contacts with airlines.
  Who built up good contacts with airlines?

- **Something** opened in 1996.
  What opened in 1996?

2 Match the questions in A with the answers in B.

A

1 Which company brings old school friends into contact with each other?
2 Who set up Friends Reunited in 1999?
3 What did they launch in 2002?
4 Which company has recently opened sites in European countries?

Object questions

- Dinesh built up good contacts with **somebody**.
  Who did Dinesh build up good contacts with?

- Customers buy tickets from **somewhere**.
  Where do customers buy tickets from?

B

a Julie, Stephen, and Jason **did**.
b Friends Reunited **does**.
c Friends Reunited **has**.
d Sites in Australia.

What kind of verb do we often use in the short answer to a subject question?

 Pocket Book p. 16

Practice

1 Look at **2.1** on p. 132. Write short answers to the questions about Friends Reunited using an auxiliary verb.

1 Who first got the idea for Friends Reunited? *Julie Pankhurst did.*
2 Who was on maternity leave? _____
3 Who is a web designer? _____
4 Who wanted to start a new company? _____
5 Who puts their details and messages on the site? _____
6 How many members were registered in 2002? _____
7 What has been launched since 2002? _____
8 How many workplaces have been added to the system? _____

2 Write three sentences (two true and one false) about things you used to do when you were younger but no longer do. Read out your sentences. The other students must try to guess which sentence is false.

Examples *I used to do karate.*
I used to live in Paris.
I used to work from home.

3 Make questions for these answers from the article about ebookers.com.

1 What _____ ?
It sells discounted flights and provides travel products.

2 Who _____ ?
Dinesh Dhamija did.

3 What _____ ?
His early experience of the industry did.

4 When _____ ?
In 1996.

5 How much _____ ?
He negotiated discounts of up to 65% on standard prices and fares.

6 Where _____ ?
It operates in eleven European countries.

7 How many _____ ?
A total of 900 staff.

8 What _____ ?
Travel is.

4 Work in Group A or Group B.

Group A   Read St Luke's datafile A and write eight questions.

Group B   Read Agora's datafile B and write eight questions.

Datafile A

St Luke's advertising agency
Headquarters in London, England

St LUKE'S

- It was founded in 1996 (on St Luke's day) as a result of an employee buy-out.
- There were originally 35 employees (or 'co-owners'). There are now 85. Each employee receives an equal financial share in the company each year.
- Each employee has a mobile phone, a locker, and a shoulder bag. Everything else is common property.
- There are no desks and no personal workspaces. You can work anywhere: in the staff café; in an area of soft seats with newspapers, fruit, and tea; in a patio area; or in a central, open area called The Hub.
- There are special Brand Rooms for St Luke's clients. Each one is decorated with a suitable theme and the client can use it to work, to hold meetings, or to socialize.
- Each month, there is a party to celebrate the work the employees have done together.
- In the employees' own words, 'Profit is like health – you need it but it is not what you live for.'

Datafile B

AGORA

Agora media company
Headquarters in Warsaw, Poland.

- The company owns *Gazeta* (Poland's first independent daily newspaper), 14 magazines, and 30 radio stations.
- Under communism, the founders of Agora used to be underground journalists. *Gazeta's* first editor, Adam Michnik, spent more than six years in jail for supporting the Solidarity union movement.
- There are 4,000 employees. Nearly all of them have shares in the company. Each year, some of the company's journalists receive shares as a bonus.
- The dress is casual – even the President of the company wears jeans. The atmosphere is very friendly. Everybody is on first-name terms.
- The offices have natural wooden floors and glass roofs. There is also a health club with a sauna and a swimming pool. On the ground floor, there is a large open-air café with gardens and trees.
- Agora runs social campaigns to make schools and hospitals better. Each year, it also gives a prize to Polish writers.
- The company's mission is to promote 'trust, tolerance, respect for human rights, and solidarity with the less fortunate'.

5 Read the other datafile. Answer the other group's questions.

6 Give your opinion of St Luke's and Agora. Explain why you would or wouldn't like to work for these companies.

7 Write down
- four things that you used to do at school (but don't do any more).

  Examples *I used to play the piano/have long hair.*
- four important events in your life.

  Examples *I got married/ran a marathon.*
- four things that you have achieved since you left school.

  Examples *I have passed university exams/learnt to drive.*

8 Discuss your lists with other students.

Work file. Dictionary skills (1)

1 Work in groups.

1 What information about words can you find in a good dictionary?
2 In a dictionary, what do the following symbols and abbreviations mean?

sb	sth
sing	pl
[U]	[C]
US (or AmE)	Brit (or BrE)

2 Use the dictionary extracts to answer the questions. Work as quickly as possible.

★**company** /ˈkʌmpəni/ *noun* (*pl* **companies**)
1 [C, with sing or pl verb] a business organization selling goods or services: *The company is/are planning to build a new factory.*
3 [U] being with a person: *I always enjoy Rachel's company.* ○ *Jeff is very good company* (= pleasant to be with).
(IDIOMS) **keep sb company** to go or be with sb so that he/she is not alone: *She was nervous so I went with her to keep her company.*

Company

1 What is the abbreviation for *company*?
2 Is *company* used with a singular or a plural verb?
3 Mark the stress in *company*.
4 Complete the sentences:
   a *I like being with her, she's _____ company.*
   b *Do you want me to _____ you company?*

★**employ** /ɪmˈplɔɪ/ *verb* [T] **1** employ sb (in/on sth); employ sb (as sth) to pay sb to work for you: *He is employed as a lorry driver.* ○ *They employ 600 workers.* ○ *Three people are employed on the task of designing a new computer system.*
➥ Look at **unemployed**.
employee /ɪmˈplɔɪiː/ *noun* [C] a person who works for sb: *The factory has 500 employees.*
employer /ɪmˈplɔɪə/ *noun* [C] a person or company that employs other people
employment /ɪmˈplɔɪmənt/ *noun* [U] **1** the state of having a paid job: *to be in/out of employment*
employment agency *noun* [C] a company that helps people to find work and other companies to find workers

Employ

1 Which of these prefixes and suffixes can be used with *employ*: in-, dis-, un-, -er, -ive, -ee, -ment, -ful?
2 Where can you go to find work?
3 Mark the stress in *employer*.
4 Complete the sentences:
   a *He is employed _____ a computer operator.*
   b *Are you employed _____ the new project?*

★**work**¹ /wɜːk/ *verb* **1** [I,T] work (as sth) (for sb); work (at/on sth); work (to do sth) to do sth which needs physical or mental effort, in order to earn money or to achieve sth: *She's working for a large firm in Glasgow.* ○ *I'd like to work as a newspaper reporter.* ○ *I hear she's working on a new novel.*
★**work**² /wɜːk/ *noun* **1** [U] the job that you do, especially in order to earn money; the place where you do your job: *It is very difficult to find work in this city.* ○ *He's been out of work* (= without a job) *for six months.*
➥ **Work** is an uncountable noun. In some contexts we must use **job**: *I've found work at the hospital.* ○ *I've got a new job at the hospital*
workaholic /ˌwɜːkəˈhɒlɪk/ *noun* [C] a person who loves work and does too much of it

Work

1 What is the difference between the nouns *work* and *job*?
2 Which phrase means *without a job*?
3 Mark the stress in *workaholic*.
4 Complete the sentences:
   a *I work _____ a large firm in London.*
   b *What are you working _____ at the moment?*

(Extracts based on *Oxford Wordpower Dictionary* 019 431 5169 © 2000)

3 Read the language areas that an English–English dictionary can help you with.

American/British English
e.g. *resumé/CV*

COLLOCATIONS
(common word combinations)
e.g. *make an appointment*

formal/informal
e.g. *colleague/workmate*

synonyms
e.g. *employ/take on*

compounds
e.g. *workplace, desktop*

prefixes
e.g. *unproductive, impossible*

4 Work in pairs. Check your answers in a dictionary.

1 Find four groups of three synonyms from the list.
2 Are there any differences of meaning between the three words in each group?
3 Use six of the new words in a phrase or sentence.

customer	buyer
establish	salary
client	set up
lay off	make redundant
income	found
fire	earnings

5 Complete these sentences with the name of a famous company and the product or service it is famous for.

Coca-Cola	makes	*soft drinks*
_____	sells	_____
_____	provides	_____
_____	produces	_____
_____	specializes in	_____

6 Which word is more informal:

a *sack* or *dismiss*?
b *benefits* or *perks*?

7 Give three examples of benefits that a company gives its employees.

8 Use *over* with each of the following words to make compounds. (It can be used at the beginning or end of the words.) Use the new compound words in sentences.

time	take	turn	heads	all

9 1 Which prefix (*un-*, *in-*, *im-*, *dis-*, *ir-*) is used with the adjectives below to make their opposites?

honest	flexible	motivated	patient
decisive	interesting	responsible	practical

2 What do the prefixes *re-* (e.g. *relaunch*) and *co-* (e.g. *co-operative*) mean?

10 Find the British English equivalents of these American English words.

bill (noun)
catalog
cellphone
eraser
internship (noun)
vacation
welfare
workstation

Company and job profile

① Work in pairs.
1 Would you like to be the Chief Executive Officer (CEO) of a company?
2 What kind of product or service would your company offer?
3 Who would be interested in buying your product or service?

② You are going to listen to an interview with Martin Leach, CEO of Maserati. Before you listen, match the words in A with the definitions in B.

A	B
1 headquarters	a a company that owns smaller companies of the same type
2 reputation	b a company that belongs to and is controlled by another larger company
3 subsidiary	c a system of machines and people in a factory that fit the parts of something together in a fixed order
4 parent company	d the place from where an organization is controlled
5 assembly line	e the opinion that people in general have about something

③ 🎧 **2.2** Listen to the first part of the interview with Martin Leach. Fill in the missing words.

Maserati

A local company with international appeal

Company history:
- Founded in Bologna in _____ [1].
- Moved _____ [2] to Modena in _____ [3].
- Fiat company bought 100% of share capital in _____ [4].
- 1997 _____ [5] by Ferrari: Maserati became a _____ [6] of Ferrari.
- Installed ultra-modern _____ [7] in 1998.
- Output in 1998 = _____ [8] cars per year
- Output now = _____ [9] cars per day
- Martin Leach appointed CEO in _____ [10].

Key features:
- tradition and _____ [11]
- attention to _____ [12]
- research and _____ [13]
- _____ [14] loyalty

4 🎧 **2.3** Listen to Martin Leach talking about his background and career. Correct the information on the press release.

Martin Leach: biodata

Position: CEO Maserati
Nationality: Italian

- Began racing go-karts at the age of seven. Won European Cup and came second in World Championships.
- Started work for Ford Car Company at the age of 19.
- Studied marketing in England.
- Worked in various departments at Ford: engineering, machinery, sales, forecasting.

1996–1999	worked in Korea for Mazda.
1999–2002	Vice-President of Marketing Development for Ford Europe
2002–2003	CEO of Ford Asia
2003–2004	Freelance consultant
	Joined Maserati as CEO in July 2004.
Languages:	English (native speaker) and Italian (fluent)

5 You are going to listen to Martin Leach talking about his job and describing a typical week. Before you listen, predict the answers to these questions.

1 What hours do you think he works?
2 Which of these activities do you think he does in a typical week?
  - check emails
  - meeting with the head of the racing department
  - arrange flights to Rome
  - tour the factory
  - meeting with the Product Marketing team
  - meeting with the directors
  - meeting with the Honorary President of the Maserati Members Club
  - give a speech to suppliers
  - have Italian language classes
  - visit regional offices
  - evaluate a prototype of a new car on the test track
  - take part in a video conference with international partners
  - fly to Rome for a ceremony with the Italian President
  - lunch with the head of Fiat

3 What do you think is the part of his job that he enjoys most?
4 What do you think is his opinion on the most important skill to have?

6 🎧 **2.4** Listen to the third part of the interview. Check your answers to **5**.

7 🎧 **2.4** Listen again and complete these sentences.

1 *I'm responsible for* _____ in Modena.
2 *It's important to* _____ of our product.
3 *It's my job to* _____ to the best of his or her ability.
4 *You need to* _____ and show people who you are and that you're interested in their work.
5 *My job involves* a lot of _____, which I like.
6 *I spend a lot of time* _____.
7 *The part of my job that I enjoy most is* _____.
8 *You have to know how to* _____ with relaxation – that's the most _____ to have.

8 Work in pairs. Interview each other about your current or previous job. In your answers, use the expressions in italics from **7**.

9 Work in groups. Discuss these questions and issues.
1 At Maserati, Martin Leach and his senior staff hold most of their meetings in English. Do you think this is a good idea?
2 Martin Leach has been able to combine one of his early interests – driving fast cars – with his career. Have you, or anyone you know, been able to do the same thing? Does it help you do a better job?
3 Maserati is a company that combines the traditional with the modern. Think of a traditional company you know, perhaps in your country or area. How could it be more modern?

Answering the phone. Making and changing appointments

1 Work in pairs. Look at standard telephone phrases 1–10. Write other phrases with the same meaning. Compare your phrases with those on p. 25–6 of the Pocket Book.

1 Claire Hallam speaking.
2 I'd like to speak to Ms Lanson, please.
3 I'm sorry, her line is engaged.
4 Would you like to leave a message?
5 Would you mind spelling that, please?
6 The reason I'm phoning is to …
7 What time would suit you?
8 Could you make it next Tuesday?
9 I'm afraid I'm not available then.
10 Yes, Thursday suits me fine.

2 Why do we often use *would* and *could* when we make requests or arrangements?

3 🎧 **2.5** Listen to Rosa Lanson telephoning Eric Carlin.

1 What does the message on Eric's answerphone ask the caller to do?
2 Why is Rosa calling Eric?

4 🎧 **2.5** Listen again and complete the missing parts of Rosa's message.

Rosa I'm calling _____[1]. Could _____[2] next week? Monday or Tuesday would be best if you _____[3] then. Could _____[4] to arrange a time? Thanks. Goodbye.

5 🎧 **2.6** Listen to Eric returning Rosa's call.

1 When isn't Eric available?
2 Why does Claire make the appointment provisional?

6 🎧 **2.6** Complete the extract from the conversation.

Claire Ah, yes, Rosa told me about it. _____[1] on Monday or Tuesday?

Eric Well, _____[2] on Monday or Tuesday morning, but Tuesday afternoon _____[3].

Claire I see. _____[4]?

Eric Yes, _____[5].

7 Read the conversation. Suggest a suitable word for each gap.

Eric Hello, Eric Carlin _____[1].

Claire Hello, Eric. It's Claire again. I'm _____[2] about the meeting next weekend. I'm sorry, but Piet isn't _____[3] at the time we arranged, he's got another _____[4]. But he's _____[5] later on. Would four o'clock be _____[6] for you?

Eric So that's four o'clock _____[7] of two fifteen?

Claire Yes. Is that time _____[8] for you?

Eric Yes, that's _____[9].

Claire Good. So, we look forward to seeing you next Tuesday, then. Goodbye, Eric.

8 🎧 **2.7** Listen to the conversation. Check your answers.

9 Work in pairs. Say what the underlined words and phrases mean.

1 I'm afraid I'm <u>tied up</u> all day on Thursday.
2 Can you <u>get back to me first thing</u> tomorrow?
3 Just a minute. I'll <u>put you through</u>.
4 We were <u>cut off</u> earlier.
5 Could you <u>read that back to me</u>?
6 The line's busy. <u>Will you hold</u>?
7 <u>There's some interference.</u> I'll <u>hang up</u> and call you again.
8 The line's very <u>faint</u>. Could you <u>speak up a bit</u>?
9 <u>Could you bear with me</u> for a minute?
10 Could we <u>put off</u> our meeting? Something important has <u>come up</u>.

10 Work in pairs, Student A and Student B. Role-play the telephone calls. See pp. 25–6 of the Pocket Book.

Student A

Situation 1
Phone Acorn Chemicals
Ask to speak to these people:
John Anderson Extension 531
Dr Rubin Research Department

Situation 2
You work for Commercial Insurance
Deal with incoming phone calls.
Sue Waite in a meeting
Mrs Johnson at lunch

Student B

Situation 1
You work for Acorn Chemicals.
Deal with incoming phone calls.
Extension 531 engaged
Dr Rubin on holiday

Situation 2
Phone Commercial Insurance.
Ask to speak to these people:
Sue Waite Customer Services Department
Mrs Johnson Marketing Department

11 Role-play.

1 Write your arrangements for next week in the diary below. Include a one-day business trip, two meetings, a business lunch, and two other appointments. Then phone two colleagues to make an appointment with each of them.

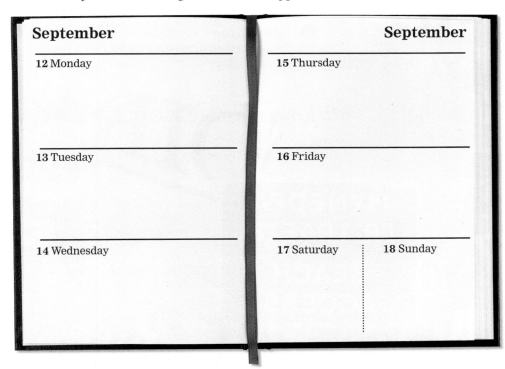

September	September
12 Monday	**15** Thursday
13 Tuesday	**16** Friday
14 Wednesday	**17** Saturday — **18** Sunday

2 Your programme has changed. Phone your two colleagues to change the appointments.

Language focus

1 Look at the table. Match the languages in the box with the countries where they are spoken. You can use one language more than once.

Country	Major languages	Number of speakers	% of population
China	Mandarin	867m	67.0%
	Wu (Shanghai)	50m	3.8%
	_____ 1	45m	3.5%
Canada	English	19m	59.3%
	_____ 2	7m	23.2%
Spain	Spanish (Castilian)	32m	74.0%
	_____ 3	7m	17.0%
	Galician	3m	7.0%
	_____ 4	850,000	2.0%
Switzerland	German	4.5m	63.7%
	_____ 5	1.4m	19.2%
	Italian	540,000	7.6%
	_____ 6	42,600	0.6%

| Basque | Cantonese | Catalan | French | Romansch |

2 Work in pairs. Say the numbers in the table in **1**. Dictate five more numbers to your partner, then check each other's answers.

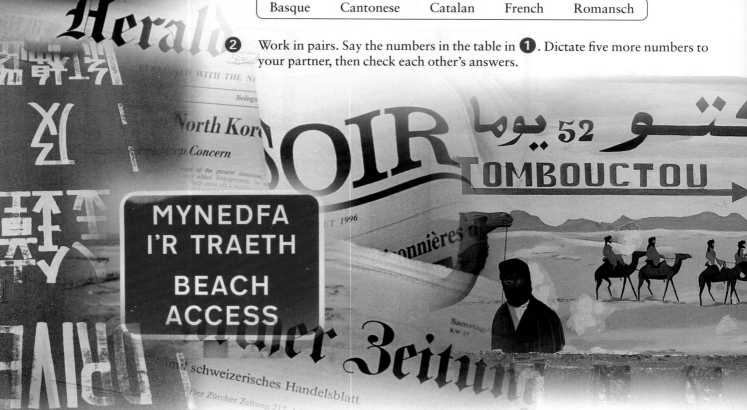

3 **3.1** Read the information about Andrea Harris. Then listen to the interview and answer the questions.

My name's Andrea Harris. I work for a large investment bank in the City, the financial district of London. I'm part of a department which arranges business trips for other companies in Europe and Asia. These are companies that want to promote themselves abroad.

I travel abroad quite a bit myself, which I love. I often have to deal with clients who don't speak English, which means I have to have other languages besides English – my mother tongue.

1 How many languages does she speak?
2 What language did she study at school?
3 Which of these things does Andrea think is more difficult:

a learning a foreign language as an adult or learning a foreign language as a child?
b learning French or learning Spanish?
c Japanese or Spanish?

4 **3.1** Listen to Andrea again and complete the sentences.

1 The first thing I realized is that learning a foreign language can be _____ _____ _____ than you think.
2 Learning a language when you're young is much _____ and _____ _____ when you're _____.
3 For me, Spanish was _____ _____ _____ than French.
4 I nearly gave up. But after a while it got _____ _____ _____.
5 Learning Spanish was one of the _____ interesting and _____ useful _____ I've ever done.
6 He's really one of the _____ and _____ _____ teachers you could hope for!
7 But then, as I said, Japanese is _____ _____ difficult than Spanish.
8 Certainly, my Japanese is not _____ _____ _____ my Spanish.

5 **Grammar quiz**

Work in pairs. Match the two halves of the sentences giving the rules for comparative and superlative adjective forms.

A
1 The opposites of *more* and *most*
2 The comparative and superlative forms of *good* and *bad*
3 We use *-er* and *-est*
4 The comparative and superlative endings of adjectives which end in *-y*
5 We use *as* + adjective + *as* or *not as* + adjective + *as*
6 To show a big difference before a comparative adjective
7 To show a small difference before a comparative adjective
8 The expression *one of the -est*

B
a as the comparative and superlative form of one- and two-syllable adjectives.
b are *less* and *least*.
c are *-ier* and *-iest* (the *y* disappears).
d we use *much* or *a lot*.
e is followed by a plural noun.
f we use *slightly* or *a little*.
g are *better, best, worse, worst*.
h to show something is or is not the same or equal.

Pocket Book pp. 2–3

Relative clauses

Read the examples. The relative clauses are underlined. Complete the rules and answer the questions.

Type A relative clauses

- I get to travel abroad quite a lot, **which** I love.
- My teacher, **who** was Japanese, was the best teacher I have ever had.
- He now lives in London, **where** we met.
- My husband, **whose** Spanish is excellent, helped me practise.

Type B relative clauses

- I'm part of a department **which** arranges business trips for other companies in Europe and Asia.
- I often have to deal with clients **who** don't speak English.

- There aren't many words in Japanese **that** are similar in English.
- I think to achieve this I would have to go and live **where** Spanish is spoken by everybody.

- Type _____ relative clauses give you extra information about the noun they refer to. They are called *non-defining relative clauses*.
- Type _____ relative clauses give you information that tells you which person, place, or thing the speaker is talking about. They are called *defining relative clauses*.

1 When can *that* replace *who* or *which*?
2 When are *where* and *whose* used?

 **Pocket Book pp. 13–14**

Practice **❶** Complete the sentences with *that*, *which*, *where*, *who*, or *whose*. Then decide if the relative clauses are defining (D) or non-defining (ND) and tick the correct column.

	D	ND
1 Andrea works for a large investment bank _____ is in London.	☐	☐
2 The head office of her company, _____ is located in the centre of the city, is only twenty minutes from her house.	☐	☐
3 She often travels to countries _____ she can practise her languages.	☐	☐
4 Her husband, _____ speaks excellent Spanish, helped her learn.	☐	☐
5 She would prefer to improve her Spanish by living _____ she can speak it on a daily basis.	☐	☐
6 The language _____ she found most difficult was Japanese.	☐	☐
7 Andrea had a teacher _____ was the best she had ever had.	☐	☐
8 The teacher, _____ first language was Japanese, was very patient.	☐	☐
9 Arabic is the language _____ she would like to learn next.	☐	☐

❷ Work in pairs. Join the facts about China to make one sentence. Use *that*, *which*, *where*, *who*, or *whose*.

Example The area of China is 9,596,960 square kilometres. It is slightly smaller than the USA.
The area of China is 9,596,960 square kilometres, which is slightly smaller than the USA.

1 The population of China is 1.3 billion. It is the highest population in the world.
2 Beijing has a population of 13 million. Beijing is the capital of China.
3 The political leader of China lives in Beijing. His title is President.
4 Badaling is a popular tourist location. You can see part of the Great Wall in Badaling.
5 China manufactures electrical goods, textiles, and clothing. They are sold throughout the world.
6 Most Chinese people are descended from the Han people. They came from North East China.

3 Work in pairs. Write similar sentences about your own country, city, or town. Compare them with your partner's.

4 1 Complete the paragraph using the information in the bar chart. Use the comparative or superlative form of a suitable adjective (e.g. *easy*, *difficult*, *hard*) and *a lot/much*, *a little/slightly*, and (*not*) *as … as* to show the degree of difference.

How difficult are these languages for an American?

| 0 = very easy |
| 10 = very difficult |

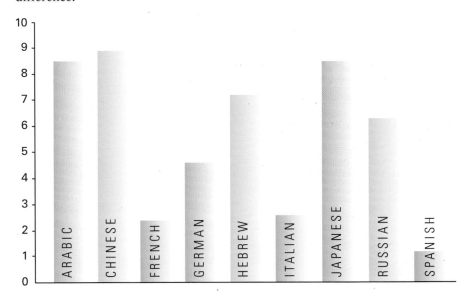

A group of students from the United States were asked which languages they found easy and difficult to learn. According to the survey, the

_____ [1] language to learn is Spanish. French is

_____ [2] difficult. Russian is _____ [3] than

Spanish. Chinese is the _____ [4] language, with Japanese and

Arabic _____ [5] difficult. Hebrew is _____ [6]

Arabic. Not surprisingly, the survey shows that for Americans, European

languages are not _____ [7] difficult to learn _____ [8] Asian languages.

2 Use the information in the bar chart to make more sentences:
- comparing Russian and Japanese
- comparing Spanish and German
- comparing all the European languages

5 Work in groups. Compare the advantages and disadvantages of the following. Say which you prefer and why.

1 Learning a language in a small group or in one-to-one lessons.
2 Learning a language with an untrained native-speaker teacher or a trained teacher from your country.
3 Using the phone or email to communicate with work colleagues.
4 Driving to work or travelling on public transport.
5 Working in an open-plan office or in individual offices.
6 Living with your parents or in your own accommodation (when you first start work).

Adjectives file. Personal attitudes and qualities

1 Make a list of the different ways in which people communicate with each other face-to-face.

Example *gestures*

2 Read the article *Understanding body language*. Underline the adjectives that describe personal attitudes and qualities.

UNDERSTANDING

BODY LANGUAGE

What you say with your body can be as important as what you say with words. In meetings, negotiations, and social situations it is important to think about body language – gesture, posture, facial expression, eye contact, and other non-verbal signals. Look at these people, for example. Which of these words would you use to describe them: *interested, bored, thoughtful, aggressive, neutral*? How did you decide?

Of course, body language can mean different things in different cultures. In western countries, crossing your arms can indicate you are suspicious or even hostile, but smiling and keeping your hands visible can indicate you are open-minded. If you play with a pen or even your hair, it can mean you are distracted; but putting your hand on your chin can show you are thoughtful. Leaning back in your chair can sometimes seem rude, but leaning forwards slightly can indicate you are attentive. Nodding gently when someone is making a point can show you are supportive and encouraging. If you stare at someone they may think you are being intrusive, but establishing good eye contact is important if you are trying to be decisive.

3 Look at the list of adjectives in the box and answer the questions.

attentive	bored	decisive	distracted	encouraging
friendly	interested	intrusive	neutral	rude	supportive

1 Find two pairs of opposite adjectives.
2 Find five adjectives whose opposites are formed by adding either *un-* or *in-*. Give the full word (e.g. *uninterested*).
3 The following words from the list do not take *un-* or *in-* to form their opposites. What are their opposites? You may need to use a dictionary.

encouraging	neutral	rude

4 Complete the sentences with a suitable adjective.

FEEDBACK ON A NEGOTIATION

1 Pierre – arms crossed for most of the meeting – not very _____ .
2 Heidi seemed _____ – constantly playing with her pen.
3 Chris kept staring at the speaker – quite _____ .
4 Sara – nodding in an _____ way during the presentation. seemed _____ .
5 Valentina – rather _____ . Didn't make good eye contact with anyone.
6 Lee didn't smile once. How _____ !
7 Neil – excellent eye contact – _____ .
8 Kati – a little _____ ? – leaning backwards slightly in her chair.

5 Replace the phrases in italics with adjectives from the box.

analytical	diplomatic	flexible	motivated	responsible
confident	enthusiastic	innovative	punctual	thorough

Employee profile

An excellent employee who is *able to be trusted* _____¹. He is *always on time* _____², and is clearly *interested in his work and works hard* _____³. His ideas are *new* _____⁴, and he is *sure about his own ability* _____⁵ when putting them forward. He is also *good at dealing with people in difficult situations* _____⁶, and is *able to change to suit new situations* _____⁷. Perhaps he needs to be a little more *logical and scientific* _____⁸ about his approach, but his reports are very *detailed* _____⁹. His best quality is that he is *excited and interested* _____¹⁰ about everything!

6 Work in pairs. Ask and answer the questions.

1 Which three adjectives would your colleagues or other students use to describe you?
2 How important is body language in your culture? How would you show you are interested, bored, thoughtful, aggressive, and neutral?
3 Do you use different body language when you speak English?
4 In business, is *what* you say more important than *how* you say it?

Past, present, and future languages

1 Do you find English easier to speak or to write?
2 What about your own language?
3 Do you know which was the earliest form of written language: Chinese, Arabic, or Hieroglyphs?

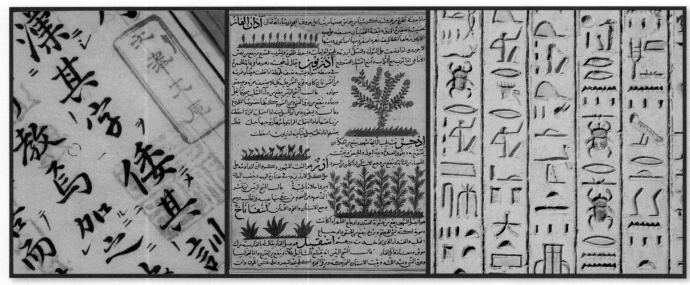

2 Read the article *The Rosetta Stone and the new Rosetta Disk*.
1 Why is the Rosetta Stone in three different scripts?
2 When was it made?
3 Who found it?
4 Where does its name come from?
5 Who deciphered the hieroglyphs?
6 Why was its discovery important?
7 What is the purpose of the new Rosetta Disk?

The Rosetta Stone and the new Rosetta Disk

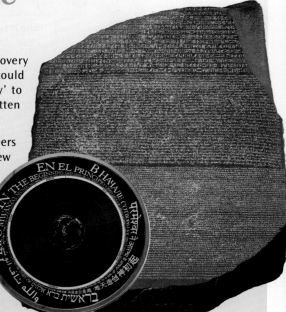

In the British Museum in London there is a black stone, called the Rosetta Stone, which measures 114 x 72 cm. It is covered with carvings in three different scripts: hieroglyphic, demotic, and Greek. The stone is written in three scripts because these were being used in Egypt at the time. It is over 2,000 years old and was found in 1799 by French soldiers who were rebuilding a fort in the town of Rosetta in Egypt.

The structure of the hieroglyphic script was very hard to work out – it was not successfully deciphered until 1822. Jean-François Champollion, a French expert in languages, discovered the text was written by a group of priests in Egypt to honour the Pharaoh. This discovery meant that the Rosetta Stone could be used as a kind of 'dictionary' to check the meaning of early written languages.

Today a small group of engineers and scientists want to build a new Rosetta 'Stone' or Disk, using the same idea of parallel texts. Many scientists predict that most of the world's languages will disappear in the next hundred years. This new stone will preserve some basic knowledge of the world's languages for future generations.

3 🎧 **3.2** Listen to part of a radio programme about the Rosetta Disk.

1 How many languages will be preserved on the disk?
2 Where is the new Rosetta Project based?
3 How many volunteers are working on the project?

4 🎧 **3.2** Listen again. Complete this FAQs (frequently asked questions) page of the Rosetta Project website.

The Rosetta Project

What is the aim of the Rosetta Project?

- To create a permanent physical archive of _____ [1] of the world's languages.

What form will the new Rosetta 'Stone' take?

- A special micro-etched _____ [2] inside a spherical _____ [3].
- An _____ [4] archive.
- A single-volume reference _____ [5].

What will be on the disk?

- A description of each language, including its _____ [6] and _____ [7] system.
- A wordlist of _____ [8] core words.
- A parallel text from the Bible, Genesis chapters _____ [9].

How will people be able to read it?

- With a _____ [10] with magnification of one thousand times.

Where will the disk be available?

- There will be lots of disks distributed throughout the _____ [11].

What is the website where people can contribute their research?

- www._____ [12].

5 Work in groups.

1 Why do you think languages disappear?
2 Do you think it is important to preserve languages, even if they are only spoken by a small number of people? Think of arguments for and against.
3 Do you speak any *dialects* (regional language variations) from your country?
4 Do you have a strong *accent* (way of pronouncing) when you speak your native language?

6 Work in pairs. Discuss the question.

Which of these reasons for learning languages do you think are relevant to people who need languages for work?

a A language is part of a people's culture and it's important to respect culture.
b If you speak the language of an international partner they will respect you more.
c It will save money on translation and interpretation services.
d It gives you an advantage over your competitors if you can speak the language of your trading partners and they can't.
e It allows you to dominate meetings with international partners.
f You can meet people from other countries and understand their way of life.
g It gives you more job opportunities.
h It's interesting and fun.

Giving opinions. Agreeing and disagreeing.
Participating in a meeting or discussion

1 🎧 **3.3** Listen to the first part of a meeting between Rosa, Piet, and Eric.

1 How many programmes will NMP finance?
2 Which countries does Eric think should be in the first three programmes?
3 Why does Piet disagree with Eric?
4 Which three countries do they agree on?

2 🎧 **3.3** Listen again. Write the phrases which Rosa, Piet, and Eric use in the meeting under the correct heading below.

Asking for opinions	Giving opinions
What are your views?	In my opinion … From a financial point of view …

Agreeing	Expressing reservations	Disagreeing
	You could be right, but …	

3 🎧 **3.4** Listen to the second part of the meeting.

1 Which two groups of people must the pilot programme impress?
2 Why does Rosa want to find a consultant for each programme?
3 What does their choice of Spain for the pilot programme depend on?

4 🎧 **3.4** Listen again. Add other phrases the speakers use under the correct headings in **2** above.

5 Work in pairs.

1 Which of the phrases in **2** would you use to give
   a a strong opinion?
   b a tentative opinion?
2 Which of the phrases would you use to agree strongly?
3 What other phrases could you use to disagree politely?

 Pocket Book p. 22

6 Some of the phrases used in the meeting are given below. Complete the list with other phrases you remember from the meeting. Check with **3.3** and **3.4** on p. 134.

Participating in a meeting or discussion

Opening

_____

Stating objectives
The aim of the meeting is to …

Beginning the discussion
(Eric), would you like to start?

Interrupting
Just a minute, (Rosa), could I just ask something?

_____

Asking for clarification

_____

Checking agreement

_____

Moving on

_____

Concluding
Well, I think that's everything. Is there anything else you want to discuss?

Summarizing

_____

Closing
Good. Let's call it a day, then.

7 Work in pairs. Compare your list of phrases. See p. 22 of the Pocket Book.

Pronunciation

1 🎧 **3.5** Listen to the same sentence, spoken twice. Tick the one which sounds polite.

  a Could you explain that again?   b Could you explain that again?

2 🎧 **3.6** Listen to five more sentences, spoken twice. Tick the one which sounds polite.

  1 a Could you begin, James?   b Could you begin, James?
  2 a Excuse me. Could I come in here? b Excuse me. Could I come in here?
  3 a Can we get back to the main point? b Can we get back to the main point?
  4 a Would you mind repeating that?   b Would you mind repeating that?
  5 a Could you go over that again?   b Could you go over that again?

3 🎧 **3.7** Listen to and repeat the polite versions of all the sentences in 2.

---

8 Work in groups. Each person chooses one of the topics below and starts a short discussion of that topic. Give your opinions and explain why you agree or disagree with your colleagues.

  1 All young people should do twelve months' military service or community service after finishing school.
  2 Public transport should be state-owned, not privatized. A public transport system can either make a profit or provide a good service. It cannot do both.
  3 University education should be free and the state should pay the cost of students' accommodation, food, and books.
  4 All employees should get a share of a company's profits, not only senior management.
  5 Unemployed people who get payments from the state should do some kind of work in exchange for the money they receive.

UNIT 4
Consumer trends

▼ **AGENDA**

▶ **Present and past trends: Present Continuous, Past Simple**

▶ **Adjectives and adverbs**

▶ **Food file. Word groups**

▶ **Ethical consumerism**

▶ **Advice and suggestions**

Language focus

1 Work in pairs.

1 What are the opening hours of most shops in the city centre in your country? Were the opening hours different when you were younger?

2 What do teenagers in your country spend most of their money on? What did you use to spend your money on when you were younger?

3 Do elderly people in your country spend or save their money? What will you do when you are older?

2 Match the phrases in A with the definitions in B.

A		B	
1	in line with	a	money spent by people in one house
2	retail outlet	b	years that someone is likely to live
3	household expenditure	c	babies born during a particular period
4	single-person household	d	money to spend after paying taxes, etc.
5	birth rate	e	child who needs financial support
6	life expectancy	f	house with one person living in it
7	dependent child	g	similar to
8	disposable income	h	shop or store

3 Read the article *Changing consumer trends in Japan*. Answer the questions.

1 What changes does the article identify in the spending habits of these groups?

- office workers
- business people in their 50s
- young single women
- senior citizens

2 What changes does the article identify in these areas?

- shop opening hours
- eating and drinking habits
- women in the workforce
- divorce rate
- proportion of elderly people

CHANGING CONSUMER TRENDS IN JAPAN

There are big changes happening in the way people spend their money in Japan. More people are shopping round the clock, single women in their 30s are now a major market force, and senior citizens are becoming known for their spending power. Changes in population, family structure, and employment practices at the end of the last century caused these new developments. The birth rate is falling, people are living longer and marrying later – and as a result they're spending more.

24-hour shopping

Consumer spending is becoming a 24-hour business – and business is booming. For example, when one men's clothing store started opening its doors round the clock ten years ago, sales immediately increased by 20%. Nowadays, one third of its annual sales are to customers who come in between 10 p.m. and 7 a.m. – and this is in line with national figures. Many customers are office workers on their way home. More retail outlets are expanding their night-time opening hours because shoppers are often more relaxed at night and spend more money. The type of goods people buy is also changing. For example, fewer people are eating traditional food and the consumption of western-style meals is increasing. People are drinking a lot less sake and a lot more red wine. They are also drinking less whisky, but more beer.

4 Find three examples of trends from the 1990s. Which tense is used? Find three examples of present trends. Which tense is used?

5 Complete this table with information from the article.

1	Proportion of sales taken in a men's clothing store between 10 p.m. and 7 a.m. _____ %	
2	Increase in telephone bills from 1995 to 2000 _____ %	
3	Proportion of women aged 20 to 39 in work in 1970 _____ %	
4	Proportion of women aged 20 to 39 in work now _____ %	
5	Increase in divorce rate from 1980 to 2000 _____ %	
6	Proportion of population aged 65+ in 1960 _____ %	
7	Proportion of population aged 65+ in 2000 _____ %	
8	Proportion of population aged 65+ in 2020 (estimated) _____ %	

6 How similar are the changes and trends described in the article to changes and trends in your own country?

7 **Grammar quiz**

Match the sentences in A with the categories in B.

A
1 I'm moving into my own apartment next week.
2 Look, he's waving at us. He probably wants to say hello.
3 The birth rate in most western countries is falling.
4 I'm cooking for myself this week because my parents have gone away.

B
a an activity happening at the moment of speaking
b a temporary activity happening around now, but perhaps not at the moment of speaking
c a future arrangement
d a present trend

Communications technology

Sales of communications technology grew dramatically in the 1990s. There was a particularly strong growth in the sale and use of mobile phones. Telephone bills rose by nearly 10% from 1995 to 2000 even though overall household expenditure fell. A lot more people are using email and the Internet on a daily basis. Business people in their 50s, for example, are spending more on communications technology because they do not want to be left behind.

Single women as a market force

Increasing numbers of women are entering the workforce. In 1970, only 33% of women in their 20s and 30s worked. Now that figure is well over 60%. Fewer young women are getting married. The proportion of single women in their 30s is rising steadily, and they are earning and spending more money than they did ten years ago. At the same time, the divorce rate more than doubled between 1980 and 2000, so there was an increase in the number of single-person households.

'The silver market'

At the other end of the scale, senior citizens are becoming big spenders. Between 1950 and 2000, there was a dramatic fall in the birth rate, and an increase in life expectancy. These trends are continuing and there are more elderly people than ever before. In 1960, 5.7% of the population was aged 65 or more. From 1960 to 2000, there was an increase of twelve percentage points to 17.7%, and by 2020 this figure is expected to be 26.8%. With no dependent children, no education costs, and low housing costs, they have a large disposable income. For example, they are spending more and more money on domestic and overseas travel.

Present and past trends

Read the examples.

- People **are drinking** | a lot less *sake*.
  | less whisky.
  | more beer.
  | a lot more red wine.

- Fewer young women **are getting** married.
- Fewer people **are eating** traditional food.
- More retail businesses **are expanding** their night-time opening hours.
- A lot more people **are using** email and the Internet on a daily basis.

- Sales | **increased** | | |
grew	by	25%.
rose		
declined	from	200 to 250.
fell		

- There was | **an increase** | | |
a growth	in	sales.
a rise		
a decline	of	25%.
a fall		

Which preposition? Write *by*, *from*, *in*, *of*, or *to*.
- We use _____ after a noun and before the amount.
- We use _____ after a noun and before the topic.
- We use _____ after a verb.
- We use _____ and _____ after a verb and before two amounts.

 Pocket Book p. 28

Practice ❶ Describe present trends in evening entertainment activities shown in the line graphs below.

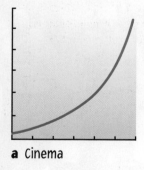
a Cinema

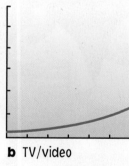
b TV/video

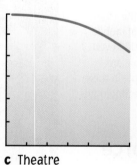
c Theatre

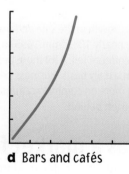
d Bars and cafés

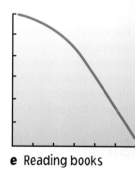
e Reading books

Example   *People are going to the cinema a lot more.*
  or   *A lot more people are going to the cinema.*

❷ Work in pairs. Describe the changes that are taking place in your country. Choose two from the list below. Give possible reasons for the changes.

- evening entertainment activities
- consumption of foods from other countries
- smoking
- car ownership
- types of shop in city centres
- use of mobile phones
- use of the Internet
- 24-hour shopping
- domestic holidays (compared to foreign holidays)

3 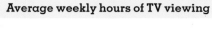 **4.1** Listen to a description of the trends in TV viewing hours in the UK last year. As you listen draw the line graph.

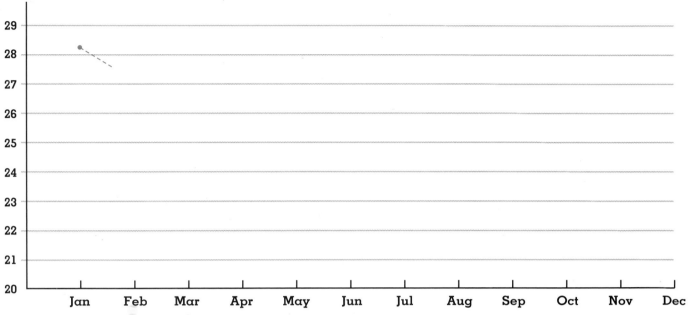

Average weekly hours of TV viewing

4 Complete the extract from the description you heard. Use suitable verbs from the box in the correct tense.

> decrease   drop   fall   fluctuate   go down/up
> increase   level off   reach   rise

> In January last year the average number of weekly viewing hours stood at 28.1. This figure _____ [1] **steadily** for the next two months, reaching 27.2 in February and 25.5 in March. The number of viewing hours then _____ [2] a little: they _____ [3] **slightly** to 26.1 in April. They then _____ [4] **dramatically** to 23.3 in May. The figure then _____ [5] **very slightly** to 23.5 in June and then more or less _____ [6] for the summer, which is traditionally the time people watch the least television. The figure _____ [7] **slightly** back to 23.3 in July and _____ [8] its lowest point in August at 23.2. Average viewing hours _____ [9] **sharply** in September to 25.3 and then _____ [10] **more gradually** for the rest of the year to 26.1 in October, and 27.4 in November. The figure _____ [11] its highest point in December at 28.2 hours per week.

5 Listen again and check your answers.

6 Work in pairs. Look at the highlighted words in the extract in **4**. Are they adjectives or adverbs? How do you know? What is the general rule for forming adverbs?

7 Write the adjectives from these adverbs. Then match the adjectives/adverbs with the type of change they show.

	Adverbs	Adjectives		Type of change
1	dramatically	_____	a	slow and regular, not sudden
2	sharply	_____	b	very small
3	steadily	_____	c	sudden, very large, and often surprising
4	gradually	_____	d	even and regular
5	slightly	_____	e	sudden and rapid

8 Work in pairs. Select information from one of the bar charts and prepare a presentation of past trends. Give your presentation to the class. Begin *This bar chart shows …* or *As you can see … .*

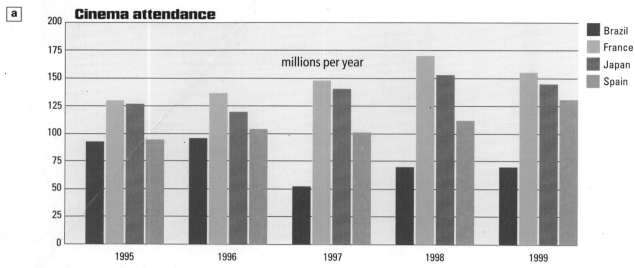

a Cinema attendance

millions per year

Brazil
France
Japan
Spain

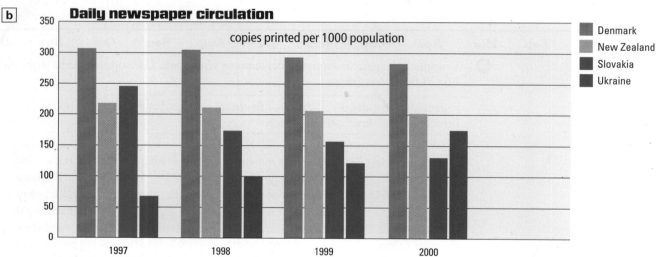

b Daily newspaper circulation

copies printed per 1000 population

Denmark
New Zealand
Slovakia
Ukraine

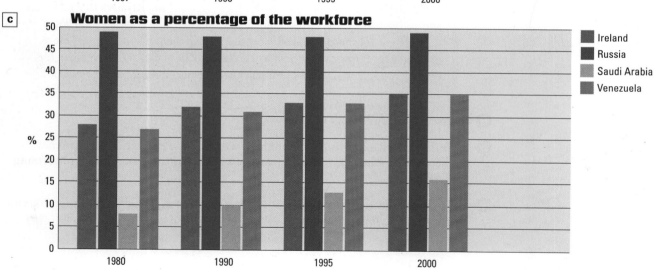

c Women as a percentage of the workforce

Ireland
Russia
Saudi Arabia
Venezuela

9 Work in groups. Discuss these questions with reference to the graphs above.

1 What were the main trends in cinema attendance, newspaper circulation, and the percentage of women in the workforce at the end of the last century?
2 Do you find any of the trends surprising?
3 How do you think they might compare with your country?
4 What do you think are the current trends in these three areas?

Food file. Word groups

❶ Match the names of four of the food and drink outlets at an international airport with their descriptions.

> 1 Trattoria ☐
> 2 Milestone self-selection restaurant ☐
> 3 Seafood island ☐
> 4 News café ☐

| a | A selection of shellfish, smoked fish, and sushi make a delicious light meal for travellers in a hurry. Meals are prepared at the bar in front of the customer and served with a glass of chilled white wine, champagne, or even *sake*. Look out for the seasonal promotions of oysters or octopus. |

| c | The best of Italian and Mediterranean cuisine. Enjoy relaxed but efficient table service. There are three-course, two-course and one-course options available, depending on your time – and your appetite! Starters include stuffed mushrooms, Greek salad (marinated feta cheese, olives, and tomatoes), and a selection of *antipasti*. There are main course specialities such as poached salmon served on a bed of spaghetti; sautéed breast of chicken served with smoked bacon, grape, and mushroom sauce; or grilled sirloin steak. |

| b | The relaxed lounge atmosphere makes this the place-to-be for the business traveller. There are hot and cold drinks, such as ground coffee and freshly-squeezed orange juice, as well as a variety of beers. Also available is a selection of snacks, pastries, and cakes. While you relax, you can make use of live news broadcasts, international newspapers, and laptop connections. |

| d | A variety of self-service international food stands. Have some deep-fried chicken or baked potatoes. Create your own salad or try the soup of the day. Enjoy a healthy breakfast of cereals, yoghurts, and fresh fruit such as apples, bananas, and grapefruit. This restaurant caters for all tastes in a fashionable setting with a magnificent view of the airport. |

❷ Find words in the texts that belong in these word groups.

1 meat	3 fruit and vegetables	5 dairy products
2 fish/seafood	4 drinks	6 other food types

❸ Think of other words for each category. Use a dictionary if necessary.

❹ Match the different methods of food preparation in A with the definitions in B.

A		B	
1	baked	a	fried quickly in a little hot fat
2	chilled	b	cooked gently in a small amount of liquid
3	deep-fried	c	cooked in an oven in dry heat
4	grilled	d	filled with something
5	ground	e	cooked in an oven by heat from above
6	marinated	f	cooked in oil that covers the food completely
7	poached	g	given a smoky flavour from a wood fire
8	sautéed	h	made into small pieces or powder
9	smoked	i	put in a mixture of oil and spices
10	stuffed	j	made very cold (but not frozen)

❺ 1 Think of other items of food that can be prepared using each of the methods in **❹**.

> **Example**   *baked   cake*

2 Think of other ways of preparing food to add to the list in **❹**. What items of food can be prepared using these methods?

> **Example**   *boiled   egg*

❻ Work in groups. Discuss the questions.

1 Is there a good selection of international restaurants in your capital city?
2 Are there different types of restaurant (e.g. fast-food, waiter service, self-service)?
3 Can you cook any dishes from other countries?
4 Where can you buy the best-quality food in your country: in street markets, small shops, or larger supermarkets?

Ethical consumerism

❶ Work in groups. Look at the pictures and discuss the questions.

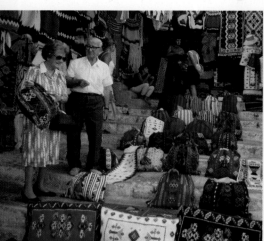 

1 Do you buy any products, such as clothes and food, which are made in other countries?
2 Do you know how they are produced?
3 What do you understand by the terms 'globalization', 'developed world', and 'developing world'?

❷ Match the words and phrases in A with the definitions in B.

A		B	
1	criteria	a	a place where people work for low wages in poor conditions
2	code of conduct	b	morally correct or acceptable
3	cosmetics	c	the percentage of total sales of a product in a particular area achieved by one company
4	dominate	d	standards or principles
5	energy-efficient	e	food produced naturally, without using artificial chemicals
6	ethical	f	a process moving in two different directions
7	exploited	g	a set of moral rules of behaviour
8	growth markets	h	treated unfairly, not receiving much in return for work
9	market share	i	to control or have a lot of influence
10	organic food	j	no waste of energy
11	sweatshop	k	markets showing an increase in investment
12	two-way process	l	products you use on your face or body to make yourself more attractive

❸ 🎧 **4.2** Read sentences 1–8 and listen to a discussion on a radio programme. Decide if, according to the speakers, the sentences are true (T) or false (F) and tick the correct column.

	T	F
1 Consumers are increasingly using the same products.	☐	☐
2 People in the developing world want many of the things that they see coming from the developed world.	☐	☐
3 The West is not very successful at persuading people to buy its products.	☐	☐
4 There are very few positive and responsible forms of trade between the developed and the developing world.	☐	☐
5 There is a falling trend in imports from the developing world.	☐	☐
6 Consumers in developed countries won't accept that products have to be made by badly-paid workers.	☐	☐
7 Local consumers in developing countries just buy what the West tells them to buy.	☐	☐
8 Fewer people in the West are becoming ethical consumers.	☐	☐

❹ 🎧 **4.2** Listen again. What information do the speakers give about

1 present trends in global production of cigarettes?
2 past trends in tobacco-related deaths in developed countries?
3 past trends in tobacco-related deaths in developing countries?
4 present trends in the Hollywood film industry?
5 present trends in the 'Bollywood' film industry?

5 Look at these statements from the discussion. Do you agree with or disagree with them? Why?

1 … globalization means some consumers can get the products they really want.
2 … people enjoy their coffee more if they know it's been produced by workers who are not exploited.

6 Read the article *The rise of the ethical consumer*. Match headings 1–4 with paragraphs a–d.

1 Ethical finance ☐
2 The ethical shopper ☐
3 The future ☐
4 Changing policies ☐

The rise of the ethical consumer

CIS = Co-operative Insurance Service
EIRS = Ethical Investment Research Service

a In the 1990s there was a big increase in 'ethical awareness' among shoppers. By 2002, shoppers in the UK for example spent £1.77 billion on organic food products, and £1.47 billion on 'green' household products such as environmentally-friendly cleaning products and energy-efficient appliances. A further £187 million was spent on cosmetics not tested on animals, while £107 million went on responsible tourism.

b Manufacturers and shops had to learn the lesson that ethical shopping was here to stay. In fact many realized that it was an opportunity for promotion and advertising. Seven of the largest supermarket chains in the UK adopted a 'code of conduct' to establish ethical policies. Manufacturers of sports shoes, such as Nike, now also have codes of conduct, particularly with regard to labour conditions. In carpet manufacturing, where child labour was a big issue, there was a successful campaign in India and Europe to introduce a 'child-friendly' labelling scheme called 'Rugmark'.

c Now the trend is moving beyond the shop and the factory into the finance and investment sector. Ordinary investors are demanding to know where their money is going, and successful investment companies are opening up decision-making to their investors. The CIS*, for example, recently invited all its members to vote on the most important ethical issues, and then invested accordingly. Turnover and profits for the CIS increased dramatically.

d The popularity of ethical investment is not slowing down. Figures from the research firm, EIRIS*, reveal that in 2003 over £4 billion was invested in funds with some sort of ethical criteria, and that there is a rate of growth of 34% per annum at a time when the general market is falling. The growth of ethical investment is increasingly becoming consumer-led. It seems that for shoppers, manufacturers, and investors alike, the future is definitely cleaner and greener.

7 Read the article again. What do the following figures relate to?

1 £1.77 billion   4 £107 million
2 £1.47 billion   5 Over £4 billion
3 £187 million   6 34% per annum

8 Work in groups.

1 Are the trends identified in the article the same in your country?
2 How practical do you think it is to be an 'ethical consumer'?
3 Do you know any companies in your country which have a 'code of conduct' to establish ethical policies?

Advice and suggestions

1 María Ferrando, a friend of Eric Carlin, has agreed to act as a consultant for NMP's programme on Spain. Read the extract from her book, *A Taste of Spain*. Why does she say '*tapas* are more than food'? What other examples of the connection between food or drink and national customs can you think of?

TAPAS *Tapas* (small portions of food served in bars) are said to have originated in Andalucía in Southern Spain, where it was the custom in the 19th century to serve customers with a glass of wine or sherry covered by a lid (*tapa*) on which there was a free slice of ham. Today, you can find an enormous variety of *tapas* in Spain: ham, sausage, squid, prawns, meatballs, salt-cod, and fried fish, to name just a few. But *tapas* are more than food, they're a way of life. In Spain you can spend a whole evening on a *tapeo*, going from one *tapas* bar to the next, sampling the variety on offer in each one.

2 🎧 **4.3** Listen to the first part of María's conversation with Rosa and Eric.

1 Which three regions of Spain does María suggest for the programme?
2 What does she say about Basque cooking?
3 What is San Sebastián famous for?

3 🎧 **4.3** Listen again. Write the phrases María, Rosa, and Eric use to ask for and give advice and suggestions under the correct headings below.

Asking for advice and suggestions	Giving advice and suggestions
	My advice would be to …

Accepting ideas	Rejecting ideas
Yes, that sounds like a good idea!	

4 What other phrases can you use to reject advice or suggestions politely? Compare your phrases with those on p. 17 of the Pocket Book.

5 🎧 **4.4** Listen to the second part of the conversation between María, Rosa, and Eric.

1 How does María describe the cuisine of Catalonia?
2 Why does she suggest Rosa and Eric go to the Penedés region of Catalonia?
3 Why does María suggest they go to Valencia?

6 🎧 **4.4** Listen again. Write other phrases the speakers use for advice and suggestions under the correct headings in **3**. Two phrases for giving advice and suggestions are tentative. Write T next to the tentative expressions.

7 Work in pairs. Match the phrases in A with a suitable ending in B.

A
1 My advice would be …
2 If I were you …
3 How about …
4 Have you thought …
5 Why don't …
6 I think you should …
7 I would suggest …

B
a filming the preparation of *paella*?
b to include a visit to some *cava* vineyards.
c explain what *tapas* are.
d I'd describe how sherry is made.
e (that) you include the Basque country.
f of including some Spanish recipes?
g you interview some Spanish chefs?

8 Work in groups. Read the letter from NMP. Choose one of the NMP projects and brainstorm ideas for the programmes. Then present your ideas to the class.

Dear Sir or Madam

We are doing some market research for the three NMP projects outlined below
and would very much like to hear your ideas and suggestions. We would be grateful if you could tell us what information and topics you think we should include in the programmes, and give us any other ideas you may have. All the programmes are designed for international audiences.

New project proposals

1 A series of ten fifteen-minute television programmes called *Improve your English*, for intermediate level adult learners.

2 Five thirty-minute television programmes about Britain, sponsored by *Visit Britain*, designed to promote tourism.

3 A series of six thirty-minute programmes for international companies called *Doing business in other cultures*, each programme about a different country.

In appreciation of your help, we would be happy to send you a copy of one of the NMP video programmes listed in the enclosed brochure. Please tell us which you would like to receive.

Yours faithfully

Rosa Lanson

NMP Project Director

REVIEW UNIT A

▼ AGENDA
▶ Grammar **1**–**5**
▶ Focus on functions **6**–**8**
▶ Vocabulary **9**

This unit reviews all the main language points from Units 1–4. Complete the exercises. Use the Pocket Book for the areas that you need to review again.

1 **Present Simple, Present Continuous, Past Simple, Present Perfect Simple, Action and state verbs**

Complete the biographical information about Vanessa Ramírez, another consultant for the *International food and drink* project. Use the correct tense and form of the verb in brackets.

Currently Vanessa Ramírez _____ ¹ (work) as the food and restaurant journalist for The International Times. Vanessa _____ ² (come) from Mexico but _____ ³ (move) to the United States in 1988, where she _____ ⁴ (study) journalism. She _____ ⁵ (live) in Los Angeles since 1994 and _____ ⁶ (work) on several newspapers at different times. Vanessa _____ ⁷ (marry) the chef, Claude Blanc, three years ago. He _____ ⁸ (own) two restaurants already and _____ ⁹ (open) his third next month. Vanessa _____ ¹⁰ (know) the world of international food and drink very well and _____ ¹¹ (build up) good contacts with many people in the industry. Unfortunately, she _____ ¹² (not like) travelling very much. She _____ ¹³ (research) a cooking programme for local TV last year. Now she _____ ¹⁴ (look) for new opportunities and _____ ¹⁵ (want) to do more consultancy work for TV.

2 **Subject and object questions**

Work in pairs. Write six questions starting with *Where, When, Who, What,* or *How many* about Vanessa's biographical information.

Examples *Where does Vanessa come from?*
Who owns two restaurants?

3 **Comparative and superlative adjectives, Relative clauses**

	Argentina	Brazil	Peru	Venezuela
Population (millions)	37.9	175.0	26.5	25.1
Birth-rate (per 1,000 population)	19.0	19.2	22.6	22.8
Cost of living (USA = 100)	90	50	66	77
Tourist attractions	Tango dancing	Rio carnival	Machu Picchu	Caribbean beaches
Main language spoken				
Capital city				
President				

1 Work in groups. Do you know the missing information in the chart?
2 Write as many sentences as possible about the four countries, using comparative and superlative adjectives, and relative clauses. Score a point for each different comparative/superlative adjective or structure, and for each relative pronoun that you use.

Examples *The population of Peru is <u>slightly larger than</u> the population of Venezuela, <u>which</u> has <u>the smallest</u> population of the four countries.* (3 points)

Peru is <u>not as expensive as</u> Venezuela, but is <u>more expensive than</u> Brazil, which is <u>the cheapest</u> place to live. (3 points only, because *which* was used in first example)

<u>One of the most famous</u> places <u>where</u> tourists visit in Peru is Machu Picchu. (2 points)

4 **Present and past trends, Adjectives and adverbs**

1 What changes are taking place in your country? Describe **present** trends in

a holiday destinations	c the crime rate	e property prices
b driving to work	d national sports teams	f your own topic

1990–2000

1 Fast food

2 Cigarettes

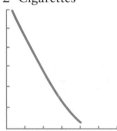

3 Alcohol

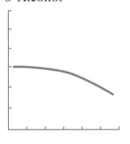

4 Fruit and vegetables

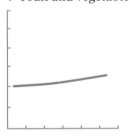

2 Look at the graphs describing trends in the consumption of various items in the 1990s. Write sentences describing **past** trends. Use different verbs, and an adjective or adverb.

Examples *The consumption of fast food rose dramatically in the 1990s.*
There was a dramatic increase in the consumption of fast food from 1990 to 2000.

5 *used to* **+ infinitive**

Work in pairs. Tell each other about your eating and drinking habits when you were younger. Ask questions if you want to clarify anything.

Example *I used to eat a lot of sweets. I didn't use to like fruit.*

6 **Introductions and greetings, Welcoming a visitor, Advice and suggestions**

A new employee or student from another country is starting at your place of work or study. What do you say in these situations?

1 Greet him/her and introduce yourself.
2 Welcome him/her by asking five questions about his/her country, journey, accommodation, interests, etc.
3 Introduce him/her to another colleague/student.
4 Give advice and suggestions on
   • how to settle in to the place of work or study
   • how to settle in to the country
   • what to do at lunch, in the evening, and at the weekend

Now role-play the situations with a partner.

7 **Answering the phone, Making and changing appointments**

What do you say in these situations?

1 Answer the phone to a friend.
2 Answer the phone in a work situation.
3 Ask to speak to someone when phoning another company.
4 Ask someone to wait while you transfer the call.
5 Make an appointment to meet a friend.
6 Make a business appointment.
7 Change an appointment.
8 Finish a business call.

8 **Giving opinions, Agreeing and disagreeing, Participating in a meeting or discussion**

In groups, have a workplace meeting to discuss these suggested changes.

1 We should write important company documents in our own language and English.
2 Everyone should work an extra hour a week unpaid for the next six months in order to improve performance and productivity.

9 **Vocabulary test**

Work in two groups, A and B. Write a vocabulary test to give to the other group. Choose ten of the words below. Write a sentence or phrase to help the other group guess the word.

Example Word *presenter*
Clue *a person who introduces a TV or radio programme*

presenter ✓	negotiate	commute	practical	fluctuate
specialize	brand	discount	ethical	maternity leave
out of work	motivated	flexible	CEO	subsidiary
accent	investment	diplomatic	retail outlet	responsible for
birth rate	consumer	workforce	chilled	body language

UNIT 5
Time for a break?

▼ **AGENDA**

▶ Passives: Present Simple, Present Continuous, Present Perfect Simple, Past Simple, *Will* Future

▶ Leisure and fitness activities file. Word combinations

▶ Fit to work

▶ Leaving recorded messages. Using mobile phones

Language focus

1 Look at the pictures of three special hotels from different parts of the world. Where do you think they are located?

2 Which of these facilities and features would you expect to find at each hotel? You might find some of them at more than one of the hotels.

- conference facilities
- fitness centre
- year-round sunshine
- satellite TV

- swimming pool
- health treatments
- air-conditioning
- moonlight camel rides

- high-speed Internet access
- private entrance to each guest room

3 Read the reviews of the three hotels.

1 Match each description with the correct picture.
2 Check your answers to **2**.

Time for a break?
Our travel correspondent, Leon Martignac, visits ...

Misión del Sol
Cuernavaca, Mexico

Have you ever been covered in volcanic mud and left to lie on a cold stone? That's one of the unusual experiences that awaits you at the Misión del Sol, situated 80 km south of Mexico City. As well as the therapeutic treatments at the hotel's health spa, guests are guaranteed year-round sunshine, and an opportunity to relax completely. A new meditation centre will also be opened next year.

The accommodation – wood and stone buildings surrounded by trees and water – is certainly relaxing. Guests are requested to wear only light-coloured clothes in natural fibres. Bedrooms are simply furnished and a telephone in each room is the only modern convenience. As Jan Heaslip, a guest from Ireland told me, 'You walk into the resort and the stress just disappears. The whole time you're there, you're not being forced to do anything. It's a wonderful feeling.'

Crowne Plaza
Coogee Beach, Sydney, Australia

A conference at a beachside hotel just a few kilometres from central Sydney doesn't sound like hard work – especially when you find out that you won't be expected to wear formal business suits, and that a full programme of entertainment has been arranged by the hotel.

The Crowne Plaza has a fully equipped business centre, which is currently being extended. The hotel's 200 rooms are designed to meet the needs of the international business traveller. All rooms have air-conditioning, satellite TV, and high-speed Internet access. There's also a pool and a spa, and a new fitness centre has recently been opened. But it's the fabulous location next to the ocean that makes the hotel special.

Conference delegates seem to agree that business and pleasure are combined perfectly. The feedback questionnaire asks, 'Were you looked after during your stay?' 'We weren't just treated like guests,' wrote one delegate from the Netherlands, 'We were treated like royalty.'

Desert Resort
Mandawa, Rajasthan, India

It was the camel ride into the desert on my first evening that convinced me I'd found somewhere fantastic. The stress of modern life was soon forgotten as my fellow guests and I were met by a group of guides and camels, and were transported into a peaceful moonlit world. 'Am I being taken back in time?' I thought.

The Desert Resort is situated in the heart of the Rajasthan Desert. Facilities are simple. The hotel was built as a tourist village with twenty-one secluded cottages, each with its own private entrance. The cottages have been fitted with modern bathrooms, and there's a swimming pool, but the resort hasn't been updated to include any unnecessary facilities. I hope this policy won't be changed. The desert, the moonlight, and the camels are all you need.

4 🎧 **5.1** Listen to part of a welcoming speech by the business manager of the Crowne Plaza hotel, welcoming a group of delegates to a conference.

What does he say about
1 another conference?
2 coffee, tea, and cold drinks?
3 lunch?
4 drinks this evening?
5 the air-conditioning?
6 the conference programme?
7 the temporary business centre?
8 breakfast?

5 🎧 **5.1** Listen again and complete the extracts.
1 Another conference _____ at the hotel at the same time as this one.
2 Coffee, tea, and cold drinks _____ all day in the café which _____ just inside the main entrance to the conference suite.
3 This evening, you _____ to join the management for drinks by the swimming pool.
4 I'm afraid it's a little warmer than usual in here because the air-conditioning in the business centre _____. However the work _____ before lunchtime.
5 Some of the rooms _____. The updated programme _____ at the moment.
6 The business service centre _____, but there is a temporary business centre, which _____ in the reception area.

Passives: Present Simple, Present Continuous, Present Perfect Simple, Past Simple, *Will* Future

Read the sentences below. Answer the questions.

a This evening you are invited to join the management for drinks by the swimming pool.
b The General Manager usually makes a short welcome speech.
c Unfortunately, one of the main speakers has cancelled her talk.
d A couple of the sessions have been cancelled or rescheduled.
e The updated programme is being printed at the moment.
f My colleague Anna is working on it.
g Will we be shown ~~show~~ round the fitness centre?
h The Fitness Centre Manager will come to the pre-dinner drinks party as well.
i My newspaper wasn't delivered to my room this morning.
j Did you request it at reception last night?

1 Match the sentences with the correct tense: Present Simple, Present Continuous, Present Perfect Simple, Past Simple, *Will* Future.

2 Which sentences are passive and which are active?

3 When do we use the passive form?

4 Find other examples of the passive in the hotel articles.

5 How do we form questions and negatives in the passive?

 Pocket Book pp. 8–9

Practice

1 Complete the sentences. Use the correct form of the verb in brackets. Decide whether the verb needs to be active or passive.

1 The manager and staff _____ (hope) you have a pleasant stay.

2 Reminder: guests _____ (ask) to place all valuables in the safety deposit box.

3 A complimentary bus service _____ (take) guests to the city centre every day.

4 Currently the main meeting room _____ (redecorate).

5 We _____ (install) another six computer terminals this week.

6 This way, madam. Breakfast _____ (serve) on the terrace.

7 Recently the meeting rooms _____ (fit) with multimedia presentation equipment.

8 We apologize, but because of the bad weather we _____ (cancel) the excursion to the mountains.

9 Your room _____ (not clean) yet.

10 There was a lot of building work going on. Every morning we _____ (wake up) by the noise.

11 The hotel _____ (build) in the year 2000.

12 The hotel _____ (open) a fitness centre in 2002.

13 When I get back next week, I _____ (ask) to write a report for my manager.

14 You _____ (give) a complete invoice tomorrow when you check out.

15 I'm sorry about that: in future the cleaning staff _____ (disturb) you in the mornings.

2 Complete questions 1–4 about Misión del Sol hotel, and questions 5–8 about Crowne Plaza hotel. Use the correct form of the verb in the passive.

1 Where / hotel / (locate)? _____
80km south of Mexico City.

2 What / open / next year? _____
A new meditation centre.

3 What / guests / (request) / to wear? _____
Light-coloured clothes in natural fibres.

4 How / bedrooms / (furnish)? _____
In a simple way.

5 What / entertainment / (arrange)? _____
A full programme.

6 What / currently / (extend)? _____
The business centre.

7 What / recently / (open)? _____
A new fitness centre.

8 How / one delegate / (treat)? _____
Like royalty.

3 Work in pairs. Make similar questions for each other about the Desert Resort hotel.

4 Read the press release about the new Metropolitan Arts and Leisure Centre. Complete the text using the correct form of the verbs in brackets.

NEW Metropolitan Arts and Leisure Centre

The Metropolitan Arts and Leisure Centre (MALC) is an exciting new riverside development. It _____ ¹ (start) five years ago, and will bring new life to a disused industrial area of the city. At the moment, work _____ ² (still continue), but when it _____ ³ (finish) in six months' time, the community _____ ⁴ (provide) with an art gallery, exhibition space, a national museum, a multiplex cinema, and a modern sports and fitness centre. A range of shops, bars, and cafés _____ ⁵ (also plan). The Centre _____ ⁶ (open) by the Mayor, who _____ ⁷ (host) a special launch party.

5 Make a list of the stages you think were involved in the MALC project.

Examples *Buy disused industrial area / Ask for government approval / Appoint the architects*

6 Work in pairs, Student A and Student B.

Student A

1 Read Datafile A below.
2 Write the questions you need to ask Student B to complete the missing information on the MALC project.
3 Ask your questions and answer Student B's.

Project update

History

buy disused industrial area	5 years ago	*e.g. When was the area bought?*
receive government approval	_____	
appoint architects	4 years ago	
construct new buildings		
start building new subway station	last year	

Recent developments (the last six months)

finish building subway station	complete	*e.g. Has the subway station been built?*
build multiplex cinema	complete	
prepare exhibition space	_____	

Work in progress (this month)

install gym equipment	yes	*e.g. Is the gym equipment being installed?*
organize museum galleries	_____	
install cinema seating	no	

Future schedule next month

print promotional material	next week	*e.g. When will the promotional material be printed?*
invite press for preview	_____	
organize launch party	next month	

Student B

1 Read Datafile B below.
2 Write the questions you need to ask Student A to complete the missing information on the MALC project.
3 Ask your questions and answer Student A's.

DATAFILE B

Project update

History

buy disused industrial area	5 years ago	e.g. *When was the area bought?*
receive government approval	4 years ago	
appoint architects	_____	
construct new buildings	18 months ago	
start building new subway station	_____	

Recent developments (the last six months)

finish building subway station	complete	e.g. *Has the subway station been built?*
build multiplex cinema	_____	
prepare exhibition space	behind schedule	

Work in progress (this month)

install gym equipment	yes	e.g. *Is the gym equipment being installed?*
organize museum galleries	yes	
install cinema seating	_____	

Future schedule

print promotional material	next week	e.g. *When will the promotional material be printed?*
invite press for preview	next week	
organize launch party	_____	

 Work in groups. Choose one of these topics.

- your place of work or study
- your home
- a town or city in your country

What changes have been made, are being made, and will be made in the topic area you have chosen? Discuss them with other members of the group. Prepare a project report with headings like the one for the MALC project in **6**.

Leisure and fitness activities file. Word combinations

1 How do you like to spend your free time after working hard? Do you do any of these activities? Which ones do you think are the most interesting? Discuss with a partner.

- I go swimming in the evenings.
- I change out of my work clothes and then go for a cycle-ride.
- I'm taking a part-time course in Japanese, so I do homework most weekends.
- I play for a local soccer team and we train once a week.
- I go to the gym. Sometimes I do a workout and sometimes I do yoga – I'm taking classes in yoga at the moment.
- I took up basketball a year ago and now I play every Saturday.
- I joined a rock-climbing club a few months ago, so on Sundays I go to a special centre with a climbing wall.
- I do a bit of acting. I'm taking part in a play at the local theatre at the moment.

2 Match the verbs in A with the nouns in B.

A	B
go	+ a club
go for	+ *an activity (gerund form)*
go to	+ a team
join	+ a hobby or interest
play	+ an action
play for	+ a play or competition
take	+ a place
take part in	+ a game
take up	+ a course

3 Match the activities in the box with the verbs and nouns in **2**.

Example go + *an activity (gerund form)*: *dancing, jogging, horse-riding, bowling*

dancing	rugby	an athletics competition	a run	netball
the driving range	t'ai chi	a local softball team	*jogging*
horse-riding	the spa	pottery classes	a walk	*bowling*
a computer course	a reading group	a new hobby	tennis

4 Work in pairs. Discuss the questions. Which of the activities in **1** and **3**

1 have you never done?
2 have you done over the last week?
3 do you think are the best for making you fit?
4 do you think are the best for relaxation?
5 exercise both body and mind?

5 Work in pairs. Make a list (using the correct verb + noun combinations) of all the leisure and fitness activities you do each week/month. Ask questions to find out more about each other's list of activities.

6 Discuss in groups.

1 What different leisure or fitness activities are popular in your country
   a with young people?
   b with older people?
   c with men?
   d with women?

2 Are there any which are not played or done in other countries?

Fit to work

1 Work in groups. Discuss the questions.

1 Do you socialize with people from your place of work or study? Do you do any sports or other activities with them?
2 Are there any organized leisure programmes or activities at your place of work or study?

2 What things to encourage health and fitness could you have or do in the workplace

- in the café/restaurant?
- inside the building in general?
- at your desk or workstation?
- outside the building?
- in the staff room/lounge?

3 Read the article *The active workplace*. Find out if the Ford Company encourage any of the things you listed in **2**.

The active workplace

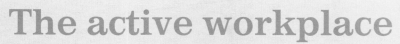

When the clock strikes twelve noon at the Ford Company's New Zealand head office, a small group of employees gathers in the main lobby. They're a mixture of men and women, old and young, office staff and shop-floor staff. They're not waiting for an interdepartmental meeting or a business training seminar. They're the 'Lunchtime walking group', and they're about to go on a thirty-minute walk in the local woods.

The Lunchtime walking group is just one of the initiatives at the Ford Company designed to make the workplace more active. Other activities include yoga courses run onsite after work. A tennis court and basketball court have been built for staff and their families to use at any time, including weekends – and staff have interdepartmental challenges at lunchtimes.

The company runs a 'Worklife week' every year, where employees are shown how to balance work and life, and where information sessions are given on men's and women's health, on aromatherapy, on t'ai chi, and on massage. Funds of up to $200 per person per year are available for life skills development such as courses in cooking, yoga, kick-boxing, and pottery, as well as conventional team sports like netball and rugby.

Sports and fitness are encouraged at all levels: from the regular 'Management versus the best-of-the-rest' sports competition, to the arrangements for staff discounts at the local gym. Teams and individuals who compete in national and local sports competitions are given paid time off work and flexible working hours and arrangements. Flexibility extends to the onsite cafeteria, where healthy meals are provided, and even made-to-order meals for weight-watchers and athletes in training.

Meanwhile, the Lunchtime walking group has set off. If they come back to work a little late, the managers won't mind too much, because they know that the employees will be more alert and rested, and will probably work more effectively in the afternoon. Ford is one of many companies who now realize that active workplaces can create a healthier and happier environment in which to work.

4 Find words or phrases in the article that mean:

1 come together in a group (verb)
2 an action which is taken to solve a problem or improve a situation (noun)
3 the use of natural oils for controlling pain or rubbing into the body (noun)
4 traditional, normal (adj.)
5 specially created to suit a particular person (adj.)
6 ready with full attention (adj.)

5 Work in groups. Discuss the questions.

1 What do you think of the Ford Company's policy on encouraging health and fitness?
2 What are the advantages
  a for the employer?
  b for the employee?
3 Can you think of any disadvantages?

6 Read the information about two businesspeople. What differences do you think there are between their lifestyles? How do you think they spend their leisure time?

Abib Cury is in his 30s and works in a marketing company in São Paolo, Brazil. He comes from a large family, but isn't married and doesn't have any children.

Gao Da Cheng is a director of a large import company in the southern city of Kaoshiung, Taiwan. He's 43 and married with one son. His wife is the manager of a local bakery.

7 🎧 **5.2** Listen to Abib Cury and Gao Da Cheung talking about their health and fitness routines. Make notes about their lifestyles under the following headings (include details of what they do, where they do it, and when they do it).

	Abib Cury	**Gao Da Cheung**
morning activities		
breakfast		
lunch		
dinner		
weekends		

8 Work in pairs and discuss the questions.

1 Which of the two men do you think has the healthier lifestyle? Why?
2 How is your lifestyle similar or different?

9 Work in groups.

1 Does your company or place of work have a staff welfare policy and programme? What activities does it include?
2 Plan a new staff welfare policy and programme for your own or an imaginary company.
3 Present your ideas to the other groups.

Leaving recorded messages. Using mobile phones

Leaving recorded messages

1 🎧 **5.3** Listen to five pre-recorded answerphone messages (1–5). Match them with the following descriptions.

a Eric Carlin's answerphone message. _____

b Rosa's answerphone message (at home). _____

c An automated voice mail message. _____

d The answerphone message from a travel company. _____

e A computer company helpline. _____

2 🎧 **5.3** Listen to the messages again. Tick the sentence you hear.

1 We'll get back to you as soon as possible. / We'll call you back as soon as possible.

2 The office is closed for a moment. / The office is closed at the moment.

3 Please talk after the tone. / Please speak after the tone.

4 The person you called is unavailable. / The person you called is not available.

5 All our operators are busy right now. / All our operators are busy just now.

3 🎧 **5.4** Listen to four recorded messages. Decide which of the answerphone messages in **1** they are replying to.

4 🎧 **5.4** Listen again and complete the messages.

1 | This is a _____ ª María Ferrando. This is Rosa Lanson. I _____ ᵇ thank you for all the help and information you gave us. I'm going to research a few things and then we'll _____ ᶜ another meeting. Thanks again.

2 | Hello, this is Rosa Lanson on _____ ª. I'm having trouble connecting up to the Internet – my computer keeps crashing. Could you _____ ᵇ soon, please? It's just after _____ ᶜ. Thanks.

3 | Hi Eric. It's Rosa. I've got _____ ª information from the Internet about the places María suggested, so we ought to have another meeting. Could you _____ ᵇ later this week? Thursday or Friday would be best if you could make it then. Call me when you _____ ᶜ. Bye!

4 | Hi, Rosa. It's Eric. I _____ ª. I'm afraid I can't make Thursday or Friday morning, but Friday afternoon's OK. How does that sound? _____ ᵇ – any time from two o'clock. _____ ᶜ. Bye.

📖 Pocket Book pp. 25–6

Pronunciation

1 🎧 **5.5** Listen to Rosa's message to Eric again. Notice how she stresses the words that carry important information.

'Hi Eric. It's <u>Rosa</u>. I've got some more <u>information</u> from the <u>Internet</u> about the places María suggested, so we ought to have another <u>meeting</u>. Could you manage later this <u>week</u>? <u>Thursday</u> or <u>Friday</u> would be best if you could make it then. <u>Call</u> me when you get a moment. Bye!'

2 In pairs practise Rosa's message, stressing the important words.

3 Look at these notes made by Eric when listening to the other messages on his answerphone. Write messages 1 and 2 as complete sentences.

Message 1 George – meet – bar of Grand Hotel – Wednesday – 6 p.m.?
Message 2 Peter – can't make – squash – tomorrow instead?

4 In pairs, practise the complete messages 1 and 2, stressing the important words.

5 Work in pairs.

1 Take turns to leave each other recorded messages. The receiver should make notes about the message, but obviously mustn't interrupt!
Here are some ideas for messages – but you can also think of your own.
- Make changes to the agenda of a meeting.
- Request information on new products/services.
- Ask about how a business trip went.
- Request a reference for a former employee.

2 For each of the messages you receive send a return message to your partner's answerphone.

Using mobile phones

1 Work in pairs.

1 What are the advantages and disadvantages of mobile phones compared to land-lines? What problems can you have when using a mobile phone?
2 What other things can mobile phones be used for apart from just talking to another person?

2 🎧 **5.6** Listen to these extracts from a conversation on a mobile phone. In each case, what problem does the speaker have?

3 🎧 **5.6** Listen again and complete the sentences.

1 _____ you.
2 You're _____ .
3 _____ to talk at the moment.
4 _____ battery's r …
5 _____ call you back?
6 I'm afraid I _____ just then.
7 _____ repeat that?
8 _____ was that?

4 Choose one of the situations from **5** above. Phone your partner. Start the conversation normally, but then introduce one of the problems identified in **2** above.

5 Change roles and repeat the activity with a different situation and problem.

UNIT 6
Home and away

▼ **AGENDA**

▶ **Past Simple, Past Continuous, Past Perfect**

▶ **Gerunds file. Personal management**

▶ **Gap years for adults**

▶ **Requests and offers. Exchanging information**

Language focus

1 Work in groups. Discuss the questions.

1 Do you know anyone who has moved to another country to live and work? Did they have any problems?
2 What difficulties might someone have when they move to another country?
3 How is living in another country different from just visiting a country for a short period?

2 Look at the photographs and read the information. In pairs, discuss the questions.

1 What problems do you think César Murillo and Chris Stewart had?
2 What do you think they like about their new lives?

César Murillo

Nationality: Spanish

César moved from Spain to a poor part of London, and became a teacher.

Chris Stewart

Nationality: British

Chris moved from England to Andalucía in southern Spain, and bought an old farm in need of repair.

3 🎧 **6.1** Listen to an interview with César Murillo. Answer the questions.

1 When did he move to London?
2 What did he do before coming to London?
3 How is teaching in London different from teaching in Spain?
4 What problems did he find?
5 What does he like about London?
6 Does he still enjoy his life in London?

4 🎧 **6.2** Listen to an interview with Chris Stewart. Tick T (true) or F (false).

	T	F
1 He was a guitarist with a band called 'Genesis'.	☐	☐
2 When he was at a party he was asked to write a travel guide to China.	☐	☐
3 He worked as a grape-picker in Seville.	☐	☐
4 He moved to Andalucía in 1988.	☐	☐
5 He had no experience of farming.	☐	☐
6 He still enjoys what he does.	☐	☐

5 🎧 **6.1, 6.2** Listen again and complete extracts 1–4.

César

1. I _____ᵃ to London in 1998. I _____ᵇ English Literature at a university in the south of Spain when I _____ᶜ the chance to come to the UK. I _____ᵈ to make a new start and London seemed like the ideal place.

2. At the beginning it was difficult. It _____ᵃ completely different from what I _____ᵇ before. The pupils came from so many different backgrounds and cultures, and a lot of them were from very poor families. There were also problems of discipline and classroom behaviour. I _____ᶜ one day when a pupil _____ᵈ and shouted, 'This is boring', and walked out. That type of thing _____ᵉ in Spain.

Chris

3. I suppose it _____ᵃ in 1973, when I _____ᵇ in France. I _____ᶜ grapes on the *vendange*, when I _____ᵈ an American woman. She told me how wonderful Seville was, especially as a place to study the guitar. When the grape-picking _____ᵉ, I immediately hitched to Seville, and fell in love with the place.

4. Ana and I _____ᵃ in England for many years when we _____ᵇ here, so we knew about sheep and farming. I _____ᶜ to shear sheep at the age of 21, for example. But there was, and still is, an awful lot to learn. They were very hard but happy days.

Past Simple, Past Continuous

Read the examples and answer the questions.
- I **was teaching** one day when a pupil **stood up** and **shouted**, 'This is boring', and **walked out**.
- I **was sitting** at home when the phone **rang**.

1. Which verbs express completed actions in the past?
2. Which verbs express an incomplete activity that was in progress over a period of time in the past?
3. Which verbs are in the Past Continuous tense?
4. How is the Past Continuous formed?

◆ Pocket Book pp. 9–10

Past Simple, Past Perfect

Read the examples and answer the questions.
- Before I **went back** to university, **I'd taught** for five years in a Catholic school.
- Ana and I **had** already **farmed** in England when we **came** here.

1. Which of the two actions happened first – *going back to university* or *teaching* in the first example, *farming* or *coming here* in the second?
2. Which verbs are in the Past Perfect tense?
3. How is the Past Perfect formed?

 Pocket Book pp. 9, 10

Find other examples of these tense combinations in the two interviews. (Look at **6.1** and **6.2** on p. 136.)

Practice **1** Complete the sentences about César Murillo. Use the verb in brackets in either the Past Simple or Past Continuous.

1 I _____ (teach) in Spain when I _____ (decide) to go back to university.

2 When I _____ (study), I _____ (meet) an English teacher from London.

3 I _____ (see) a poster advertising cheap flights to the UK while I _____ (wait) at the train station.

4 I _____ (live) in Kent when I _____ (have) an offer of a job in London.

5 When I _____ (arrive), schools in London _____ (go through) a difficult time.

6 I _____ really _____ (enjoy) my first lesson when the bell _____ (ring).

7 When I _____ (start) my teaching job, I _____ (live) in temporary accommodation.

8 While I _____ (read) the newspaper, I _____ (see) an advert for a flat-share.

2 Look at the biographical information about Alison MacDonald, a Scottish engineer who settled in Canada. Use the Past Simple and Past Perfect to write sentences about Alison's life.

Examples *When Alison was born, her parents had already brought up two other children.*
Her family had moved to Glasgow by the time she started school.

1970	born Isle of Skye, Scotland (two older brothers, born 1956 and 1958)
1972	family moved to Glasgow, Scotland
1974	started school
1988	finished school, passed all her Higher exams
1988	worked on a farm in Australia for a year
1989	started Glasgow University; studied Civil Engineering
1992	took her Master's degree, Macquarie University, Canada
1993	married her boyfriend (Stewart); settled in Vancouver, Canada
1994	started work for a Canadian engineering company
1996	son born (Callum)
1997	returned to work
1998	promoted to a senior management position
2001	daughter born (Moira)
2002	visited Scotland for a 3-month vacation with family

3 Work in pairs. Write similar biographical information about yourself (or someone you know well). Make sentences about each other's lives using the Past Simple and Past Perfect.

4 Read the extract from Chris Stewart's book about life on his farm in Andalucía. Complete the sentences using the correct tense of the verb in brackets.

ONE DAY, I decided to become a writer. The idea _____ [1] (come) to me when I _____ [2] (walk) back from a neighbour's farm. A few hours before, I _____ [3] (visit) Domingo and his wife Antonia. Domingo _____ [4] (work) as a farmer, but at the same time he _____ [5] (make) sculptures of animals. He _____ [6] (teach) himself, and some of them were really quite good. While he _____ [7] (show) me his work, I _____ [8] (think) that I should do something creative too.

The next day the sun _____ [9] (shine) when I _____ [10] (get up). By 7 o'clock I _____ [11] (have) breakfast. By 8 o'clock I _____ [12] (feed) the chickens. By 10 o'clock I _____ [13] (finish) all my usual morning tasks – so I was able to get everything ready to start my new career. When Ana _____ [14] (come) back from the market, everything was ready. I _____ [15] (prepare) pens, pencils, and paper, and I _____ [16] (sit) down, ready to write.

I _____ [17] (write) my first words, when I _____ [18] (hear) Ana scream, and through the window I _____ [19] (see) a sheep on the strawberry patch. It _____ [20] (escape) from the field, and _____ [21] (enjoy) a feast of our fruit and vegetables. I dropped my pen and rushed out to drive the sheep away. By the time the sheep was back in the field, I was exhausted and I _____ [22] (lose) the desire to write. So much for my first morning as a writer!

5 Work in groups. Take turns to think of as many strange and amusing explanations for these events as you can. Use the Past Perfect to describe them.

Example I missed the meeting *because I had gone to the wrong company.*

1 I didn't hear the phone …
2 I missed the last bus home …
3 His manager wanted to talk to him …
4 The conference was cancelled …
5 She was invited to meet the President …
6 The airport was closed …
7 My desk wasn't where it usually is …
8 The computer crashed …

6 Work in groups. Think of something you were doing at a particular time last week. Tell the others in the group the time only. They have six questions to try to guess the activity.

Examples *Between 7 p.m. and 8 p.m. last night.*
Were you cooking dinner?
Were you working out at the gym?

7 Think about an important decision that you have made in your life – for example, about education, work, or relationships.

1 Where were you and what were you doing when you made the decision?
2 How did your life change as a result of the decision?
3 What had your life been like before you made it?

Describe your important decision to a partner.

Gerunds file. Personal management

❶ 1 Personal Management Solutions is a company that helps people make positive changes in the way they manage their lives. Look at the advertisement. What main piece of advice does it give? Do you think it's good advice?

2 Find examples of verb + gerund and verb + preposition + gerund. Write them in columns 1 and 2 of the table opposite.

Personal management

Too much paperwork? • Is your desk covered with documents?

It may just be your personal management that needs improving. We recommend following some basic rules.

That's just one simple example. We can suggest doing many other things. If you're not very *good at planning* how to manage your personal time, or if you're just interested in finding out about personal management, then contact us. If you don't mind answering a few simple questions about your job, we can help you – and you can look forward to living and working in a more positive environment.

For example – write a 'destruction date' on every unimportant document. Maybe you're used to keeping every piece of paper you receive. But how much time do you *spend looking* for things because your desk is untidy and your filing cabinet is full? Here's a simple piece of advice: avoid filing a task you've finished working on without writing a date when you can throw it away. Maybe the 'destruction date' is one week, one month, or one year in the future. When you next open your filing cabinet and the date has passed, you can enjoy throwing useless paperwork away. You'll need a bigger office if you keep putting it off!

Don't delay!
Call Personal Management Solutions on 0443 897676

❷ 1 Read another of Personal Management Solutions' advertisements. What main idea does it give about positive change? Do you think the idea is helpful?

2 Find examples of verb + infinitive or gerund. Write them in column 3 of the table opposite.

Positive change

Do you ever *stop to think* how you could make a positive change?

It's amazing how many people seem to complain about their situation. They would like to be different – more interesting, exciting, or attractive – but they can't find a way to make it happen. Maybe it's because they remember being told by their parents or teachers that 'you are who you are'. They remember to turn on the computer in the morning, but they don't remember to think creatively about themselves.

Well, now you can stop worrying. You don't need to put up with being the same forever. We have the solution. We *love thinking* of creative analogies that suit individuals, and we would love to help you.

It's easy really. For example, just answer these questions: Are you a Mini but would like to be a Mercedes? Do you like thinking of yourself as light blue, but feel you're actually dark grey? We can help you make a positive change by looking at how to take the steps in between. How many steps you can take in the right direction will be up to you!

Act now!
Call Personal Management Solutions on 0443 897676

1 Verb + gerund	2 Verb + preposition + gerund	3 Verb + gerund or infinitive
spend looking	*be good at planning*	*stop to think*
		love thinking

3 Which column do you think these verbs go into?

> prefer   would prefer   hate   would hate

❸ Grammar quiz

Complete the rules. Write *gerund* or *infinitive*.

1 When we use *would* with *love, like, hate,* and *prefer,* the form of the verb which follows is usually the _____.

2 When we use *love, like, hate,* and *prefer* to refer to a general situation, the form of the verb which follows is usually the _____.

3 With *remember*, when the remembering happens before the action it is followed by the _____.

4 When the remembering happens after the action it is followed by the _____.

5 When *stop* means *not do any longer*, it is followed by the _____.

6 When *stop* means *interrupt one activity in order to do another*, it is followed by the _____.

 Pocket Book p. 7

❹ Complete the sentences. Write the gerund or infinitive form of the verb in brackets.

1 Do you remember _____ him when we were in Copenhagen? (see)

2 Will you remember _____ and confirm the meeting for next Tuesday? (write)

3 After working on the new project all morning, he stopped _____ lunch. (have)

4 I don't play football any more. I stopped _____ five years ago. (play)

❺ Work in groups. Discuss the questions.

1 What things do you remember doing when you were younger?
2 What activities did you do in the past, but have now stopped doing?

❻ Work in pairs. Prepare eight questions about personal management using verbs from the table. Then change pairs and interview your partner.

Examples *How much time do you spend tidying your desk each week?*
What are you particularly good at doing in your job or study?
How would you love to be different?

Gap years for adults

1 Work in pairs. Ask and answer the questions.

1 What did you do after school or university, and before starting work?
2 What is the best time of life to travel or spend time in another country?
3 What is the longest holiday you have ever taken from work? What did you do?

2 Read the article *What is a gap year for adults?* and the three adverts. Work in pairs and answer the questions.

1 How is a gap year for adults different from a traditional gap year?
2 Why do employers think gap years are a good idea?
3 Would you like to take a gap year as an adult? If yes, what would you like to do? Where would you like to go?
4 Which, if any, of the three areas a, b, or c would you choose? Give reasons for your choice.

What is a gap year for adults?

A gap year for adults is constructive time out – it can be anywhere, doing anything and everything. You could be travelling round the world, building a school in Chile, doing alternative work experience, lying on a beach in Fiji, or simply having a new look at your life.

Traditionally a gap year was viewed as a student activity, taking an extended break before university. It usually involved travel and, as a result, was only done by people from wealthy families able to pay for the experience. In the UK, both Princes William and Harry took gap years before starting university or military training.

However, a gap year now offers something for everyone: for young people, or for older people reaching retirement; for people who don't want a career, but just want to take life one stage at a time, or for people in steady careers. Many top companies regard 'portfolio careers' of this kind as a very positive thing. If your CV has an interesting range of activities it can often make you more employable.

a **Improve your job skills!**

Taking time out to work in another country is a rewarding experience. It can also be a chance to gain new qualifications and learn new skills; all of which will improve your job prospects when you return. Doctors, nurses, teachers, nearly everyone can benefit – and others will benefit from your knowledge and skill.

b **Save the planet!**

There are thousands of conservation projects running globally from close to home to the deepest darkest corner of the Amazon. YOU can volunteer and help make a difference.

Opportunities range from working on wildlife reserves in South Africa to conserving the coral reefs of Malaysia.

See the world!

Round-the-world tickets are flexible and can be cheaper than you think. Decide on the places you really want to visit and then build your itinerary around them. If you include some work experience as you go, you'll not only see the sights but you'll live the culture.

c

3 🎧 **6.3** Listen to these interviews with three people who took a gap year. Make notes to complete the first part of the table.

	Dean Douglas	Alicia Rubio	Hortense Robert
Which type of gap year did they choose (a, b, or c from **2**)?			
What was their previous job?			
How old were they when they took a gap year?			
Why did they take a gap year?			
Where did they go?			
What was the best bit?			
What was the worst bit?			
What do they do now?			

4 🎧 **6.3** Listen again and make notes to complete the second part of the table.

5 Work in pairs. Sort the adjectives in the box into six pairs with opposite meanings. Use a dictionary if necessary.

> adventurous   ambitious   cautious   hard-working
> lazy   optimistic   pessimistic   reckless   relaxed
> unadventurous   unambitious   uptight

Now answer these questions.
1 Which of the adjectives best describe Dean, Alicia, and Hortense?
2 Which of the adjectives best describe you?
3 Think of people you know who you could describe with each of the adjectives. Tell your partner about them.

6 Work in groups. Design the perfect gap year for each other. Think about the adjectives in **5** and use the suggestions below.

- travel round the world (Which route? Which countries?)
- voluntary work in an developing country (Doing what exactly? Which country?)
- learn a completely different skill (What skill? Where?)
- study a foreign language in the host country (Which language? Which country?)

Present your ideas to the rest of the class.

Requests and offers. Exchanging information

> Can you … ?
> Would you mind …
>   (+ -ing)?
> Do you think you
>   could … ?
> Could you … ?
> I'd like you to …
> Do you mind …
>   (+ -ing)?

1 Work in pairs. Which of the phrases in the box would you use to make the requests below? Give reasons for your choice.

Ask

1 a colleague to translate a letter for you.
2 a friend to do some supermarket shopping for you.
3 your secretary to work three hours overtime this week.
4 a colleague to give you a lift to the train station.
5 your secretary to make some photocopies.
6 your son or daughter to tidy their bedroom.
7 a colleague to help you move some office furniture.
8 a friend to water your houseplants whileyou're on holiday.

2 🎧 **6.4** Listen to a conversation between Rosa and Claire. Write the information Rosa asks Claire to get.

3 🎧 **6.4** Listen again. Write other phrases Rosa and Claire use under the correct heading below.

Requests and offers

Requesting	Agreeing
Could you … ?	Yes, of course.

Offering	Accepting	Declining
Would you like me to … ?	Yes, if you could.	Thanks, but you needn't bother.

4 What phrases can you use to refuse a request? How do we begin a refusal and what do we add to sound polite?

5 Work in pairs. You are colleagues. Practise making and responding to requests. Add two more requests each. Give a reason when you refuse a request.

Student A	**Student B**
Ask Student B	
1 to help you translate a document.	Agree.
2 to give you a lift to the airport.	Refuse.
Student B	**Student A**
Ask Student A to	
1 explain a new computer system.	Agree.
2 look after a visitor next week.	Refuse.

6 Work in pairs. You are preparing for a seminar. Practise making and responding to offers. Give a reason when you decline an offer. Add one more request each.

Student A	**Student B**
Offer	
1 to set up the audio-visual equipment.	Accept.
2 to check the number of participants.	Decline.
Student B	**Student A**
Offer	
1 to open the windows.	Decline.
2 to get supplies of stationery.	Accept.

7 🎧 **6.5** Listen to the phone call Claire makes to Executive Travel Services. Write the times of flights in her notebook.

FLIGHTS

From	To	Day/Date	Departure	Arrival
London	Bilbao	Sunday 2nd		
Bilbao	Seville	Tuesday 4th		
Seville	Valencia	Friday 7th		
Valencia	Barcelona	Saturday 8th		
		Sunday 9th		

8 🎧 **6.5** Listen again. Write the other phrases Claire and Jan use under the correct heading below.

Exchanging information

Asking	**Checking**
I'd like some information on …	That's … is it?

Confirming	**Correcting**	**Showing understanding**
Yes, that's right.		

Pronunciation

1 🎧 **6.6** Listen to the corrections. Which word is emphasized?

1 No, not the 7th, the 17th.
2 No, not Málaga, Madrid.
3 No, not 10.35, 10.25.

2 🎧 **6.7** Listen to the corrections. Circle the correct information.

1 4th 14th
2 30th 13th
3 Zürich Geneva
4 Frankfurt Berlin
5 12.45 12.30
6 07.30 07.20

3 🎧 **6.8** Look at the examples of corrections and then listen.

a So, travelling on the 7th … (5th)
   No, not the 7th, the 5th.

b So, departing at 11.45 … (11.35)
   No, not 11.45, 11.35.

4 🎧 **6.9** Listen and correct the mistakes you hear using the information below. You will then hear the correction.

1 30th   4 Toronto
2 19th   5 13.45
3 Rome   6 15.50

---

9 Rewrite the indirect questions as direct questions.

1 Could you tell me what time the 10.30 flight from Paris will arrive?
2 Do you know if there are any cancellations on the 8 a.m. flight to Moscow?
3 I'd like to know where I can get some foreign currency.
4 Can you tell me where you bought your tax-free goods?

10 Compare the indirect and direct questions in **9**. Answer the questions.

1 What is the difference in the form of the verb and the word order?
2 Which are usually more polite: direct or indirect questions?
3 Which do we use more at the beginning of a conversation?

11 Rewrite the direct questions as indirect questions. Use introductory phrases from **9**.

1 Are there any seats available on that flight?
2 Has the plane from London Heathrow arrived yet?
3 Is there a connecting flight to Manchester?
4 Which terminal should I go to?

UNIT 7
Bridging the culture gap

▼ AGENDA

▶ Modal verbs: *must/mustn't/needn't*, *have to/need to*

▶ City descriptions file.
British English and American English

▶ International outsourcing

▶ Giving talks and presentations

Language focus

1 Look at the heading from a conference programme. Imagine you are going to this conference.

> **MOSCONE CENTER SOUTH • SAN FRANCISCO**
> ## 'Doing business in different countries and cultures'
> A convention for international businesses
> **SEPTEMBER 5–8**

1 What topics do you expect to be on the programme?
2 What practical information do you need about attending the conference?

2 Read the extract from the conference advice sheets. Check your answers to question 2 in **1**.

> **Arrival and registration**
>
> Your hotel will advise you on public transportation from your hotel to the Moscone Conference Center. Alternatively, you can call the following toll-free taxicab numbers: 626 2345, 648 4444, or 673 1414.
>
> Conference registration opens at 10.00 on September 5th at Desk B of the Moscone Center South. Please bring your registration documents with you.

3 You are going to listen to a conversation between a young Chinese businessman and his English language teacher. Wu Chao is about to leave for the conference in San Francisco and Mike Millard is Canadian, but is now based in China.

Before you listen discuss what advice you think Mike will give Wu Chao on these topics about doing business with Americans.

- speed of negotiation
- sensitivity to cultural differences
- individual initiative and achievement
- making decisions
- periods of silence in meetings
- social formalities

4 🎧 **7.1** Listen to the first part of the conversation and check your answers in **3**.

5 🎧 **7.1** Listen again. Complete the sentences.

1 I know I _____ be prepared for things to be very different.

2 You _____ expect the way of doing business to be the same.

3 You _____ remember that American business culture is largely individualistic.

4 You _____ think clearly and quickly when you're doing business.

5 You _____ worry. In American business culture, they stick to the rules.

6 You _____ spend a long time on social formalities.

6 🎧 **7.2** Listen to the second part of the conversation. What advice or information does Mike give Wu Chao about

1 general conversation topics?
2 asking personal questions?
3 if you don't understand what someone is saying to you?
4 being on time?

7 🎧 **7.2** Listen again. Complete the sentences.

1 You _____ ask about a person's job in general terms.
2 You _____ ask a person how old they are.
3 You _____ ask a few questions about her husband and children.
4 You _____ find you don't understand everything people are saying.
5 You _____ stop the person you're talking to and ask for clarification.
6 You _____ be invited for a round of golf.
7 You _____ practise your golf before you go.

8 Write the modal verbs from **5** and **7** next to the appropriate meaning.

1 it's necessary/obligatory _____
2 it's not necessary/obligatory _____
3 it's necessary/obligatory *not* to do it _____
4 it's possible _____
5 it's permitted _____
6 it's advisable _____
7 it's not advisable _____

Modal verbs, *have to/need to*

Read the examples. Answer the questions and complete the rules.

must/mustn't/needn't

- I **must** go and pack.
- What else **must** I be careful about?
- You **mustn't** ask questions that are too personal.
- You **needn't** worry. In American business culture, they stick to the rules.

have to/need to

- You **have to** be on time for meetings and business appointments.
- You **need to** think clearly and quickly.
- **Do** I **have to** be on time for everything?
- **Do** I **need to** know about American popular culture?
- You **don't have to** arrive exactly on time for parties and social occasions.
- You **don't need to** spend a long time on social formalities.

1 How do we make questions with *must*?
2 How do we make questions and negatives with other modal verbs, e.g. *can, could, may, might, should*?
3 How do we make questions and negatives with *have to* and *need to*?
4 What is the Past Simple form of *have to*?

Write *mustn't* or *needn't*.

- _____ is used to express no necessity or obligation to do something.
- _____ is used to express a necessity or obligation not to do something.

Write *have to, need to,* or *must*.

- _____ usually expresses the personal opinion of the speaker about what is necessary or obligatory.
- _____ usually expresses a general obligation outside the control of the speaker, or an obligation based on a rule or law.
- _____ is used in both contexts to express necessity.

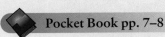 Pocket Book pp. 7–8

Practice **1** Read this email from the Human Resources department of a company to their delegate for the San Francisco conference. Choose the best alternatives.

From	Glenys Garbett	To	John R Livitsky
Subject	San Francisco conference		

John,

Just a few last-minute reminders about the conference. According to the schedule, you *have to/must*[1] register at the conference at 10 o'clock.

I know you're very interested in Argentina, so you *have to/must*[2] sign up for the optional session on South America. As far as the other sessions are concerned, you *don't need to/mustn't worry*[3] – you can choose. The Managing Director would like you to meet with Jacques Pétain. It *mustn't/needn't*[4] *be* a formal meeting – a chat in the bar is OK if you want. However, you *mustn't/needn't*[5] tell him about our plans in Argentina, as they're highly confidential.

You *don't have to/mustn't*[6] take any brochures, but you can take a few if you want.

On a more personal note, as I know you haven't been to San Francisco before, you *must/have to*[7] pack some warm clothes. It can get quite cool in the evenings. Also smoking: you *don't need to/mustn't*[8] smoke anywhere in public buildings – they're very strict about it. One last thing – you *don't have to/mustn't*[9] forget your registration form!

Good luck! Glenys

Pronunciation

1 🎧 **7.3** Listen and write the number of words you hear in the sentences. Count contractions (e.g. *don't*) as one word.

1 _____   3 _____   5 _____   7 _____

2 _____   4 _____   6 _____   8 _____

2 🎧 **7.3** Listen again and complete the sentences.

1 I _____ go to the talk.

2 You _____ be late.

3 You _____ about me.

4 You _____ take an umbrella.

5 We _____ to ask him.

6 Do _____ early tomorrow?

7 He _____ very hard.

8 What _____ should do?

3 🎧 **7.3** Listen again and repeat after each sentence.

2 🎧 **7.4** Listen to some recorded information about driving and parking in San Francisco.

1 Complete the sentences with words from the box.

| allowed |
| obligatory |
| recommended |
| forbidden |
| permitted |
| required |

a A full international driving license and auto insurance are _____ for all drivers.

b The wearing of seat belts is _____ .

c It is _____ to drive under the influence of drugs or alcohol.

d It is _____ to stop or park at red curbs at any time.

e Only commercial vehicles are _____ to load at yellow curbs.

f All vehicles are _____ to stop at green curbs for a maximum of ten minutes.

g The following tips are _____ for tourists driving in the Bay Area.

2 Which sentences express: permission, advice, obligation, obligation not to do something?

3 Rephrase each extract as if you were speaking directly to the person.

4 What advice about driving would you give people visiting your country? Think about vehicle safety and general driving etiquette, as well as driving and parking laws.

3 Rewrite these sentences where necessary so they are true for your country.

1 Everyone has to have an identity card.

2 Smoking in restaurants and bars is forbidden.

3 You mustn't use mobile phones in public places like restaurants and museums or art galleries.

4 You are not allowed to go into a bar serving alcohol if you are under 18.

5 You have to buy a ticket before you get on a bus.

6 People from other countries do not need a visa to enter the country.

7 You have to pay for your tuition fees if you go to university.

8 You are not allowed to own a gun without a special licence.

4 Work in pairs. Ask your partner questions about the activities in the box, or other activities. Use *have to* in different tenses. Then complete sentences 1–8.

Examples *Do you have to work at the weekends?*
Did you have to use your English yesterday?
Will you have to work late tomorrow?

| work long hours |
| make a long journey to work |
| use your spoken English at work |
| send emails in English |
| use a computer a lot |
| get up early |
| do the housework |
| go abroad in business |
| make a lot of phone calls |
| do repairs around the house |

My partner

1 has to _____

2 doesn't have to _____

3 had to _____

4 didn't have to _____

5 has had to _____

6 hasn't had to _____

7 will have to _____

8 won't have to _____

City descriptions file. British English and American English

❶ What do you know about San Francisco? Look at the photographs to help you. Make notes under the headings in the box.

- Geography/climate
- Transport
- Culture/entertainment
- Eating/drinking
- Business/industry

❷ 1 Read the description of San Francisco. Add information to the five headings in **❶**.

2 Find places and things that are also in your town or city.

Examples *beach, skyscrapers, financial district*

3 Which places and things mentioned in the text are not in your town or city?

San Francisco

Situated on a 120-square-kilometre peninsula – bounded in the west by the Pacific Ocean, the north by the Golden Gate Strait, and the north-east by the Bay – San Francisco was once a small Spanish fishing village. It has now grown into a lively and cosmopolitan city and one of the main business and tourist centers in California. The population is over 800,000 in the city, with a total of nearly seven million inhabitants living in the wider metropolitan area. The climate is never too hot and never too cold – although it can get chilly and foggy at times.

Dramatic hills, stunning beaches, soaring skyscrapers, peaceful parks, and interesting architecture help to make San Francisco one of America's most visited cities. San Francisco is also a very safe and clean city. Tourism is the main industry, with visitors enjoying the famous tourist attractions such as the Golden Gate Bridge and Alcatraz, as well as the museums and art galleries, concert halls, and theaters. There is an extensive range of retail outlets in the shopping malls and streets of the city, and a wide variety of eating establishments, especially in the exciting ethnic neighborhoods such as China Town, North Beach (Italian), and the Mission (Mexican).

There are many other businesses in San Francisco. Although the 1990s boom of the dot com industries has now passed, the computer industry and new media in general are still big businesses, helped by the proximity of Silicon Valley. The financial district in downtown San Francisco is also full of banking, insurance, and other corporate enterprises.

The public transportation system makes all areas of the city accessible, and getting around is reasonably quick and cheap. There are buses, a subway system, and of course the famous cable cars. But probably the best way to experience the rich variety of this fascinating city is on foot.

small
foggy
cosmopolitan
hot
cold
dramatic
accessible
safe
stunning
famous
fascinating
peaceful
lively
extensive
interesting
exciting
quick
clean
chilly
cheap
soaring

3 What do each of the adjectives in the box describe in the text?

Example *small – fishing village*

4 Match these adjectives in the box with their opposites in the box in **3**.

| dirty | dangerous | dull | boring |
| noisy | warm | limited | expensive |

5 1 Look at these pairs of words. Which one is American English and which one is British English? Use an English–English dictionary to help you.

a downtown/city centre
b shopping mall/shopping centre
c pavement/sidewalk
d flat/apartment
e elevator/lift
f taxi/cab
g freeway/motorway
h gas/petrol

2 American English and British English spelling is sometimes different, e.g. *center* (AmE) and *centre* (BrE). Can you find any other examples of American English spelling in the San Francisco text?

3 Do you know any other differences between American English and British English?

6 Work in pairs. Describe the town or city where you live to each other. Use words and phrases in **2**, **3**, and **4**.

7 Look at the list of common questions asked by visitors when they are in a city for the first time.

- I'm only in the city for a day. What can I do?
- Where can I get the best view of the city?
- How do I get to (*name of famous attraction*)?
- Is there a discount travel pass?
- Who do I call for hotel reservations?
- What's the nightlife like?
- What type of food and restaurants do you recommend?
- Where are the main shopping areas?

1 Which of the questions do you think would be asked by a business visitor?
2 How would you reply to a business visitor to your city or town asking these questions? Role-play with a partner.

The outsourcing option – the way to save your company money

500 jobs lost as bank relocates call centre to India

1 Work in pairs. Look at the photograph and headlines.

1 What do you think is meant by 'international outsourcing'?
2 What is a *call centre*?
3 Why do some businesses have call centres based in other countries?
4 What good or bad experiences have you had phoning call centres?

2 Read the article and check your answers to questions 1 and 2 in **1**. Then answer these questions.

1 In which countries are call centres often based?
2 Why is the number of international call centres increasing?
3 What characteristics and skills does a good call centre operative need?
4 List the ways in which call centre operatives are helped to relate to callers from different countries.

Indians learn to be Brad and Britney

Elocution lessons are helping staff at call centres in India to lose their accents and make them more effective when speaking to customers from the UK and the USA.

Many western companies now use international outsourcing as part of their business operation. Outsourcing is when a company uses a different company, often in another country, to manage some of their business tasks, particularly telephone help and information lines – known as 'call centres'.

Most English-speaking countries outsource to call centres in countries like India, where English is spoken. India in fact accounts for 66% of international call centre outsourcing. But other countries, such as the Philippines, Sri Lanka, Mexico, Poland, Russia, and Romania, are also used by western companies.

Advances in technology, the falling cost of international phone calls, and the big differences in labour costs mean that international call centres are booming. It is estimated that soon there will be more than two million call centre operatives in India.

Call centre operatives have to be polite, friendly, and helpful and they need to be able to give information clearly and respond to customer questions. They also need to sympathize with callers and understand their problems. Call centres go to great lengths to make their staff sound like they are from the country of the person they are speaking to.

Zia Sheikh, head and co-founder of Infowavz International in Mumbai said, 'There are definitely challenges about bridging the culture gap between someone sitting in Denver and someone supporting them from India who's probably never travelled outside the country. We believe that it's important that the caller should feel like they're talking to someone next door. They mustn't know that the voice at the other end of the line is from the other side of the world.'

Staff are sometimes given Western pseudonyms to use such as 'Brad' or 'Britney' instead of their real names. They also watch films from the UK and US to learn about how people live their lives. One call centre operative, 'James', who has never been to the UK, attended a crash course in British culture. His course taught him that 'what English people like most is going to the pub, and they love horse racing and obviously football, and they like food such as puddings and fish and chips.'

Call centres also have clocks set to the time of the countries that are calling them so they know whether the caller has just got up, or is about to have dinner, or go out. They have regular weather reports, so that they can make conversation about the weather and other topics of small talk.

So the next time you phone to ask for information about train times or because you have a problem with your computer, you might be talking to someone on the other side of the world. But will you actually know?

③ Find words or phrases in the text that mean

1 the ability to speak clearly and correctly, especially in public.
2 a way of pronouncing words connected with the country, area, or social class that you come from.
3 progress or developments in something.
4 understand and share someone's feelings or problem.
5 make more effort than usual in order to achieve something.
6 new and difficult things that force you to make a lot of effort.
7 a name that you use professionally that is not your real name.
8 a course which gives you a lot of information in a very short time.
9 desserts, often sweet and heavy.

④ 🎧 **7.5** Listen to this discussion from a business meeting. Complete the table.

	Advantages	**Disadvantages**
1 companies		
2 home countries		
3 countries where call centres are located		

⑤ Work in groups. Give your own opinion of the advantages and disadvantages of call centres and international outsourcing in general. Compare your views with the other groups.

⑥ Work in groups. Produce a training guide for call centre staff dealing with callers from all over the world, with specific advice about callers from your country. Include the following areas:

A practical guide for call centre staff

- General advice on being polite and friendly, on how to answer the phone, and on how to address the caller.

- General advice on speech delivery, accent, and phone manner.

- Suitable pseudonyms to adopt when talking to people from particular countries (including your own).

- Topics for conversation and small talk. What would callers from your country want to talk about?

- Cultural differences. Are there any particular cultural differences that you think call centre operatives should be made aware of?

Compare your guide with other groups.

Giving talks and presentations

1 Work in groups. Make a list of what you need to do to give a successful talk or presentation.

2 Carol Hunt is a freelance consultant for NMP. She gives talks and presentations on a variety of subjects.

1 What is the title of her talk?
2 What do you think is meant by 'signposting language'?

NMP BUSINESS TRAINING SEMINAR   Carol Hunt

 Communication skills at work

Giving talks and presentations

- Preparation
- 'Signposting language'
- Delivery

NMP BUSINESS TRAINING SEMINAR   Carol Hunt

 Communication skills at work

Preparation: six key points

- Objectives
- Audience
- Content
- Organization
- Visual information
- Practice

---

3 Which of the six key points on Preparation do you think these questions refer to?

1 Who are you talking to?
2 What is the aim of your talk?
3 Is the talk clear and logical?
4 Have you practised giving the talk?
5 What is the important information to get across?
6 What do you want to achieve?
7 Have you checked the timing?
8 Can you use the visual display equipment correctly?
9 Are you using 'signposting language' that makes the talk easy to follow?
10 Are you showing too much information on the screen or slide?
11 What do they need to know?
12 Are you sure what you are saying is interesting?

4 **7.6** Listen to the first part of Carol Hunt's talk and check your answers in **3**.

5 Carol Hunt gives a handout on 'Signposting language'. Write the correct heading for each extract.

Introducing each section   Referring backwards and forwards
Referring to questions   Concluding
Summarizing a section   Referring to visual information
Introducing the topic   Referring to common knowledge
Dealing with questions   Checking understanding

Signposting language

1 _____

| This morning | I'm going to … (*talk about …*) |
| Today | I'd like to … (*describe …*) |

The aim of my presentation this morning is to … (*explain …*)

| I've divided my presentation into … | (*three parts*). |
| My talk will be in … | |

First,	I'd like to … (*give you an overview of …*)	
Second,	I'll	move on to …
Then		focus on …
After that,	we'll	deal with …
Finally,		consider …

2 _____

| Feel free to | interrupt me if there's anything |
| | you don't understand. |

If you don't mind, we'll leave questions till the end.

3 _____

So, let's start with … (*objectives …*)
Now let's move on to … (*the next part …*)
Let's turn our attention to … (*the question of …*)
This leads me to … (*my third point …*)
Finally … (*let's consider …*)

4 _____

That completes my … (*description of …*)
So, to summarize … (*There are five key points …*)

5 _____

I mentioned earlier … (*the importance of …*)
I'll say more about this later.
We'll come back to this point later.

6 _____

Is that clear?
Are there any questions?

7 _____

This screen shows … (*a diagram*).
If you look at this graph you can see …
What is interesting in this slide is …
I'd like to draw your attention to … (*this chart …*)

8 _____

As you know …
As I'm sure you're aware …

9 _____

That concludes my talk.
That brings me to the end of my presentation.
If you have any questions I'd be pleased/I'll do my best to answer them.
Thank you for your attention.

10 _____

That's a good point.
I'm glad you asked that question.
Can I get back to you on that later? I'm afraid I don't have … (*the information at present*).
I'm afraid I'm not the right person to answer that.

6 🎧 **7.7** Listen to the last part of Carol Hunt's presentation. Complete the key points about delivery on the screen.

NMP BUSINESS TRAINING SEMINAR   Carol Hunt

Communication skills at work

Delivery – key points

1 *nerves*
2 _____
3 _____
4 _____
5 _____

7 🎧 **7.7** Listen again. Make notes to help you remember what the presenter says about the five areas. Then compare notes with a partner.

8 Work in groups or individually.

1 Prepare a talk or presentation on a topic of your choice. Use the information in this section to think about how you will organize your talk – e.g. how many sections, what visual aids, what visual information systems, how to deal with questions, what signposting language to use.
2 Give your talk or presentation to the rest of the class.

UNIT 8
On a global scale

▼ AGENDA

▶ Arrangements and intentions:
Present Continuous, *be going to* +
infinitive, *will* + infinitive

▶ Money and finance file. Collocations

▶ Hosting a major event

▶ Types of business communication.
Texting

Language focus

1 What problem is illustrated in the photograph below? What can be done to solve problems like this? How can companies and businesses help?

2 Match the words in A with the definitions in B.

A	B
1 sanitation	a urgent request for something that is needed
2 hygiene	b system for keeping places clean
3 sustainable	c keeping things free from disease
4 voluntary	d removing human waste
5 appeal (noun)	e done willingly, not because you have to do it; unpaid
6 sewage disposal	f able to continue for a long time

3 Look at the information on WaterAid.

1 What are WaterAid's general aims?
2 Who are they trying to help?
3 What are their main sources of funds?
4 Which of the six aims for WaterAid Ethiopia do you think are most important?
5 Which of the statistics in the Ethiopia factfile do you find most surprising?

Vision and mission

WaterAid's vision is of a world where everyone has access to safe water and effective sanitation.

Our mission is

- to provide safe domestic water, sanitation, and hygiene education to the world's poorest people.
- to help local organizations set up low-cost, sustainable projects using appropriate technology that can be managed by the community itself.
- to influence the policies of key organizations such as governments.

WaterAid is independent and relies heavily on voluntary support. Over 70% of our funds come from individuals, businesses, appeals, and special events.

WaterAid Ethiopia

Ethiopia is one of WaterAid's areas of operation. Our aims are

- to improve water supply, sanitation, and hygiene.
- to raise awareness among local people.
- to work in both rural and urban areas.
- to establish a range of projects, run by on-site project managers.
- to work with local communities and local organizations.
- to continue work on data collection and surveys.

Ethiopia factfile

Capital:	Addis Ababa
Population:	68.6m
Population below poverty line:	44.2%
Life expectancy:	42 years
Water supply coverage:	24%
Sanitation coverage:	12%

4 🎧 **8.1** WaterAid is organizing a trip to Ethiopia for businesses which raise money for them. Listen to the first part of a meeting between a representative of WaterAid and the business delegates.

1 Complete the flight dates and times.

	Date	Time
Arrive Addis Ababa		
Return London		

2 Match the following itinerary arrangements with the correct date: 4th, 5th, 6th, 7th, and 8th March.

   a meet local community leaders
   b transfer to hotel, check in, reception at Government offices
   c meet *woreda* and *kebele* leaders, meet women's group
   d free day
   e travel to rural village in the east

5 🎧 **8.2** Listen to the second part of the meeting. Where are the group visiting on

   a 9th March   _____ harvesting project
   b 10th March   _____ scheme
   c 11th March   _____ building sewage disposal systems
   d 12th March   redevelopment project in _____ areas

6 🎧 **8.3** Listen again and complete the sentences.

1 **D2** Sorry, what time _____ the flight get into Addis Ababa?

   WA It _____ at 15.00 on the 4th, then _____ to the hotel, checking-in, and getting ready for the reception at the Government offices. You can see that it's _____ a tiring day. We're _____ anything on the 5th, so there's time to rest before the main itinerary.

2 **D1** Are we _____ any professional interpreters? My Human Resources department has a good contact if we need to take an interpreter.

   WA No, we're _____ interpreters – I'm afraid it's too expensive. We _____ local interpreters from our volunteers already working out there. I think _____ them good enough.

   D1 That's fine. I _____ contact our HR people.

3 **D2** Can I just ask about publicity – are we _____ a photographer for example?

   WA We're _____ a small TV crew and our own photographer for publicity and press coverage.

   D2 I don't know if you're interested, but _____ with my wife, who's a professional photographer. She's interested in doing the publicity shots if you want.

   WA Fantastic! In that case _____ leave our photographer behind. Are you sure it's OK?

   D2 _____ with her, but yeah I'm sure.

❼ Grammar quiz

Match these sentences from the listening in A with the descriptions in B.

A

1 The flight gets in at 15.00.
2 I'm going to send all the travel documents on to you.
3 I think you'll find them good enough.
4 A number of senior ministers are coming.
5 In that case we'll leave our photographer behind.
6 You can see that it's going to be a tiring day.

B

a A timetabled regular event in the future.
b A definite arrangement in the future.
c A planned intention (decision already made).
d A spontaneous decision (made at the time of speaking).
e A future prediction based on present evidence.
f A future prediction in general.

Identify the tense or form in each case (e.g. Present Simple, *be going to* + infinitive).

Arrangements and intentions: Present Continuous, *be going to* + infinitive, *will* + infinitive

Look at these sentences from the listening. Complete the rules and answer the question.

Present Continuous
- I'm **coming** with my wife, who's a professional photographer.
- We're **not doing** anything on the 5th.
- Unfortunately, the President of Ethiopia isn't available so he **isn't coming**.
- When **are** we **visiting** one of the projects?

be going to + infinitive
- You can see that it's **going to be** a tiring day.
- Are we **going to take** any interpreters?
- No, we're **not going to take** any interpreters.

will + infinitive
- In that case we**'ll leave** our photographer behind.
- That's fine. I **won't contact** our HR people.

- We use _____ for a future intention when the decision has been made in the past.
- We use _____ for a definite arrangement (one that is written in a diary for example).
- We use _____ for a spontaneous decision about a future action.
- The contracted form of *will* is _____.
- The negative (contracted) form of *will* is _____.
- How do we form questions for the Present Continuous and *be going to* forms?

 Pocket Book pp. 5–6

Practice

1 Choose the best verb form to complete the sentences.

1 A The flight *leaves/will leave* at 10, so what time *do you leave/are you leaving* for the airport?
  B I'm *booking/going to book* a taxi to pick me up at 8.

2 A You have to check in two hours before the flight.
  B I thought it was one. In that case, I'*ll book/I'm going to* book the taxi for an hour earlier.

3 A Can you bring me back a souvenir?
  B I'*m not having/I'm not going to have* much time for shopping, but OK, I'*ll try/I'm going to try*.

4 A What time *does/will* the return flight *land*?
  B Eight in the evening. *Do you meet/Are you going to meet* me?

2 Complete these sentences with the correct form of the verbs in brackets.

1 A Would you like to join the delegation to Ethiopia?
  B I'd love to, but I _____ (travel) to New York on an important business trip.

2 A Which airport _____ (fly) to?
  B JFK. I _____ (attend) a conference in a hotel near the airport, and the flight _____ (get in) at just the right time on the 4th.

3 A Are you _____ (have) any time to relax?
  B Probably not. After the conference I _____ (meet) clients on the 7th, 8th, and 9th.

4 A Did you know that our ex-boss _____ (be) in New York at the same time? He _____ (stay) at the Plaza.
  B No, I didn't know that. In that case I _____ (not go) there for a meal – I don't want to run into him when I'm on business!

3 Make new plans as a result of discovering these situations.

Example I haven't been paid. *I won't go out for dinner tonight.*

1 The email isn't working.
2 My phone bill is enormous.
3 My boss wants to see me now.
4 I've lost my dictionary.
5 All the tickets are booked for today's New York flight.
6 I can't start my car.

4 Work in pairs. Take turns to think of more examples for each question. Ask each other questions for more details.

1 What regular timetabled events are there in your country in the next year or two?

  Example *The President opens Parliament in November.*

2 What definite arrangements have you made for next week?

  Example *I'm flying to Paris on Friday.*

3 What intentions and plans do you have for next year?

  Example *I'm going to pass my English exam.*

Money and finance file. Collocations

1 Which of these methods of payment do you use? When do you use them? Do you use any others?

- cash
- credit card
- debit card

- cheque
- traveller's cheque
- bank-to-bank transfer

2 Which of these banking and insurance products and services do you use? Do you use any others?

- online banking
- mortgage
- loan
- pension

- home insurance
- car insurance
- investment advice
- foreign currency

3 One of these phrases is already complete. Complete the others with the correct preposition from the box. One phrase does not need a preposition.

back	*by*	for	off

1 pay *by* credit card or cheque
2 pay _____ a bill or invoice
3 pay _____ goods or services
4 pay _____ money you borrowed
5 pay _____ a loan or debt

4 Complete the sentences with the correct preposition from the box. Then decide if it is good advice or not.

back	by	for	from	in	into	off	on	out	to

1 Never lend money _____ a friend.
2 Never borrow money _____ a friend.
3 Always pay _____ any money you've borrowed as soon as possible.
4 If you take _____ a loan, make sure you pay it _____ on time.
5 Always pay _____ holidays _____ credit card.
6 Always choose a bank that pays interest _____ its accounts.
7 Always have your salary paid directly _____ your bank account.
8 If you get the chance, always invest _____ shares.

5 Look at the underlined words in the leaflet *Internet banking – at your fingertips*. Match them with the definitions.

1 give (money) back
2 put (money) into a bank account
3 instructions to your bank to make regular payments of the same amount from your account
4 taking money dishonestly
5 take (money) out of a bank account
6 secret Personal Identification Number
7 list of all the money going into and out of your bank account
8 the amount of money in your bank account
9 pieces of business done
10 money lent by your bank, so you can spend more than is in your account
11 the local office of your bank, where you keep your account
12 instructions to your bank to transfer money automatically from your account as a way of paying bills, etc. The amount is often different each time.

6 Read the leaflet *Internet banking – at your fingertips*. Answer the questions.

1 When is the Internet banking service open?
2 How much does it cost?
3 How can you be sure that the information is confidential and secure?

Internet banking – at your fingertips

With over two million customers, our Internet banking service is a safe and easy way to access your personal bank accounts at a time that suits you, seven days a week. And it's free. All you pay are your usual charges for accessing the Internet.

There is no need to open any new accounts. Internet banking is simply another way of accessing your existing ones. You'll still be free to call into your branch or phone us whenever you need to talk to someone in person. And you can of course withdraw or deposit money in the normal way.

You can:

- check your balance and recent transactions
- apply for a new overdraft or increase your existing one
- transfer money between your bank accounts
- pay money to another person's bank account
- print or download your online statement
- pay bills, such as credit card or utility bills
- set up, amend, or cancel standing orders
- order foreign currency or traveller's cheques
- view or cancel direct debits or standing orders.

And you can feel secure doing it, because we ensure that all details transferred between us remain confidential. We use industry-standard levels of security, protecting you against fraud. However, in the unlikely event of fraud, we will refund your money. Of course, as with PIN numbers, you must be careful to keep your security information secret at all times, especially when using shared PCs or those in public places.

7 Match verbs in A and nouns or phrases in B to make collocations. Sometimes more than one match is possible.

Example *check (your) balance*

A

print	amend	access
cancel	check	pay off
set up	pay	transfer
download	order	apply for
open		

B

bank account	loan
balance	foreign currency
money between accounts	statement
bills	standing order
overdraft	travellers' cheques

8 Complete the questionnaire by ticking the boxes.

Are you sensible with your money?

	Always	Often	Sometimes	Not very often	Never
1 I only use Internet banking on my private PC at home.	☐	☐	☐	☐	☐
2 I keep my password and PIN number secret.	☐	☐	☐	☐	☐
3 I check my bank statements regularly and keep my own personal record.	☐	☐	☐	☐	☐
4 I pay bills on time.	☐	☐	☐	☐	☐
5 I have direct debits or standing orders so that my bills are paid on time.	☐	☐	☐	☐	☐
6 I save some money every month.	☐	☐	☐	☐	☐
7 I keep to a weekly budget.	☐	☐	☐	☐	☐
8 I keep a good balance in my account.	☐	☐	☐	☐	☐
9 I clear my credit card balance at the end of every month.	☐	☐	☐	☐	☐
10 I make sure I'm getting the best possible interest rate on my savings.	☐	☐	☐	☐	☐

9 Compare your answers with your partner. Do you think your partner is sensible with money? Why/Why not? Can you give your partner any advice?

Hosting a major event

1
1 Has your city or country ever hosted a major event, e.g. the Olympic Games, a political summit?
2 What preparation is required to host such an event?
3 What changes or improvements to a city continue after the event has finished?

2 Use an English–English dictionary to check the meaning of these words.

> construction industry   environmentally friendly
> estimate   GDP   infrastructure   recession
> solar-powered   urban renewal   water conservation

3 Work in pairs, Student A and Student B.

Student A

1 Read about Barcelona.
2 Tell Student B about the effect of hosting the 1992 Olympic Games on Barcelona. Include information about

  a 2002
  b the recession
  c Barcelona's airport
  d 12.5 %
  e 12,500 new jobs
  f eight years
  g $8bn
  h $2.4bn

3 Student B will tell you about Sydney. Ask questions if you don't understand anything.

Barcelona

Barcelona enjoyed hosting the 1992 Olympics so much that 40,000 people gathered in the Montjuïc stadium in 2002 to celebrate the tenth anniversary of the Games. They had a lot to celebrate: it was not only a sporting triumph, it was also a lasting social and economic success. Despite a recession that lasted until the mid-1990s, Barcelona was able to grow, building on its Olympic achievement. The city used the Games to introduce an imaginative urban renewal plan that transformed its decaying industrial areas into the gorgeous seaside city which tourists and visitors love.

Barcelona's airport handled 2.9 million passengers in 1991; this figure has now risen to over 21 million. Tourism, which accounted for less than 2% of the city's pre-Olympic GDP, is now worth 12.5%. The increase in hotel beds as a result of the Games has produced 12,500 new jobs. Barcelona estimated that in eight years it had built infrastructure that would usually take fifty years. They invested $8 billion in a ring road, a new airport, a telecommunications system, and an improved sewage system. The filthy harbour and port area were transformed by a $2.4 billion waterfront development, with the two tallest towers in Spain, one a luxurious hotel, the other an office building.

Student B

1 Read about Sydney.
2 Student A will tell you about Barcelona. Ask questions if you don't understand anything.
3 Tell Student B about the effect of hosting the 2000 Olympic Games on Sydney. Include information about

   a 11%
   b the major beneficiaries
   c Homebush Bay
   d 137m Australian dollars
   e the athletes' village
   f the green and golden bell frog
   g Stadium Australia
   h recycled water

Sydney

Sydney, with the 2000 Olympics, put itself firmly on the tourist map. Tourism now accounts for nearly 5% of Australia's economy, and the number of visitors rose 11% in 2000. The major beneficiaries, other than tourism, were the convention and construction industries, and the 'eco-industry'. Many environmentally-friendly policies developed as a result of the Games. The Olympic Park was built on a disused industrial estate, Homebush Bay, which had been a salt mine, a brick factory, an arms depot, and a general waste dump. The government spent 137 million Australian dollars cleaning up chemical waste before they could begin construction. This included using plants to filter and feed on waste.

As well as the clean-up of Homebush, the construction programme included many environmental initiatives, such as the preservation of the endangered green and golden bell frog, which now has a population six times greater than before the Games. The main priority was energy and water conservation. The athletes' village was the world's largest solar-powered suburb and became ordinary homes after the event. Stadium Australia, the main arena, uses 30% less energy than conventional designs. The water is recycled from sewage, cutting drinking water consumption by 50%. Sydney's communications manager, Michael Bland, claimed that the city could be proud of its effort to conserve energy, water, and the environment while minimizing waste and pollution.

4 🎧 **8.4** Listen to part of a press conference given by a company of consultants describing their estimate of the income and expenditure if London hosts the Olympic Games. Answer the questions.

  1 Why have they not allocated much money for infrastructure improvements?
  2 How large is the new stadium going to be?
  3 What is the estimate for total expenditure?
  4 What is the final estimated profit figure?
  5 What other benefits are mentioned?

5 🎧 **8.4** Listen to the press conference again. Match the numbers in the box with the correct item on the income and expenditure account.

50m	127m
403m	500m
100m	679m
430m	810m
106m	325m
436m	864m

Expenditure	£	Income	£
Building of new facilities		Ticket sales	
Buying of land		Other direct revenue	
Staging the event		Contribution from the IOC*	
Security		Sponsorship and advertising	
Improving the team		Resale of land	
Unforeseen risks		Tourism and tax from jobs	
Total	1.69bn	Total	3.14bn

IOC = International Olympic Committee

6 Work in groups.

  1 Think of a city that you know well. Which of these events could be hosted there?

    • an international sporting event   • an international tourism convention
    • a meeting of world leaders   • any other event
    • a cultural festival

  2 Choose one of the events and plan what the city will need to do before, during, and after the event to make it successful.

  3 Discuss your plans and opinions with another group.

Types of business communication. Texting

Types of business communication

1 Work in pairs.

1 Which of these ways of communicating do you use at work? Do you use any other ways?

- face-to-face
- letter
- fax
- telephone
- memo
- text message
- email

2 What different situations do you use them for? Give examples.
3 Which do you use most?

2 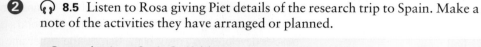 **8.5** Listen to Rosa giving Piet details of the research trip to Spain. Make a note of the activities they have arranged or planned.

Research trip to Spain 2–11 May

Place	Date	Activities
San Sebastián	2–4 May	_____
Seville	4–7 May	_____
Valencia	7 May?	_____
Barcelona	7/8–11 May	_____

3 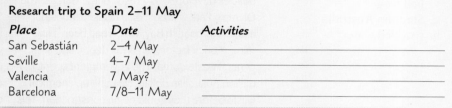 **8.5**

1 Listen to the conversation again. Complete the table with the type of communication used (e.g. phone message, email, etc.).

From	To	Message	Type of communication
Hotel	Rosa	confirm booking	
Rosa	Claire	check flight times	
Rosa/María	chef in San Sebastián	request for interview	
chef in San Sebastián	Rosa/María	accept request for interview	
Rosa	NMP	team feedback on visits	
Piet	Eric	invite for lunch	
Rosa	María	invite for lunch	

2 Which type of communication is not mentioned? Could it be used for any of the messages above?

4 **8.5** Listen to the conversation again. Complete the missing parts of extracts 1–4.

1
Well, _____ ᵃ in two weeks, on 2nd May. _____ ᵇ to San Sebastián first, so _____ ᶜ a flight to Bịlbao on the 2nd. In San Sebastián _____ ᵈ to interview the chef of one of Spain's top restaurants.

2
Then on the 4th, _____ ᵃ to Seville and _____ ᵇ until the 7th. _____ ᶜ to the bar where the custom of *tapas* began and _____ ᵈ a convent where traditional Spanish confectionery is made. If we have enough time, _____ ᵉ to Jerez de la Frontera and find out all about sherry production. From Seville either _____ ᶠ straight to Barcelona or _____ ᵍ to Valencia.

3
And on the 9th _____ ᵃ to spend the day visiting vineyards in the Penedés area of Catalonia, talking to cava producers. Then _____ ᵇ on Tuesday. I'm _____ ᶜ a full report on all the visits for the editorial and production team – _____ ᵈ you in of course.

4
I think she said she's out of the office all morning. I know, _____ ᵃ her and tell her where _____ ᵇ.

5 Work in groups. Take turns to describe a future arrangement, plan, or intention which may or may not be true. The other students can ask a maximum of six questions to guess if what you say is true or not.

Example **A** *I'm going to buy a new car next month.*
                 B *Really? What make are you going to buy?*

Texting

1 How often do you send or receive text messages? Have you ever sent any

  a in a work situation?   b in English?

2 Look at Rosa's text message to María, and María's reply.

If they speak to each other, how will they say the same messages?

3 Look at these abbreviations and symbols often used in informal text messages. What do you think they stand for?

1 asap	6 tmrw/2moro
2 b4	7 2nite
3 c u l8r	8 :)
4 gr8!	9 :(
5 r u coming?	

4 Convert these messages into text messages. Try to be as brief as possible.

  1 Shall we meet for a coffee at the Grand Café at 11 o'clock?
  2 Can you bring your laptop computer to work tomorrow?
  3 Are you coming to the seminar tonight?
  4 I need to talk to you urgently. Can you call me as soon as possible?

5 Write some messages of your own – either in full or as a text message. Get your partner to 'convert' them.

REVIEW UNIT B

This unit reviews all the main language points from Units 5–8. Complete the exercises. Use the Pocket Book for areas that you need to review again.

❶ Passives: Present Simple, Present Continuous, Present Perfect Simple, Past Simple, *Will* Future

1 Complete the description of the Social and welfare programme of Julie Voelckel's company. Use the correct tense and form of the verb in brackets. Be careful: five of the verb forms are active rather than passive.

Our Social and welfare programme _____¹ (introduce) ten years ago. A Social and welfare co-ordinator _____² (appoint), and since then the job _____³ (do) by four different people. The company _____⁴ (develop) the programme over the years. In the early days they _____⁵ (organize) reading groups and yoga classes, but recently lots of sports events _____⁶ (arrange). Last year I _____⁷ (play for) the company basketball team. We also go running regularly, and at the moment we _____⁸ (encourage) to take part in next year's marathon. We _____⁹ (take) on a ten-kilometre run every Friday by our fitness coach. All our training equipment _____¹⁰ (provide) by the company, and we _____¹¹ (give) time off to train. I enjoy it but I'm not very fast, so perhaps I _____¹² (not pick) for the final team next year, but I _____¹³ (support) my colleagues. The Social and welfare programme is a very important part of our working life. It's enjoyable and I _____¹⁴ (learn) new skills, but most of all we all feel that we _____¹⁵ (not treat) as just workers, but as people.

2 Write six questions about the programme based on the text. Use a range of tenses, some active and some passive.

Example *When was the programme introduced?*

❷ Past Simple, Past Continuous, Past Perfect

Work in pairs. Complete the sentences. Use the Past Simple of the verb in brackets. Then continue the sentence in two ways, using the Past Continuous and the Past Perfect.

Example *I felt* (feel) embarrassed at the wedding reception *because I was wearing jeans / I had forgotten to buy a present.*

1 When I _____ (leave) home this morning …
2 She _____ (choose) to work in another country because …
3 He _____ (write) a letter of apology to the client because …
4 When I _____ (begin) this course …
5 The company _____ (take over) one of it's competitors when …
6 They _____ (want) to take a break because …

❸ Modal verbs

Complete the table below with verbs from the box.

must
could
have to
don't have to
needn't
may
shouldn't
can
mustn't
should
might

1 Necessity/Obligation	2 No necessity/obligation	3 Necessity/Obligation <u>not</u> to do something
need to		is/are forbidden
is/are required	don't need to	is/are prohibited
4 Advice	**5 Possibility**	**6 Permission**
	can	
	may	
		is/are permitted
is/are recommended		is/are allowed

④ Arrangements and intentions: Present Continuous, *be going to* + infinitive, *will* + infinitive

Complete the sentences with the correct form of the verb in brackets.

1 I'm afraid I can't come to the conference. I _____ (fly) to Paris then.
2 According to the timetable, the train _____ (leave) at exactly 12.05.
3 I've decided I want to do that training course so I _____ (ask) the Human Resources Manager to send me.
4 The email's not working again! I _____ (have to) fax this document instead.
5 We can meet next Tuesday if you want. I _____ (give) a presentation in the afternoon, but I _____ (not do) anything in the morning.
6 I see from the schedule that you _____ (take) your holiday in August. In that case, I _____ (not take) mine until September.

For each sentence, ask for clarification.

Example   1 *Sorry? Where are you flying to?*

⑤ Gerunds and infinitives

be good at
enjoy
decide
like
would love
want
be used to
don't mind
be interested in
remember
manage
stop
look forward to

1 Write eight sentences about your personal attitude to work or study. Choose from the verbs in the box.

Example   *I'm quite good at organizing things.*

2 Ask your partner questions to find out if they have a similar attitude to work or study.

Example   *Are you good at organizing things?*

⑥ Leaving recorded messages, Requests and offers, Exchanging information, Texting

1 Write recorded messages to leave on someone's answerphone.
  • two requests to do something
  • two offers to do something
  • two asking for information
2 Work in pairs. Say the messages to each other. Make notes on the messages you receive.
3 Respond to the messages by leaving a return message.
4 Write a mobile text message for two of the messages.

⑦ Types of business communication, Giving talks and presentations

1 How many different types of communication have you used in the last week in your place of work or study?
2 Tell your partner about the different types and explain why you used each one.
3 Prepare a presentation on the advantages and disadvantages of different types of business communication.
4 Give the presentation to the other students.

⑧ Vocabulary test

Work in two groups, A and B. Write a vocabulary test to give to the other group. Choose ten of the words below. Write a sentence or phrase to help the other group guess the word.

Example   Word *ambitious*
             Clue   *keen to achieve things and do well*

ambitious ✓	delegate	GDP	initiative	air-conditioning
outsourcing	allocate	fitness centre	crash	crash course
cosmopolitan	updated	conservation	stressful	install
itinerary	direct debit	uptight	accessible	early retirement
infrastructure	volunteer	small talk	fund-raising	shopping mall

Language focus

1 Work in groups.

1 How will the world be different in the year 2030? Make predictions about these areas.

- energy supplies
- the relationship between different generations of people
- the role of women in society

2 Compare your predictions with other groups. How likely or unlikely do you think each other's predictions are?

2 Read the article '*What if ... ?*' – *Scenario 2030* about the UK.

1 Are any of your predictions in **1** mentioned in the article?
2 What other predictions are made?
3 How likely or unlikely do you think the predictions are?

'What if ... ?' SCENARIO 2030

Sky-trains, space travel for the masses, and food pills? Future predictions haven't always been accurate. But now governments and businesses are increasingly using 'scenario planning' to help them plan policies and make decisions.

1 What if the power fails?

SCENARIO

In 2030, the UK will have problems generating enough energy and will be dependent on imported sources of fuel. It is easy to imagine a terrorist attack on a major pipeline. As soon as the pipeline is attacked, energy supplies will drop by 40%. Emergency supplies will not be enough. The logical consequence is that by the evening rush-hour, whole sections of the country will lose power. There will be traffic gridlock, trains will stop, and airports will close. Essential services won't be able to move and lives will be put at risk. After the government introduces emergency powers, the army will control daily life.

COMMENT

'If we covered just part of the Sahara Desert with solar panels, it would provide all the world's electricity. The UK government has set a target of 30% renewable sources (such as solar energy and wind power) by 2030. It's true – if we don't meet that target, then we'll have to use either nuclear power or imports of natural coal, oil, and gas. The pipelines that carry some of these imports will certainly be at risk of terrorist attack as well as mechanical failure.'

Professor Rees Wilson, Institute of Energy Management

Time clauses

Read the examples and answer the questions. The time clauses are underlined.

- **As soon as** the pipeline **is attacked**, energy supplies will drop by 40%.
- **Before** the strike **is a week old**, the transport and financial systems will collapse.

1 Which tense is used after *as soon as* and *before*?
2 Find other examples of time clauses beginning with *when*, *after*, *as soon as*, and *(not) … until* in the article in ❷. Do they refer to present or future time?
3 Which tense is used in the time clauses?

1st Conditional

Read the examples and answer the questions.

- If we **don't meet** that target, then we**'ll have to use** either nuclear power or imports of natural coal, oil, and gas.
- If current trends **continue**, the number of elderly people **will** more than **double** in the next 25 years.

1 Do the sentences refer to present or future time?
2 Which form of the verb is used in the *if* clause?
3 Which form of the verb is used in the result clause?
4 Is the event in the *if* clause likely to happen?
5 What are the negative and question forms of 1st Conditional sentences?

2nd Conditional

Read the examples and answer the questions.

- If we **covered** just part of the Sahara Desert with solar panels, it **would provide** all the world's electricity.
- If women **had** control, there**'d be** fewer conflicts.

1 What is the uncontracted form of *there'd* in the second sentence?
2 Which form of the verb is used in the *if* clause?
3 Which form of the verb is used in the result clause?
4 Is the event or situation in the *if* clause (a) likely, or (b) unlikely or impossible?
5 What are the negative and question forms of 2nd Conditional sentences?

 Pocket Book pp. 3–4

2 What if the money runs out?

SCENARIO

In 2030, the number of retired people in the UK will be higher than the number of working people. The pressure on the Government to find money to provide the services and facilities needed by this ageing population will be enormous. There's a chance that the government might decide to increase taxes dramatically on the younger population. If this happens, there will be demonstrations, perhaps even riots. People will continue to protest until the government starts to listen. If they don't abandon their plans, a national strike will be called. Before the strike is a week old, the transport and financial systems will collapse. The country will be divided: generation against generation.

COMMENT

'The developed world is definitely getting older. If current trends continue, the number of elderly people will more than double in the next twenty-five years. At the same time, the number of workers expected to pay for everyone's pensions and services will increase by only 10%. It's a fact that governments will need to look for alternative sources of labour if they want to avoid conflict between the generations over tax and other financial issues.'

Sean Cope, UK Economics Forum

3 What if women have control?

SCENARIO

By 2030, it is possible that nearly all the senior positions at work will be taken by women. The leading female politicians of the day will help to end wars by dialogue and discussion. The world will be a more peaceful and co-operative place. Families, too, will be dominated by women, and men will have a smaller part to play in bringing up their children. Men could be marginalized and have fewer rights. But what if they decided to fight back against this situation? If men demanded a return of their rights, it could lead to a fresh gender battle. Men's groups would be formed to help protect the new 'weaker sex'.

COMMENT

'The 21st century will be the century of women. By 2030, when the workplace is "feminized", traditional working structures and hours will be a thing of the past. At the same time, I agree that families will change so there will be less need for men as soon as their biological function is complete. If women had control, there'd be fewer conflicts. Dialogue, discussion, and compromise would be the main features of international relations.'

Kim Harmer, Gender Studies Initiatives

Practice

1 Complete the sentences. Use *when, before, after, as soon as,* or *(not) … until.*

Example   I'll call you *as soon as I get to the airport.*

1 I'll send you an email _____ .

2 _____ , I'll explain what I'd like you to do.

3 I probably won't leave the office _____ .

4 _____ , I'll text you.

5 I need this document sent urgently. Will you be able to send it _____ ?

6 I won't book a table _____ .

7 Could you log off _____ ?

8 _____ , I'll get us some coffee.

2 Complete the sentences using the verbs in brackets. Decide whether the predictions are likely, or unlikely or impossible, and use 1st and 2nd Conditional forms as appropriate.

1 If fuel consumption _____ (increase), we _____ (need) to look for more energy resources.

2 If everyone in the world _____ (use) their cars less, the demand for petrol and gas _____ (fall).

3 If life expectancy in the West _____ (continue) to rise, there _____ (be) more older people.

4 If people _____ (work) until the age of 90, they _____ (not need) to have a state pension.

5 If women _____ (take) more positions of power in business, some traditional practices _____ (change).

6 If men _____ (disappear) completely, the human race _____ (become) extinct.

3 Work in pairs. Look at the events in the box. Decide

1 how likely or unlikely they are to happen to you in the future.
2 your course of action.

Make conditional sentences.

Examples *If it rains at the weekend, I'll go to the cinema.*
If I became a top politician, I'd …

rain at the weekend
become a top politician
see my friends tonight
get promotion
have a day off next week
have six months' holiday
oversleep tomorrow
buy a new car
get the offer of a job abroad
speak five languages

4   🎧 **9.1** Listen to an interview with three young working adults: Peter, Jola, and Yves. They are discussing three predictions. As you listen, tick to show how probable they think the predictions are.

Prediction		Definite	Likely	Possible	Unlikely	Definitely not
1 The family will disappear as the main social unit.	Peter					
	Yves					
2 People will move away from the parental home earlier.	Jola					
	Peter					
3 There will be cheaper, independent accommodation for young people and key workers (e.g. teachers and nurses).	Yves					
	Jola					

5 🎧 **9.2** Listen to the extracts and complete the different ways of expressing probability.

1 **Peter** I'm _____ . The family is far too important. I _____ that it will become a little less important – _____ – but it won't disappear.

2 **Yves** I'm not so sure. I _____ that the family as we know it will disappear – eventually.

3 **Jola** I _____ .

4 **Peter** Yes, I agree with Jola. There _____ a move away from the family for young working people – for financial reasons as much as anything.

5 **Yves** _____ . Society needs young people to work in the centres of cities, for example – in businesses, in hospitals, in schools and so on. I'm _____ cheaper accommodation for young working people, and key workers in general – maybe smaller and less comfortable, but affordable.

6 **Jola** I _____ , because, as Yves says, society needs it. But _____ to mean the end of the family.

6 Write the phrases they use to express different degrees of probability in the table.

Definite		
Likely		
Possible		
Unlikely		
Definitely not		

7 Work in groups. Discuss the following predictions using the phrases in **6**.

1 The family will disappear as the main social unit.
2 People will move away from the parental home earlier.
3 There will be cheaper, independent accommodation for young people and key workers.
4 We'll have to spend more time looking after our elderly relatives.
5 People will work from home more.
6 Employees will be expected to work a minimum of six days a week.

8 Decide what the results will be if the predictions in **7** come true. Use the 1st or 2nd Conditional as appropriate.

Examples (5) *If people work from home more, there will be less need to commute to work, and the roads and transport system will be better.*
(6) *If employees were expected to work a minimum of six days a week, they would go on strike.*

9 Work in groups.

1 Think of possible future events in your place of work or study. Choose some likely and some unlikely events. Think about new developments, building improvements, technology, staff changes, relocation, training, exams, etc.
2 How will/would you react if these events happen/happened?

Examples *I think it's likely that my company will open a branch in another country. If they do, I'll …*
I doubt if I'll pass my exams. If I did, I'd …

Phrasal verbs. Dictionary skills (2)

Phrasal verbs (also called multi-word verbs) consist of two, or sometimes three, words. The first word is a verb and it is followed by an adverb (*put away*) or a preposition (*look after*) or both (*put up with*). The adverbs and prepositions are sometimes called particles.

① Work in pairs. Read the instructions for a first-time computer user. What do you think the underlined phrasal verbs mean?

Getting started

1 First of all, check you have <u>plugged in</u> all the connections in the correct colour-coded sockets. Then <u>turn on</u> the power. 'Matt Mouse', the on-screen computer assistant, will <u>come up</u> on your screen.

2 Matt provides simple tutorials where you can <u>find out</u> about the different functions of your computer. He'll show you how to <u>set up</u> a password, which you will need every time you <u>log on</u>. Remember, if you write your password anywhere, do it in a secret way so that no one else can <u>work it out</u>.

3 If you've got a report to <u>write up</u> or a memo to type, Matt will show you how to do it, how to save it, and how to <u>print it off</u>. If you want to use the Internet, Matt will also show you how to <u>set up</u> an email address and how to download information and files. You'll be shown how to send an email, and attach documents.

It couldn't be easier! And if there's a problem you can't <u>sort out</u> with the help of Matt, or if your computer <u>breaks down</u>, then you can always call our 24-hour helpline. Our free mouse mat has all our details on it – so you won't need to waste time <u>looking up</u> our number.

② Match the phrasal verbs in **①** with the definitions below.

1 find the answer
2 appear
3 deal with a problem
4 connect to an electricity supply
5 transfer from computer to paper
6 search for information in a book

7 establish for the first time
8 write something in a final form
9 move the switch to start
10 discover information
11 stop working
12 type your password to start

③ Which of the phrasal verbs from the instructions in **①** can take an object, and which of them can't?

④ Read the extracts from the *Oxford Advanced Learner's Dictionary*. Answer the questions.

1 Which verb has two particles?
2 Which verb does not take an object?
3 Do you know another meaning for *take off*?
4 What do you think the symbol ↔ means?
5 Which of the example sentences is in the passive?

'**come across sb/sth** to meet or find sb/sth by chance: *I came across children sleeping under bridges.* ◊ *She came across some old photographs in a drawer.*

,**put sth↔'off** to change sth to a later time or date: *We've had to put off our wedding until September.*

,**take 'off 3** (of an idea, a product, etc.) to become successful or popular very quickly or suddenly: *The new magazine has really taken off.*

,**get 'on with sb** to have a friendly relationship with sb: *She's never really got on with her sister.*

,**take sb↔'on 1** to employ sb: *to take on new staff* ◊ *She was taken on as a trainee.*

(Extracts based on *Oxford Advanced Learner's Dictionary* 7th edition 019 431 6068 ©2005)

Phrasal verbs which take an object

Type 1 Phrasal verbs with an object which has two possible positions ('separable')

- Did you **take on** any new staff?
- Did you **take** any new staff **on**?

When the object is a pronoun (*it/me/her/them*, etc.) only one position is possible.

- Did you **take** him **on**?
- ~~Did you take on him?~~

Type 2 Phrasal verbs with an object which has one position only ('inseparable')

- I came across an old friend.
- ~~I came an old friend across.~~
- I came across him.
- ~~I came him across.~~

How do the dictionary extracts show if the object is separable or inseparable?

 Pocket Book p. 10

5 Match the phrasal verbs in A with suitable objects in B.

A	B
1 take on	a a new receptionist
2 put off	b your holidays
3 come across	c my new colleagues
4 get on with	d an old diary
5 look after	e a difficult decision
6 look forward to	f my sister's children

6 Build short question and answer dialogues using the phrasal verbs in **5**.

Example A *Has your company taken on any new staff recently?*
B *Yes, we've taken on a new Sales Assistant, Lisa Kitano.*
A *When did you take her on?*

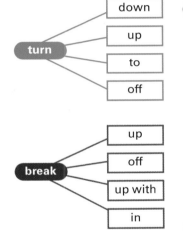

7 Complete the sentences with the correct form of the phrasal verbs below. Check the meaning in a dictionary.

1 On my first day at work I was completely lost. I didn't know who to _____ for help.
2 I was talking to my boss on my mobile when I went into a tunnel and he started to _____.
3 The door of my flat was damaged. Someone had _____ and stolen my TV.
4 I didn't do very well at the interview, so they _____ me _____.
5 I was so late that the meeting was almost over when I eventually _____.
6 I started giving my presentation, but suddenly _____ when I realized that I didn't have my notes.
7 I _____ the computer by mistake and lost all the work I'd done.
8 I _____ my partner last week. We were just about to go on holiday together.

8 Have any of the situations in **7** happened to you? Change the sentences so that they are true for you. Tell your partner about the situation and what happened. Ask each other questions to find out more details.

Pronunciation

1 🎧 **9.3** Listen to the examples. Notice the stress on the adverb/preposition of a phrasal verb.
a My car has broken dówn.
b We've put the meeting óff.

2 🎧 **9.4** Listen to the sentences. Mark the adverbs/prepositions that are stressed.

1 What time do you usually get up?
2 Did you turn on the TV?
3 Shall I turn it off?
4 Could you fill in this form?
5 They've managed to put the fire out.
6 Has the plane taken off?
7 I've just sorted out the problem.
8 What time did they set off?

Complete the rules. Write *stressed* or *unstressed*.

- The adverb/preposition of a phrasal verb which doesn't take an object is _____.
- The adverb/preposition of a phrasal verb which takes an object is _____ when it is separated from the verb, and _____ when it is not separated.

3 🎧 **9.4** Listen again. Repeat each sentence twice quietly to yourself after the tape.

Urban living

1 Work in groups.

1 Look at the photographs. What problems do you associate with urban living? Can you add any to the list?
- crowded living conditions
- not enough services and facilities (e.g. health care and schools)
- high rents for businesses
- inadequate sanitation
- shortage of affordable accommodation for key workers

2 Do any of these problems occur in your town or city?

2 Work in pairs.

1 Describe the place where you live to your partner, e.g. the kind of accommodation, the number of rooms, the size of the rooms, any special features.

2 Which of these features do you think
  a you must have
  b it would be nice if you had
  c you can live without?

- a bed
- a shower
- a bath
- high ceilings
- a balcony with a nice view
- plenty of natural light

- well-insulated walls
- a large kitchen
- modern furniture and fittings
- polished wooden floors
- space to entertain friends (e.g. for a dinner party)

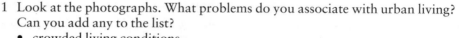

3 Look at this plan of a 'microflat', which provides accommodation in a city centre.

1 What rooms and features are there?
2 Which type of person do you think it is suitable for?
3 Would you like to live in it?

4 Before reading the article *Living in a shop window*, discuss who you think would live in a shop window and why.

Now read the article and answer the questions.

1 Where is the microflat?
2 Which type of person is the microflat designed to help?
3 Which of the features in **2** does the microflat have?

Living in a shop window

A 24-year-old bank clerk has begun a week-long stay in a 'microflat' specially constructed in a shop window on London's Oxford Street. A small crowd cheered as Warren Bevis arrived, suitcase in hand, for his experiment in cheap inner-city living. 'I'm really looking forward to living here,' he announced cheerfully.

The event is aimed at promoting a way of allowing young people and key workers to beat rising real estate prices. 'There's enough space for Warren to invite friends round for a dinner party,' said Richard Conner, of Piercy Conner, architects of the flat. 'He can even put a friend up for the night if he wants!'

Organizers insist that the living window-display in Selfridges store is not another reality-TV show. 'This sort of micro-living has been happening in countries like Japan for several years, but it hasn't happened here before. The aim is to help young professionals get a foot on the property ladder,' Conner told Reuters on Monday. 'The microflat is about two-thirds of the size of the average London flat. But everything's been resized so it doesn't feel very small,' he said of the 32-square-metre flat.

Features include a double bedroom, a tiny pod with a toilet and shower, some storage space, and a kitchen/living room with access to a small balcony. Ceilings are high (2.8 m) to introduce natural lighting and a feeling of space, the walls are well-insulated to keep heat in and noise out, and the interiors are attractively fitted with the latest fashions and styles.

The project will run for a fortnight and Bevis will be replaced after a week by a young woman, Hélène Cacace, who also wants to move to London but cannot afford the high house prices. The price of the flat will be about a quarter of an ordinary one-bedroom flat.

Onlookers were divided on the attractions of living in a shop window. Marka Peake, 14, waited two hours to see the flat revealed – with its glistening stainless steel kitchen and polished wooden floors. 'It's cool. I'd love to do it if I was sure you couldn't be seen in the bathroom,' he said. Student Corine Smith wasn't so convinced. 'Do I want to live in a glass box? Twenty-four hours a day – eating, sleeping, and washing in front of the whole of Oxford Street? No way,' she said.

But, who knows – it may be the answer to housing problems for lots of young working people in cities throughout the world.

5 Read the article again and complete the table.

	Who are they?	What's their opinion of the microflat?
1 Warren Bevis		
2 Richard Conner		
3 Hélène Cacace		
4 Marka Peake		
5 Corine Smith		

6 Work in groups and discuss these questions.

1 Is there a problem finding enough affordable accommodation for young working people in the cities of your country?
2 Would the microflat solution be a good idea in your country?
3 What other ways of solving city centre accommodation problems can you think of?

Writing emails

1 Work in pairs.

1 Have you ever written emails in English? If so, what problems did you have?
2 What are the similarities and differences between the language used in emails, letters, and phone communication?

2 Look at the phrases in the box.

1 Are they from an email, a letter, or a phone conversation? (Note they could be from more than one.)
2 Are they formal, informal, or neutral?
3 Are they used at the start or the end of the email?

Dear Rosa	It was good to talk to you the other day.
Hi Eric	I can't talk to you right now.
See you later.	Bye.
Yours sincerely	Kind regards
OK, I'll see you soon.	Dear Mr van Els
Is that you Claire?	I look forward to hearing from you.
Cc. Marketing Manager	I'm looking forward to seeing you at the weekend.
Get back to me asap.	

3 Read the email from Rosa Lanson to María Ferrando concerning her research trip to Spain.

1 What is the purpose of the email?
2 Who else will read the email?
3 What information does Rosa want from María?

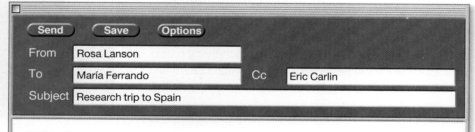

Send	Save	Options		
From	Rosa Lanson			
To	María Ferrando		Cc	Eric Carlin
Subject	Research trip to Spain			

Hi María

It was good to see you for lunch the other day.

I thought I'd just give you a few details of our itinerary, in case you've got any last-minute suggestions.

- 2nd May – San Sebastián: interview the chef we wrote to

- 4th May – Seville: *tapas* bar, convent where confectionery made (possibly visit Jerez)

- 7th May – Valencia?: try *paella valenciana*

- 8th May – Barcelona: meet your friend; visit *tapas* bars and vineyards

- 11th May – return

Can you forward me the contact details of your friend in Barcelona? Also, do you have any idea what she might like as a present?

Could you get back to me asap? We've only got a few days left!

Regards

Rosa

4   Read the list of email guidelines.

1   Identify examples of good practice in Rosa's email to María.

Email guidelines

▶ Clearly state the purpose of the email

▶ Make sure the subject line is updated each time you reply

▶ Copy in any relevant people

▶ Don't use capitals (it's like shouting)

▶ Personalize the greeting and reply in the same style

▶ Get to the point quickly (keep social 'chat' brief)

▶ Use short sentences

▶ Make sure grammar and spelling are accurate

▶ Abbreviations are acceptable (if you're sure the reader understands them)

▶ Use bullet points and headings

2   Are the guidelines the same in your country and your language?

5   Work in pairs. Write the following emails.

1   The Travel agent to Rosa, confirming details of a flight change (and where to collect the tickets at the airport).
2   Rosa to Eric, arranging where to meet for the trip to the airport.
3   Rosa (in Spain) to her husband, Colin, telling him how the trip is going.

6   Work in groups of four or five. Sit in a circle. You are going to write short emails from Rosa Lanson to some of the following people or companies:

- Piet van Els
- Eric Carlin
- a restaurant or food producer in another country
- a travel agent
- the production department of NMP
- a friend of Rosa's
- the owner of a specialist food shop

1   Choose one of the people and start an email from Rosa related to the subject of 'The food and drink project'. Only write the headings (*From, To, Date, Cc, Subject*).
2   Pass your email to the person on your left. Write the next stage of the email you receive from the person on your right (greeting and social chat, if appropriate).
3   Continue passing the emails round, adding one stage at a time in the following order: the purpose of the email, the main message (including bullet points), any questions you have, a quick closing summary and final 'signature'.
4   The last person to receive each email should check it, and then put it up on the wall for other groups to read.

UNIT 10
Transitions

Language focus

1 Look at the photographs.

1 What happened in Russia in 1991?

2 What do you know about economic and political developments in Russia since 1991?

2 Match the words in A with the definitions in B.

A		B	
1	co-operative	a	official document that shows permission to do, own, or use something
2	entrepreneur	b	business owned and run by the staff
3	devaluation	c	supplies of coal, oil, wood, etc.
4	market economy	d	reduction in value, e.g. when a currency's exchange rate falls
5	bureaucracy	e	economic system based on the principle of buying and selling goods for profit
6	shopping mall	f	(AmE) a group of shops under one roof, closed to traffic
7	natural resources	g	a complicated system of official rules and ways of doing things
8	licence	h	a person who makes money by starting a business

The 'second Russian revolution'

In a recent survey of the Forty richest people aged under 40, five of the ten richest people came from Russia. This may seem surprising for a country that spent most of the last century under communist rule. But anyone who has been following developments in Russia since the fall of communism in 1991 won't be too surprised.

Even before 1991 it was legal for people to start private companies and co-operatives. Since then the values of capitalism and a market economy have been emerging. In the mid-1990s, Russia's vast state oil and mining companies were sold off and many young entrepreneurs took the opportunity to start successful businesses. These companies have now expanded into other areas of industry, such as banking, telecommunications, retail, and the arts.

At the same time, the number of smaller businesses has increased dramatically. More money has been coming into the economy. The devaluation of the rouble after the 1998 economic crisis actually helped to promote a mini-boom. Real wages fell, which encouraged small enterprises to expand. Imports became too expensive for the average Russian, so local production increased. As a result, a new middle class has emerged with money to spend on consumer goods. It's all part of the new market economy.

International companies have also been investing in Russia since the fall of communism. Companies like McDonald's, Rolls Royce, Ferrari, and IKEA have opened businesses such as shops, showrooms, and factories. Russian entrepreneurs themselves have made significant investments outside Russia – for example Roman Abramovich, who has invested some of his fortune in the London football club Chelsea.

As one observer put it: 'The speed of what's been happening in Russia since 1991 is remarkable – in many ways they've seen a "second Russian revolution".' ■

3 Read the article *The 'second Russian revolution'* and answer the questions.

1 When did the communist system fall in Russia?
2 When did private companies and co-operatives become legal?
3 What event in the mid-1990s helped young entrepreneurs to emerge?
4 What effect did the devaluation of the rouble have in 1998?
5 Which international companies have invested in Russia?
6 Can you name one Russian entrepreneur who has invested outside Russia?
7 Do you think the changes represent a 'second Russian revolution'?

4 🎧 **10.1** Listen to the first part of an interview with Lennart Dahlgren, the General Director of the Russian section of the Swedish furniture and home furnishings company IKEA. Complete the factsheet.

1	**IKEA started in Russia:**	*1998*
2	**First store opened:**	_____
3	**Number of stores at present:**	_____
4	**Year 1 sales:**	_____
5	**Resources from Russia:**	*wood,* _____ ,
		_____

5 🎧 **10.1** Listen again and complete extracts 1–4.

1 Mr Dahlgren, IKEA _____ a in Russia for several years, and you arrived at the start. How long _____ b in Russia?

I _____ c since 1998. That's when IKEA _____ d operations in Russia.

2 How many stores _____ a?

We _____ b five stores so far, and we _____ c several large shopping malls in the last few years.

3 Consumer demand _____ a steadily since we _____ b the first store.

4 We _____ a the percentage of our global supply that comes from Russia for a number of years. We _____ b several factories throughout Russia – near St Petersburg, Moscow, and Karelia.

6 🎧 **10.2** Listen to the second part of the interview.

1 What two problems has IKEA faced in Russia?
2 Who are IKEA's management training programmes designed to help?

7 🎧 **10.2** Listen again and complete extracts 1 and 2.

1 But bureaucratic problems _____ fewer recently. For example, the Government _____ the number of licences that are needed for a new company to set up.

2 However, we _____ a number of things in the time we _____ here. We _____ management training programmes to help new Russian entrepreneurs. We _____ to show how a modern company has to work to survive in the international market.

8 Grammar quiz

Read these sentences from the article and the interview, and answer the questions below.

a Young entrepreneurs took the opportunity to start successful businesses.
b Imports became too expensive for the average Russian.
c Consumer demand has been growing steadily.
d We've opened five stores so far.
e Why do you think it's been successful?

1 Which sentences refer to a period of time completely in the past?
2 Which sentences refer to a period of time from the past to the present?
3 What are the full forms of *We've opened* and *it's been* in sentences d and e?
4 Match the verbs in the sentences with the tenses: Past Simple, Present Perfect Simple, Present Perfect Continuous.

Present Perfect Simple and Present Perfect Continuous

Read the sentences and answer the questions.

a International companies **have** also **been investing** in Russia since the fall of communism.
b Companies like McDonald's, Rolls Royce, Ferrari, and IKEA, **have opened** businesses such as shops, showrooms, and factories.
c How long **have you been living** in Russia?
d I've **been living** here since 1998.
e How many stores **have** you **established**?
f We've **opened** five stores so far, and we've also **built** several large shopping malls in the last few years.
g Bureaucratic problems **have been getting fewer** recently.
h The government **has reduced** the number of licences that are needed for a new company to set up.

1 Which sentences focus on the result or completion of the action?
2 Which sentences focus on the activity itself?
3 Which sentences are in the Present Perfect Simple and which are in the Present Perfect Continuous?
4 Find other examples of the Present Perfect Simple and Present Perfect Continuous in the article, and in **10.1** and **10.2** on p. 140. Why is the simple or the continuous form used?

 Pocket Book pp. 12–13

Time phrases

Complete the gaps in the following groups of time phrases with *for*, *in*, or *since*.

1 _____	the fall of communism
	1998
	we opened the first store

| 2 _____ | several years |
| | a number of years |

| 3 _____ | the mid-1990s |
| | the last few years |

Find other time phrases in the text and interview extracts.

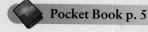 Pocket Book p. 5

Practice

❶ Complete the sentences with either the Present Perfect Simple or the Present Perfect Continuous of the verb in brackets.

1 How long have you _____ (work) in China?
2 I _____ (work) here for two years.
3 Our company _____ (invest) in China for several years.
4 We _____ (open) ten shops in Beijing and Shanghai, but we _____ (not move) into southern China.
5 You look tired. What have you _____ (do)?
6 I _____ (write) a report all day.
7 Have you _____ (finish) the report?
8 Not yet. I _____ (write) about two-thirds.
9 He _____ (study) accounts management for six months.
10 He _____ (not learn) how to do spreadsheets.
11 Has the computer _____ (crash) again?
12 It _____ (do) that all week.

❷ Complete the following article. Use the most appropriate tense of the verb in brackets: Past Simple, Present Perfect Simple, or Present Perfect Continuous.

The return of the young Russians

In the 1990s, as many as one million young Russians _____ ¹ (go) abroad to look for better opportunities. But in the new millennium, people like Pavel Doshlov and Tatyana Leonova _____ ² (decide) to return to the 'new' Russia.

Pavel is a 28-year-old economist, currently living in Budapest.

'I'm back in Russia on holiday at the moment. I _____ ³ (travel) abroad in 1996 to study. I _____ ⁴ (see) a lot of the world. I _____ ⁵ (live) in China, England, and Hungary. I _____ ⁶ (work) in Budapest for the last year. But since I _____ ⁷ (arrive) here a month ago, I _____ ⁸ (make) a decision to move back to Russia. So much _____ ⁹ (change) since I lived here before. It's exciting, dynamic, and there's so much opportunity.'

Tatyana, aged 29, is a sales manager for Nestlé's Moscow region.

'I _____ ¹⁰ (come back) two years ago and I _____ ¹¹ (not regret) it. I _____ ¹² (work) for Nestlé for two years. I'm very happy with my job and my standard of living. I _____ already _____ ¹³ (have) three promotions, and recently I _____ ¹⁴ (move) into an apartment in the centre of Moscow. Last year, I _____ ¹⁵ (win) an award as Young businesswoman of the year!'

❸ 1 Work in groups. Prepare a questionnaire on work and jobs, or studies. Write six questions to find out about other student's experiences.

Examples *How many different jobs have you had?*
What books have you been studying recently?

2 Use the questionnaire to interview a student from another group.
3 Report back to the class.

Job descriptions file. Collocations. Word-building

1 Work in pairs. Discuss the questions.

1 Do you enjoy your job? What keeps you motivated?
2 How can employers motivate their staff?

2 Read the article *Morale boosting*. Find ways in which staff can be motivated.

Example *create a sociable environment*

Morale boosting

A motivated workforce is a great business asset that can help you get ahead of the competition. Consider what motivates your staff. This could be the opportunity for new challenges. You may need to create a more sociable environment or encourage a feeling of satisfaction for a job well done and recognition by peers.

Initially, some people may show resistance to change. But this will disappear if you explain why you are changing things and if you make it clear what your expectations are and the contributions you are looking for from your employees.

There are some particular ways you can do this. People enjoy trying to reach a goal or exceed a target. However, goals and targets must be agreed with the employee, not imposed from above. There should also be a clear reward associated with achieving the goal. This might be public praise for a job well done, promotion to a more senior role, or a pay bonus.

Regular feedback is essential. This could be formal appraisal sessions, as well as informal comment on current work and achievements. Criticism should not be avoided if it is necessary. Staff who feel that one individual is getting away with poor performance can quickly become demotivated. Dismissing persistent poor performers generally boosts the morale of co-workers.

Bonus schemes can be set up in ways that link final pay to individual or team performance. To be effective, goals must be clearly defined, achievable but not too easy, and set for specified periods. Bonuses are particularly relevant for sales-related roles. Some employees may be highly motivated by basic pay if there is a high bonus element. In general, staff need to believe that the salaries paid to themselves and colleagues are fair.

3 Does your company, or a company you know, use any of these techniques? If so, are they successful? If not, do you think they could be successful at your company?

4 Make the verbs in the box into nouns by adding the appropriate suffix: *-ment*, *-tion*, *-ance*, or *-al*. Write the nouns in the correct columns in the table. Check meanings and spellings in a dictionary.

agree	commit	disappear	expect	perform
appear	contribute	dismiss	explain	promote
appraise	define	encourage	improve	resist
assist	develop	establish	pay	satisfy

-ment	-tion	-ance	-al

Pronunciation

1 🎧 **10.3** Listen to the different stress patterns of the three words.

• ● •   • ● • •   • • ● •

a performance   b encouragement   c satisfaction

2 🎧 **10.4** Mark the stress pattern of the following words. Write *a*, *b*, or *c*.

1 appearance _____
2 definition _____
3 development _____
4 dismissal _____

5 establishment _____
6 expectation _____
7 explanation _____

8 improvement _____
9 promotion _____
10 resistance _____

3 🎧 **10.4** Listen again and say each word twice quietly to yourself.

4 What do you notice about the stress pattern of the words that end in *-tion*?

5 Are there any other patterns in the way these nouns are stressed? Look at the other words in **4** to help you.

5 Complete the sentences with one of the nouns from the table in **4**.

1 I want to feel I'm doing something useful, so job _____ is important for me.
2 I want to progress in my career, so I want a job with opportunities for _____ .
3 I sometimes lack confidence, so any _____ my managers and colleagues can give me is very important.
4 I want to find out what my managers think of my performance, so I think a staff _____ scheme is very important.

6 1 Make the nouns in the box into adjectives by adding an appropriate suffix. Choose from *-able*, *-ing*, *-y*, *-ous*, *-ful*. Check the meaning and spelling in a dictionary.

2 Mark the stress pattern of each adjective.

adventure
challenge
danger
health
profit
resource
reward
success
value
wealth

7 1 Complete the table.

Verb	Noun	Adjective
achieve	*achievement*	*achievable*
compete		
fulfil		
motivate		
recognize		

2 Mark the stress pattern of each word. Then check in a dictionary.

8 Match the words in A and B to make compounds and collocations.

A	B
full-time	experience
annual	employment
careers	pay
flexible	workforce
job	appraisal
keyboard	hours
motivated	advice
profit-related	satisfaction
formal	salary
work	skills

9 Work in groups.

1 List as many positive job/career characteristics as you can.

   Examples *new challenges, regular feedback, profit-related pay*

2 In your opinion, what are the five most important characteristics of a job?

Getting your ideal job

❶ Read the quotes from Clare and Albert.

1 What jobs do they have?
2 Why do they like their jobs?

Do you have your ideal job?

Clare and Albert think they do.

Clare Montgomery, from Scotland:

'I'm the marketing manager for a big international company. I love my job – I get to use my training, travel, and I meet people from all over the world. I love working with people from other cultures, and understanding their way of doing business. I like winning new clients – I've signed three big contracts this year already!'

Albert Lerus, from France:

'I worked as a chef in a successful restaurant until 2002. That's when I won the lottery. But I didn't want to stop working. Instead, I bought the restaurant from my boss and I've been running it ever since. I've also opened some other restaurants. I'm still a chef and I still do everything in my business. My life is cooking. I couldn't be happier.'

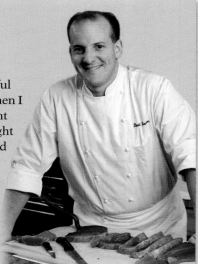

❷ Work in pairs. Answer the questions about your job.

1 Have you been doing interesting and exciting things over the last year?
2 Have you achieved everything you wanted to over the last year?
3 Do you want to be doing the same job in five years' time?
4 Is everything exactly how you want it in your job?

❸ Read the title and opening quotation from an article giving careers advice on finding your ideal job. What advice and information do you think the article will give on the following questions?

1 What do you want work to do for you?
2 What do you have to offer?
3 Where can you look for your ideal job?
4 What's involved in the application process?

❹ Read the article and check your answers in **❸**.

Finding your ideal job – it's all about

Firstly, what do you want work to do for you?

Be prepared to ask yourself deep and direct questions about what you really want from a career. Right now, you might be thinking that all you want is a big salary or to do something worthwhile. But is that really what will motivate you on a daily basis?

Looking for a career is like looking for a new partner – your life goals need to match. Ask yourself what you want

from life. You will need to analyse yourself closely: put yourself and your lifestyle preferences under the microscope. Think about what you enjoy doing the most with your time. Take a look around you – note down particular jobs and fields that inspire you.

Secondly, what do you have to offer?

Any sales rep will tell you that you have to know your product inside out to sell it effectively. In job-hunting, the product is YOU. You need to identify

your strengths and weaknesses. Asking close friends can be one way, but you have to be sure they're being honest. Think about achievements and successes you've had, and analyse what you did to make them happen. Do the same for failures and disappointments. Decide if any of your weaknesses will get in the way of your perfect job. If they will, then set about addressing your weaknesses immediately.

5 Explain the meaning of these expressions from the article.

1 do something worthwhile
2 put your lifestyle preferences under the microscope
3 know your product inside out
4 set about addressing your weaknesses immediately
5 look at the bigger picture
6 seize the opportunity
7 tailor your CV
8 first and foremost

6 Work in pairs. Discuss the questions and advice in the article, and try them out on each other.

Examples   *What do you enjoy doing most with your time?*
           What achievements and successes have you had?

7 Work in pairs.

1 What was the last interview you had?
2 What type of questions and tasks were you given?

8 🎧 **10.5** Listen to the first part of an interview with Rob Yeung, a business psychologist, talking about how to succeed at job interviews. Answer the questions.

1 How have job interviewers changed recently, according to Rob?
2 What does he say is the purpose of each of the following interview questions, and how should you answer them?
   a Could you tell me what sort of animal you'd like to be?
   b Do you know how many cars there are in Australia?
   c Would you mind if I recorded this interview?

9 🎧 **10.6** Listen to the second part of the interview. Answer the questions.

1 What three interview assessment tasks does Rob Yeung mention?
2 What skills is the in-tray exercise designed to test?
3 What three piles does Rob Yeung recommend applicants separate the in-tray information into?
4 Which job applicants might be given these tests:
   a a keyboard exercise?
   b a memory test?
5 What questions can an applicant be asked to test memory?
6 What does Rob Yeung think is the most important piece of advice to give someone going for a job interview? Do you agree?

10 If you were recruiting someone for your own job (or a job that you know well) what interview questions and tests or tasks would you set? What would be the ideal answers?

.you

'The best careers advice is quite simple: find out what you like doing best, then get someone to pay you for doing it.'

The next question: where can you find the ideal job?

The ideal job won't just suddenly arrive – you'll have to work hard to find it. There are the traditional ways: newspaper advertisements, trade press, company websites, internet searches, and recruitment agencies. But also look at the bigger picture. The best, most fulfilling jobs often come to those who spot opportunities before they are advertised. Look around you. What trends have been happening in the industry or sector you're interested in? What changes and developments are going to happen? How can you be part of them? Don't be frightened to seize the opportunity – it may change your life for the better.

And finally: what's involved in the application process?

The different stages of applying for a job are fairly well-known: prepare a basic CV, research the job details and company background, tailor your CV, write a personalized covering letter, send it … and then start preparing for the interview. However, the important thing to remember is that each stage is an opportunity for you to show your potential employer what you can offer.

One final piece of advice: enjoy the process. If you're enjoying it, then there's more of you involved – and that ideal job is first and foremost about YOU.

Describing a process. Interviewing techniques

Describing a process

1 🎧 **10.7** Listen to Eric Carlin interviewing Javier Pérez, a sherry producer in Spain. Tick T (true), or F (false).

	T	F
1 Sherry is produced in several different areas of Spain.	☐	☐
2 Nearly three-quarters of the production is exported.	☐	☐
3 Britain is the biggest export market today.	☐	☐
4 Most of the big sherry companies are Spanish-owned.	☐	☐
5 The sherry producers want to attract younger markets.	☐	☐

2 🎧 **10.8** Listen to a later part of the interview. Answer the questions.

1 In which row of barrels in the *solera* is the oldest wine?
2 How long does it take for a premium sherry to progress through the *solera* system?

3 Work in pairs. Use the verbs in the box to complete the following extract from the interview. Use the appropriate passive form of the verb for describing a process.

add
fill
keep
need
reach
take
take on
top

> When wine _____ ¹ for bottling, it _____ ² from the barrels on the bottom row, and these barrels _____ ³ with an equal amount of wine from the next row up. Then, the barrels on that row _____ ⁴ up with wine from the row above and that process continues until the top row _____ ⁵. Finally, at the end of the process, new wine _____ ⁶ to the barrels on the top row. In this way, the characteristics of the older wine _____ ⁷ by the younger wine and the quality of the wine _____ ⁸ consistent.

4 🎧 **10.8** Listen again. Check your answers.

5 Number the stages below to show the correct order in which olive oil is made.

The making of olive oil

☐ **a** After that we take the olives to an olive press. Before pressing the olives we wash them and remove the leaves.

☐ **b** We spread a large net or canvas sheet under the olive tree, and we shake the tree to make the olives fall.

☐ **c** Then we collect the olives and put them into large baskets.

☐ **d** We harvest the olives at the end of autumn.

☐ **e** We make virgin olive oil from the first pressing. To qualify as virgin olive oil, we have to press the olives within seventy-two hours of harvesting.

☐ **f** We use two types of olive press: the preparatory press, which we use to extract the first oil from the olives, and the final press, which we use to press the olives more thoroughly.

☐ **g** We refine and blend the oil which we obtain from the final pressing, and then sell it as blended olive oil.

6 Work in pairs. Write a description of how olive oil is produced. Use the passive form of the verb to describe the stages in the production process. Begin *The olives are harvested at the end of autumn … .*

Interviewing techniques

1 Read the interview questions and phrases Eric uses in his interview with Javier Pérez. Add other interview questions and phrases you know under the appropriate headings.

Introducing a topic
Could I start by asking you about … ?
Could we talk about … ?

_____

_____

Asking for clarification
By (*DO wine*), do you mean (*the wine produced in classified areas*)?

_____

_____

Checking understanding
So (*all sherry comes from this area*)?
So if (*70% is exported*), then (*only 30% is drunk in Spain*)?

_____

_____

Showing understanding
Yes, I understand.
I see. Thank you.

_____

_____

Asking for more information
Now I imagine (*a lot of the sherry is exported*). Is that the case?
You say (*tastes are beginning to change*). Could you explain in what way?
Earlier (*you referred to …*). Could you describe how (*the* solera *system works*)?

_____

_____

Thanking
Thank you very much, (*Señor Pérez*).
It's been most interesting.

_____

_____

2 Work in pairs. Give your partner an interesting topic, e.g. a leisure interest, foreign travel, etc. Make a list of questions about this topic, then interview him/her. Answer your partner's questions.

UNIT 11
Critical incidents

▼ **AGENDA**

▶ **3rd Conditional**

▶ *should have (done)/shouldn't have (done)*

▶ **Culture file. Confusing words. Dictionary skills (3)**

▶ **A tough choice**

▶ **Business correspondence**

Language focus

1 Work in groups. Discuss the questions.

1 What cross-cultural problems do companies face when they work with companies from other countries?
2 Can you give any examples of cross-cultural problems from your own experience, either at work or when visiting other countries?

2 Work in pairs. Discuss the questions.

1 What problems could there be in these three situations?
  a a parent company investigating a serious mistake by an employee at one of its subsidiaries in another country
  b two companies of different nationalities competing for a sales contract in a third country
  c a foreign employee who, by chance, meets his boss shopping with his family at the weekend

2 Match situations a–c above with case studies 1–3.

CASE STUDY 1

A British company and a Swedish company were competing for a sales contract in Argentina. The British sales team knew their product was superior. They went to Argentina, gave a very good modern presentation, and returned to the UK the next day, confident that they had won the contract. The Swedish sales team spent a week in Argentina and didn't talk about the product for the first five days. Instead, they used the first five days to get to know the Argentinian company. It was only on the last day that they introduced their product. Even though it was less attractive and slightly higher-priced than the British product, they got the contract. The disappointed leader of the British sales team later asked, 'What did we do wrong?'

CASE STUDY 2

An Australian employee was working in Germany. One Saturday, he saw the German Director of the company in a car showroom in the city centre. The Director was with his family and was trying to buy a car. He was having some problems deciding which model to buy. The employee knew about that particular car because he had just bought one himself. He had only met the Director once before and was keen to make a good impression, so he walked into the showroom, smiled, and said 'Hi, Mr Langer. Is this your wife and children? Nice to meet you. I can see you're having a few problems. Perhaps I can help. The important thing to know is how many kilometres you need to drive in an average week.' The Director didn't look pleased, and after a quick 'Thank you', he walked out with his family following behind. The amazed Australian later asked, 'What did I do wrong?'

CASE STUDY 3

An American boss was sent to look into a serious mistake made by a Japanese worker. The mistake happened at the Japanese subsidiary of a US multinational company. During production, a machine component had been inserted upside down and the entire batch was lost. The cost of this was very high. The boss insisted on finding out exactly which worker had made the mistake. The Japanese production manager said he didn't know but that the entire team would take responsibility. Despite this, the American boss continued her enquiries until eventually she discovered the individual responsible. She gave a public warning to the worker and made sure that he was closely monitored in future. 'If I hadn't done this,' she explained, 'the rest of the workforce would have thought it's acceptable to make mistakes, and production would have become less efficient.' However, as a result of her actions, production actually got worse, not better. The frustrated American boss later asked, 'What did I do wrong?'

3 What do you think they did wrong in each situation? What advice or explanation would you give to the British team leader, the Australian employee, and the American boss?

4 **11.1** Listen to an expert on cross-cultural communication giving his advice and analysis.

1 Match analyses a–c with case studies 1–3.
2 Do you agree with his advice?

5 **11.1** Listen again and complete extracts 1–3.

1 The Australian employee _____ ᵃ a little more formal, and he _____ ᵇ to be introduced to the Director's family. Also, he _____ ᶜ that he knew more than his boss about cars, especially in front of his family. If _____ ᵈ for the Director to speak to him, he _____ ᵉ for his opinion. That way, he _____ ᶠ a good impression.

2 She _____ ᵃ the worker in public. It _____ ᵇ if she _____ ᶜ the facts, expressed her concern, and then let them deal with it themselves. The Japanese production team _____ ᵈ the worker responsible, and made sure he didn't make mistakes in the future.

3 They _____ ᵃ more time to get to know the company. They _____ ᵇ so quickly to the business side of things. Also, perhaps they were over-confident. If they _____ ᶜ a good personal relationship with their potential clients, the British sales team _____ ᵈ the contract.

3rd Conditional

Read the examples and answer the questions.
- If he'**d waited** for the Director to speak to him, he **might have asked** for his opinion.
- It **would have been** better **if** she'**d** just **found out** the facts.
- **If** they'**d built up** a good personal relationship with their potential clients, the British sales team **would have won** the contract.

1 What time does the 3rd Conditional refer to, present or past?
2 Which tense is used in the *if* clause?
3 Which form of the verb follows *would have/might have* in the result clause?
4 What is the difference in meaning between *would have* and *might have*?

📖 Pocket Book pp. 4–5

should have (done)/shouldn't have (done)

Read the examples and answer the questions.
- He **should have waited** to be introduced.

1 Did he wait to be introduced?
2 Did he do the right thing?

- She **shouldn't have criticized** the worker in public.

1 Did she criticize the worker in public?
2 Did she do the right thing?

Complete the rules.
- We use _____ and the _____ form of the verb when something was the best thing to do, but the subject didn't do it.
- We use _____ and the _____ form of the verb when the subject did the wrong thing.

📖 Pocket Book p. 16

Practice **1** Work in pairs. What did these people do wrong? Write sentences using *should have* and *shouldn't have*. Give a reason why you think the action was wrong.

1 A businessman visiting a company in Saudi Arabia offered his business card with his left hand.

> **Example** *He shouldn't have offered it with his left hand.*
> *He should have used his right hand.*
> *The left hand is considered unclean.*

2 A tourist didn't take his shoes off when he went into a temple in India.
3 A tired businesswoman travelling on the metro in Seoul yawned loudly without putting her hand over her mouth.
4 A British boss scheduled dinner for a visiting Spanish delegation at 6 p.m.
5 A Chinese visitor with a cold kept sniffing during a meeting in the US.
6 A woman sat next to a Buddhist monk on a crowded bus in Thailand.
7 A hotel guest in Finland went into the hotel sauna wearing shorts and a tee-shirt.
8 A European diner in Japan left his chopsticks sticking up out of a bowl of rice when he'd finished eating.

Pronunciation

1 🎧 **11.2** Listen to these two sentences from the expert's advice in **4** again. Note the pronunciation of *should have* and *shouldn't have*.

a He should have waited to be introduced.
b They shouldn't have rushed so quickly.

2 Repeat the sentences. Practise the other *should* sentences in **4** (**11.1** on p. 141).

3 🎧 **11.3** Listen to this 3rd Conditional sentence. Note the stressed words and the rhythm.

If they'd built up a good relationship, they would have won the contract.

4 Practise saying these sentences.

1 If they'd done more research, they wouldn't have made the mistake.
2 If they hadn't been over-confident, they wouldn't have lost the contract.
3 If they'd spent longer in the country, they would have understood the culture.

2 Complete the sentences. Say what you *would* or *might have* (done).

1 If I'd had a day off last week, _____.
2 If I'd got a bonus last month, _____.
3 If I'd chosen a different career, _____.
4 If I hadn't decided to learn English, _____.
5 If I'd been born a different nationality, _____.
6 If I'd known about _____.

3 Read the memo and the article about the company Comptek. What mistakes did the company make? What should they have done?

Example   *Comptek didn't follow their own advice.*
They should have followed their own advice.

MEMO TO ALL STAFF

I saw this story in a magazine.
Can you believe it?!

Karl Svensson

IT Operations Manager

The computer distribution company that got its IT security wrong

Comptek were responsible for advising their clients on aspects of computer hardware and software, including security and anti-virus protection. But it turns out the company weren't following their own advice.

For a start, they didn't have a proper firewall to protect their own servers. They hadn't even installed some of the basic anti-virus software they stocked themselves. On top of this, they had a relaxed attitude to staff sending personal emails, and downloading files and programmes from the Internet. As a result of this, the system crashed regularly, operational time was slowed, and orders were lost.

But the real disaster struck with the latest international 'worm' virus. Within seconds of an employee opening the attachment on one of his emails, the whole system was down, the main database was destroyed, and the virus was being sent out to all the addresses on the Comptek mailing lists. Luckily for most of the recipients, they had already installed the correct protection. It was too late for Comptek however – they went out of business overnight!

---

4 Work in pairs. Discuss the questions.

1 Make 3rd Conditional sentences with *would* and *might* about Comptek.

    Example   *If they had followed their own advice, they might have avoided the damaging effects of the 'worm' virus.*

2 Have you ever made any mistakes when using computers, such as forgetting to make a back-up copy of a document? What were the consequences?

5 Work in pairs. Ask and answer questions about important decisions you've made in your life, e.g. about your studies, career, etc. Say how your life would have been different if you had made different decisions.

Culture file. Confusing words. Dictionary skills (3)

1 Work in pairs. Which of the types of culture listed below do you think influences you most?

Types of culture

When we use the word *culture* we do not just mean national culture, but the whole range of different types of culture. These include:

- corporate culture (for example, the culture of Microsoft)
- professional culture (for example, the culture of lawyers or doctors)
- gender (the different cultures of men and women)
- age (the different cultures of young, middle-aged, and elderly people)
- religious culture (for example, Catholicism, Protestantism, Islam)
- regional culture (for example, Northern and Southern Italy)
- class culture (working class, middle class, and upper class)

From *International Business Communication* by Robert Gibson 2002

2 Read the dictionary extracts and complete the sentences with the correct word or phrase.

cul·tural /ˈkʌltʃərəl/ *adj.* [usually before noun] **1** connected with the culture of a particular society or group, its customs, beliefs, etc.

cul·tured /ˈkʌltʃəd; *NAmE* -tʃərd/ *adj.* **1** (of people) well educated and able to understand and enjoy art, literature, etc.

multi·cul·tural /ˌmʌltiˈkʌltʃərəl/ *adj.* for or including people of several different races, religions, languages and traditions

cul·ture /ˈkʌltʃə(r)/ *noun* **1** [U] the customs and beliefs, art, way of life and social organization of a particular country or group

'culture shock *noun* [C, U] a feeling of confusion and anxiety that sb may feel when they live in or visit another country

(Extracts based on *Oxford Advanced Learner's Dictionary* 7th edition 019 431 6068 ©2005)

1 A lot of problems in international business are caused by _____ differences and misunderstandings.
2 She's an extremely _____ woman and knows a lot about literature and art.
3 As a journalist on the new magazine for teenagers you'll need to have a good understanding of youth _____ .
4 I come from a _____ city with lots of people from different countries and different religions.
5 When I first went to China, I suffered from _____ : everything was so different.

3 Work in pairs. Discuss the questions.

1 Have you ever experienced *culture shock*?
2 Do you think of yourself as a *cultured* person?
3 Is the city or country where you live *multicultural*?
4 How would you define the culture of
- your country?
- your region?
- your age group?
- your place of work or study?

4 Work in groups. Do you think that the place where you work has a corporate culture? Discuss these questions. Use a dictionary to check the meaning of the underlined words and phrases.

1 Is your working environment open-plan, or are there separate offices and work-stations?
2 Does the management operate an open-door policy?
3 Are most policy decisions made by individuals at senior level, or are they collective, with consultation of all staff?
4 Is there an organigram of your company and staff structure? Does it show a hierarchical approach?
5 Do you work mainly in teams or as individuals?
6 Does your company employ secretaries or administrators?
7 Are you encouraged to see new tasks as problems or challenges?
8 Is there a dress-code or a dress-down day?

5 Describe the main features of your corporate culture to students from other groups. Compare the differences.

Confusing words

1 Choose the correct word.

1 The meeting started promptly because there was a long *agenda/itinerary/ schedule* to get through.
2 Halfway through, we *adjourned/cancelled/postponed* the meeting for coffee.
3 Sorry, I can't make 10 o'clock tomorrow. I've got a doctor's *meeting/ appointment/arrangement*.
4 My colleagues were arguing so much that I had to *intercept/interfere/ intervene*.
5 Have you seen the weather *forecast/plan/prediction*?
6 I've got an exam tomorrow, so I need to *review/rehearse/revise* tonight.

2 Write sentences using the words you didn't choose in **1**. Use a dictionary to help you.

3 In the sentences below, one word is not correct. Identify the word and replace it with the correct word.

1 He was so angry with the decision that he retired immediately.
2 I had to work hardly to get the job finished on time.
3 She makes a good counsellor because she's so sensible to people's problems.
4 After we'd got on the train, the inspector controlled everyone's ticket.
5 The directors accused the bad exchange rate for the fall in profits.
6 Despite loosing some of our best sales staff, we still reached our targets.
7 His raise from the position of Sales Assistant to Chief Executive in less than five years was spectacular.
8 There's an opportunity that I might be asked to go to Hong Kong for a conference.

4 Work in groups. Choose two of these word groups and discuss the questions.

a salary, wage, earnings
b recruit, employ, apply
c student, trainee, pupil
d answer, feedback, reply
e staff, workforce, employees
f make redundant, dismiss, lay off

1 What is the difference between each of the three words? Use a dictionary to help you.
2 Write sentences to show the difference.
3 Explain the differences between the words to students from another group.

5 Work in groups. Discuss the questions.

1 Have you ever confused any of the words in this section?
2 What other words have you confused during this course? Look back at some of the previous units.
3 Are there any words in your own language that seem similar to English words but have a different meaning ('false friends')?
4 Are there any English words which are used in your language? Is the meaning different from the meaning in English?

A tough choice

1 Leah Pattison was recently awarded the title of 'Woman of the Year' for her charity work in India with women who have leprosy. Before you listen to an interview with her, discuss these questions.

1 What do you know about leprosy?
2 How do you think women suffering from leprosy in India are regarded?
3 What help do they need?

2 🎧 **11.4** Listen to the first part of the interview with Leah Pattison. Check your answers to **1**.

3 🎧 **11.4** Listen to the first part again. Answer the questions.

1 What is the name of the charity Leah has co-founded?
2 Can all victims of leprosy be cured?
3 Why do many women with leprosy hide their condition?
4 What did Leah study before she went to India?
5 What job did she go to India to do?
6 What was her initial reaction to the leprosy patients, and how did it change?

4 🎧 **11.5** Listen to the second part of the interview. What happened to Leah? What tough choice did she have to make?

5 🎧 **11.5** Listen to the second part again and tick T (True) or F (False).

	T	F
1 Leah was worried she might catch leprosy.	☐	☐
2 Leprosy is a difficult disease to catch.	☐	☐
3 Leah decided to return to the UK for treatment.	☐	☐
4 Leah found it a very tough choice to make.	☐	☐
5 Her friend caught leprosy at the same time.	☐	☐
6 Leah made a full recovery.	☐	☐
7 At first, the women patients are often difficult to communicate with.	☐	☐
8 The interviewer thinks Leah's decision was very brave.	☐	☐

6 Work in groups. Discuss the questions.

1 What is your reaction to Leah Pattison's story? Do you think you would have done the same as her? Would you have stayed and had the treatment in India?
2 What other charities do you know that help disadvantaged people? What are the needs of the people who the charities are trying to help?
3 Have you ever had to make a tough choice that affected a close friend or your family, either in a positive or a negative way?

Business correspondence

1 Work in pairs. Do the correspondence quiz. Look at the letters to help you.

Correspondence quiz

1 How many of the letters have a letterhead? What information does it contain?
2 How do you close a letter that begins *Dear Sir or Madam*?
3 How do you close a letter that begins with the recipient's name, e.g. *Dear Claire, Dear Ms Lanson*?
4 When do you use *Ms* before a woman's name?
5 What do the following abbreviations mean?
   a encs   b no   c plc   d pp   e Rd   f St
6 Which expression is sometimes used to a business contact before closing?

31 Aylston Rd
London NW6 5PR

Ms R Lanson
Project Director
Network Multimedia Productions
Network House
30 Portland Terrace
London W1A 6RU

23 March 2005

Dear Ms Lanson

Thank you for your letter of 17 March. I apologize for not replying sooner but I have just returned from holiday.
I would be delighted to act as consultant for the *Food and Drink in Spain* programme in your new video project. The project sounds extremely interesting, and I will be very pleased to help you in any way I can.
I am afraid I will not be able to meet you next week owing to prior commitments, but I will be available during the first week of April.
I enclose a copy of my book *A Taste of Spain*, which I hope you will find useful.
I look forward to meeting you and Eric next month.

Yours sincerely

María Ferrando

María Ferrando

ets Executive Travel Services
28 Chiltern St
London W1M 2LH

Tel 020 7486 9740 • Fax 020 7487 4432
enquiries@ets.com

Ms C Hallan
Network Multimedia Productions
Network House
30 Portland Terrace
London W1A 6RU

25 April 2005

Dear Claire

Please find enclosed airline tickets for Ms R Lanson and Mr E Carlin.
Would you kindly check the tickets to make sure all the bookings are correct?
Unfortunately, the hotel you requested in Barcelona is fully booked due to an international convention taking place at that time. I am awaiting confirmation of a booking at the Hotel Feria Palace.
Please let me know if you require any information on hotels in Valencia.

With best wishes
Yours sincerely

Jan Tate

Jan Tate
encs

NMP

13 May 2005

Dear Sr Pérez

It was a pleasure meeting you in Jerez last week. Mr Carlin and I would like to thank you for a very interesting and informative visit, and for giving us so much of your time.

We are delighted that you have agreed to a further interview, to be filmed for inclusion in our programme *Food and Drink in Spain*. We will contact you shortly to finalize arrangements for filming the interview.

Please give our kind regards to Señor Corzón.

Mr Carlin and I very much look forward to meeting you again soon.

Your sincerely

Rosa Lanson

Rosa Lanson
Project Director

NMP | Network House, 30 Portland Terrace, Lo
Tel 020 7243 2673 | Fax 020 7243 0531 | enq

Welco✚
Pharmaceuticals plc

Redwood Park
Maidenhead
Berks SL7 2RL
messages@welcophar.com

Fax cover letter

To: NMP

From: G Burnett

Subject: Video order

Date: 17 June 2005

No of pages: 1

Dear Sir or Madam

Further to our telephone enquiry, would you please send us the following video training courses?

No of copies	Code	Title
1	NMP 601	Communication skills at work
1	NMP 603	Doing business in other cultures
3	NMP 608	Motivating your workforce

We would appreciate it if you could send us information about new training courses as they become available.

Yours faithfully

J McLaren

pp G Burnett
Human Resources Manager
Welco Pharmaceuticals plc

2 Look at the standard phrases from business correspondence. Find more examples of standard phrases in the letters and fax on pp. 117–118. Use them to complete the table.

Explaining the reason for writing
I am writing to | enquire about …
               | inform you that …
               | confirm …
	Giving good news
	I am pleased to inform you that …
	I am delighted to tell you that …

Making reference With reference to your letter of … It was a pleasure meeting you … _____ _____	**Giving bad news** _____ _____
Apologizing I am sorry about … _____	**Enclosing documents** _____ _____
Requesting We would appreciate it if you could … _____ _____ _____	**Closing remarks** Please pass on my best wishes to … _____ _____
Agreeing to requests I would be delighted to … _____	**Referring to future contact** We very much look forward to meeting you again … Please contact us again if we can help in any way. _____
Explaining reasons This is | the result of … | due to … _____	◆ Pocket Book pp. 17–18

3 Work in pairs. Choose two of the following.

1 Write a fax to the Hotel Majestic, Passeig de Gràcia 70, 08007 Barcelona, Fax: +34 93 215 77 73, confirming a reservation for Ms Lanson and Mr Carlin from 8–10 May.

2 Write a letter to Mme Martine Granget, 95 Gloucester Place, London W1A 5SP, asking her if she would be willing to act as a consultant for the programme *Food and drink in France*. Describe briefly the aim and content of the series of programmes. Suggest a meeting to discuss the matter in more detail.

3 Write a letter to Piet van Els and Rosa Lanson. Offer to act as a consultant for a programme about the food and drink of your country.

4 Write a typical letter you may need to send out in your own work or studies.

UNIT 12
Hard news, soft news

Language focus

e-vote warning

Fishing disaster

Workers face more stress

1 Work in pairs.

1 What do you think the following 'hard' or serious news headlines are about?
2 In which news items do you think the words and phrases in the box will appear? Use a dictionary to help if necessary.

apathy	bacteria	clinical depression	downsizing
dumping of waste	environmental disaster	fraud	lay-offs
local election	pollution	sick leave	turnout

2 Read the articles and check your answers to **1**.

a

Plans to introduce electronic voting for the next national elections are likely to be delayed after a world expert in e-voting warned that the system was still not secure. Rebecca Mercuri, a computer science expert, said that e-voting gave an opportunity for fraud and said that she couldn't believe that anyone was even considering using the Internet for national elections. Mercuri told reporters it would be at least ten years before systems were safe enough. Governments throughout the world see Internet and text-message voting as a way of beating apathy and getting more people to vote. The turnout in the recent local elections was as low as 15% in some parts of the country. A government official confirmed that they had decided to wait for further reports before introducing e-voting.

b

Government officials are still trying to find out the cause of the environmental disaster that has led to 2,000 tonnes of dead fish being washed ashore in the last few weeks.

Scientists think mystery bacteria may be responsible. One scientist told reporters that he thought the exceptionally hot weather in August had caused the bacteria to spread. He explained that a similar problem had occurred at the same time the previous year. Other scientists maintain that pollution caused by the dumping of waste from the oil industry may be responsible.

The Government announced that they would introduce a special aid programme to help the 4,000 fishermen affected.

c

A United Nations report out today reveals that workplace stress is rising at an alarming rate and is costing employers billions of dollars in sick leave and lost working time.

The study by the UN's International Labour Organization (ILO) looked at problems of stress and mental illness at work in the United States, Germany, the UK, Finland, and Poland. In the United States, one in ten workers suffers from clinical depression, and 200 million working days are lost every year because of stress. But the problem is worst in Finland where more than half the workforce have stress-related problems.

The report blamed a number of factors for the dramatic rise: downsizing, lay-offs, mergers, short-term contracts, and higher demands. The ILO said that 50 years ago these problems hadn't existed but in the present day there was much less security in work. The report added that companies were making more demands on their staff. A spokesperson for the Employers' Association explained that many companies had made improvements in recent years. He believed that employees could expect to see more help and support schemes in the future.

3 Who made the following statements in the newspaper articles? Choose from the list in the box.

  a 'Fifty years ago these problems didn't exist.'
  b 'I can't believe that anyone is even considering using the Internet for national elections.'
  c 'Many companies have made improvements in recent years.'
  d 'I think the exceptionally hot weather in August caused the bacteria to spread.'
  e 'It'll be at least ten years before systems are safe enough.'

> a government official   the US Congress
> the ILO   a computer science expert
> a reporter   a scientist
> a spokesperson for the Employers' Association   a fisherman

4 Work in pairs. Answer the questions.

  1 Compare the direct statements in **3** with the reported statements in the newspaper articles. What happens to the verb when a direct statement becomes a reported statement?
  2 What always immediately follows the verb *tell*? What other reporting verbs are used in the articles, e.g. *say* (*said*)?
  3 Find other examples of reported statements in the articles. What are the direct statements?

Reporting spoken language

Complete the table to show how the verb changes in reported speech when the reporting verb is in the past tense. Answer the questions.

Direct statement	Reported statement
Present Simple 'There **is** much less security in work.'	*Past Simple* The ILO said that there **was** much less security in work.
Present Continuous 'Companies **are making** more demands of their staff.'	a _____ The report added that companies **were making** more demands of their staff.
Past Simple 'A similar problem **occurred** at the same time last year.'	b _____ He explained that a similar problem **had occurred** at the same time the previous year.
Present Perfect 'We **have decided** to wait for further reports before introducing e-voting.'	c _____ A government official confirmed that they **had decided** to wait for further reports before introducing e-voting.
will 'We **will** introduce a special aid programme to help the 4,000 fishermen affected.'	d _____ The Government announced that they **would** introduce a special aid programme to help the 4,000 fishermen affected.
can 'Employees **can** expect to see more help and support schemes in the future.'	e _____ He believed that employees **could** expect to see more help and support schemes in the future.

1 What happens to pronouns *I, we, you, my, our, your* in reported speech?
2 What happens to expressions such as *last year, yesterday, today, tomorrow, next year* in reported speech?

 Pocket Book pp. 14–15

Practice

❶ Complete the reported statements.

1 'We've looked at problems of stress and mental illness at work in five countries.'

A spokesperson told reporters _____.

2 'We're planning to employ a professional counsellor to help our staff.'

The Director announced _____.

3 'I don't know if I'll be able to survive until next year.'

A fisherman said _____.

4 'It can't be oil pollution because we have very strict controls.'

A spokesperson for the oil industry told us _____.

5 'Our party lost the last election because the turnout was low.'

One politician claimed _____.

❷ Work in pairs. Complete the list of direct questions from the reported questions.

Reported question	Direct question
1 The unions wanted to know how the employers planned to deal with workplace stress in the future.	*'How do you plan to deal with workplace stress in the future?'*
2 The reporter wanted to know if the problem was just as bad in other countries.	_____ _____
3 The fishermen asked the Government when they could expect more financial aid.	_____ _____
4 The fishermen asked the Government what they were doing to prevent another environmental disaster.	_____ _____
5 The reporter asked Professor Mercuri if she thought e-voting would be introduced in her lifetime.	_____ _____
6 The journalist asked Professor Mercuri if there had ever been any cases of fraud in electronic voting.	_____ _____

❸ Look at the reported questions in **❷**.

1 How is the verb form in a reported question different from the verb form in a direct question?
2 What differences are there in the word order between reported questions and direct questions?
3 When is *if* used in a reported question?

 Pocket Book p. 15

4 Work in pairs.

1 Write six questions that a reporter might ask one of the fishermen affected by the environmental disaster.

Examples *How long have you been a fisherman?*
Do you have any other jobs?

2 For each of the direct questions write the reported question form.

Examples *The reporter asked how long he had been a fisherman.*
The reporter asked if he had any other jobs.

5 Write the reported orders and requests as in the example.

Example 'Check your pollution controls,' the Government ordered the oil refineries.
The Government ordered the oil refineries to check their pollution controls.

1 'Could you speak up a bit please?' the professor asked the reporter.

_____

2 'Don't dump waste in the sea,' the Government warned representatives of the oil industry.

_____

3 'Can I finish my point?' the speaker asked the reporter.

_____

4 'Don't make too many demands of your staff,' the presenter told the companies.

_____

5 'Could you email us a copy of the report?' she asked the speaker.

_____

6 'You must re-count all the votes,' the official told them.

_____

6 Work in groups.

1 Write six questions to ask another student about workplace stress. You can include questions on:
• their experience of stress in their job, or the jobs of anyone they know
• how their company, or companies they know, deal with stress
• their opinion of workplace stress as a current problem, and how it can be avoided

2 Interview a person from another group. Then answer their questions.
3 Report back to your group on the interview.

Examples *She said that she ...*
She asked me if I ...

Newsdesk International

politics

sport

health

science/nature

technology

business

entertainment

education

Item 1
Government announces financial plans in spring _____ [1]

The national share index rose by several points as the _____ [2] reacted positively to measures announced yesterday by the Finance _____ [3] in his speech to _____ [4]. He said that he hoped that a period of economic growth would now replace the years of _____ [5]. He also commented that prices had become settled and that he expected the rate of _____ [6] to remain at 2% for the coming year. Wage-earners will be pleased that there are no plans to increase _____ [7]. At the same time the National Bank confirmed that _____ [8] would be reduced by a quarter of a per cent. [More details …]

Item 2
UN reveals _____ [1] for African state

Plans for a new National Assembly for the Central African Republic (CAR) have been revealed. _____ [2] will be held in six months' time. The Secretary-General of the United Nations also announced a lifting of _____ [3]. Many countries who broke off _____ [4] a year ago are preparing to re-open their _____ [5]. They are also preparing a programme of _____ [6], which will allow the CAR to increase _____ [7] on housing, schools, and hospitals. [More details …]

Around the world

Africa:	UN <u>peacekeeping</u>[1] force arrives to end <u>civil war</u>[2]. [More details …]
Americas:	Democratic and Liberal <u>parties</u>[3] join to form <u>coalition</u>[4] government. [More details …]
Asia Pacific:	Heads of Government arrive for <u>summit</u>[5] in Singapore. [More details …]
Europe:	Socialist Party <u>manifesto</u>[6] reveals plans for <u>nationalization</u>[7] of railways. [More details …]
Middle East:	Religious leader to stand as <u>candidate</u>[8] in first <u>democratic</u>[9] election. [More details …]
South Asia:	Explosion increases fears of <u>terrorism</u>[10]. [More details …]

local news   national news   international news   breaking news

1 Read the home page of the news website. Complete the sentences in item 1 with a word or phrase from the box.

budget
recession
interest rates
stock market
Minister
taxation
parliament
inflation

2 Match words from A with words from B to make collocations. Use the collocations to complete the sentences in item 2.

A	B
new	spending
foreign	constitution
fresh	relations
diplomatic	sanctions
economic	aid
public	elections
international	embassies

3 Match the underlined words in *Around the world* with their definitions.

a   having equal voting rights for all people (adj)
b   the killing of ordinary people for political purposes (n)
c   someone who wants to be elected to a position (n)
d   an important meeting between the leaders of two or more countries (n)
e   a group of people who have the same political aims and ideas (n)
f   intended to help keep the peace and prevent violence (adj)
g   putting a company or organization under the control of the Government (n)
h   a government formed by two or more political parties working together (n)
i   a war between groups of people who live in the same country (n)
j   a written statement that explains what a political party wants to do if it becomes the government in the future (n)

4 Work in groups. Discuss the questions.

1 Does the government announce budgets in your country? What measures were announced in the last one? What measures would you like to see in the next one?
2 Does your country have close international relations with any other countries? If so, which ones?

5 🎧 **12.1**

1 Listen to an audio-guide explaining the layout of a parliamentary chamber. Label the parts of the diagram.

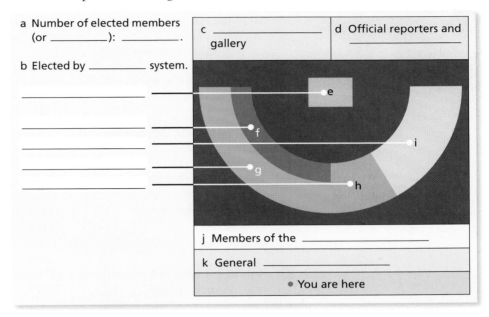

a Number of elected members (or _____): _____ .

b Elected by _____ system.

c _____ gallery

d Official reporters and _____

e

f

g

h

i

j Members of the _____

k General _____

● You are here

2 Can you say how the parliamentary chamber in your country is different from the diagram?

6 Work in pairs. Discuss the questions.

1 How is the political system organized in your country?
2 Would you like to change the political system in your country? How?

7 Match words in A with words in B to make pairs of opposites.

A	B
boom	minority
privatization	opposition
majority	dictatorship
government	right-wing
left-wing	recession
democracy	nationalization

8 Complete the table. Mark the stress for each word.

Noun (subject)	Noun (person)	Adjective
politics		
	economist	
		diplomatic
	democrat	

9 Work in groups. Complete one of these sentences, and discuss your answer.

• If I were Prime Minister/President of my country …
• If I were Secretary-General of the United Nations …

Compare your views with other groups.

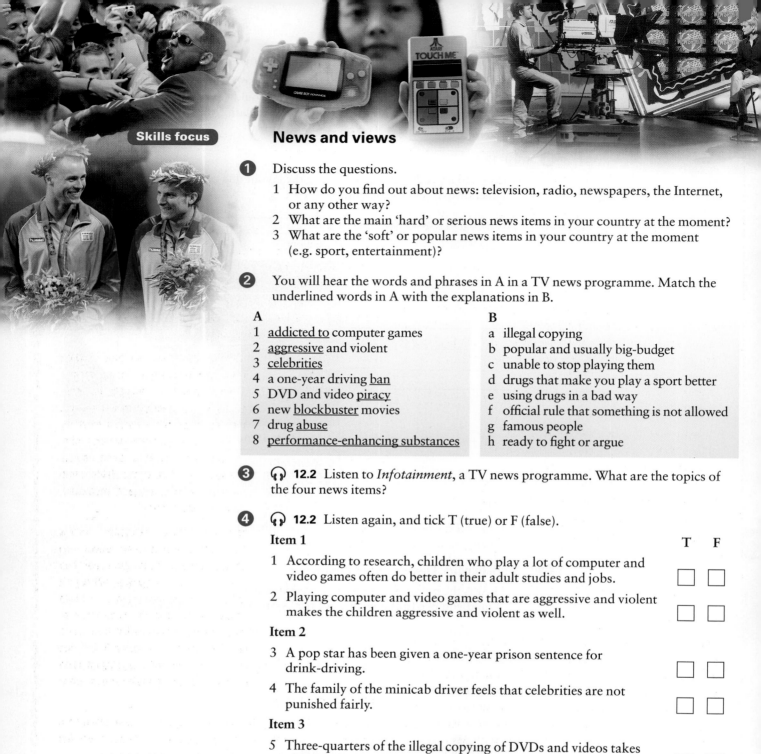

News and views

1 Discuss the questions.

1 How do you find out about news: television, radio, newspapers, the Internet, or any other way?
2 What are the main 'hard' or serious news items in your country at the moment?
3 What are the 'soft' or popular news items in your country at the moment (e.g. sport, entertainment)?

2 You will hear the words and phrases in A in a TV news programme. Match the underlined words in A with the explanations in B.

A	B
1 <u>addicted to</u> computer games	a illegal copying
2 <u>aggressive</u> and violent	b popular and usually big-budget
3 <u>celebrities</u>	c unable to stop playing them
4 a one-year driving <u>ban</u>	d drugs that make you play a sport better
5 DVD and video <u>piracy</u>	e using drugs in a bad way
6 new <u>blockbuster</u> movies	f official rule that something is not allowed
7 drug <u>abuse</u>	g famous people
8 <u>performance-enhancing substances</u>	h ready to fight or argue

3 🎧 **12.2** Listen to *Infotainment*, a TV news programme. What are the topics of the four news items?

4 🎧 **12.2** Listen again, and tick T (true) or F (false).

Item 1   T   F

1 According to research, children who play a lot of computer and video games often do better in their adult studies and jobs. ☐ ☐

2 Playing computer and video games that are aggressive and violent makes the children aggressive and violent as well. ☐ ☐

Item 2

3 A pop star has been given a one-year prison sentence for drink-driving. ☐ ☐

4 The family of the minicab driver feels that celebrities are not punished fairly. ☐ ☐

Item 3

5 Three-quarters of the illegal copying of DVDs and videos takes place in Asia. ☐ ☐

6 Illegal copies become available as soon as a major film is released. ☐ ☐

Item 4

7 A footballer has been banned for one year for using drugs. ☐ ☐

8 It is difficult to tell the difference between illegal drugs and ordinary supplements. ☐ ☐

5 Work in groups. Discuss these issues from the last three news items.

1 Drink-driving offences should carry automatic prison sentences.
2 Celebrities should be punished more strictly for things they do wrong, as an example to the general public.
3 If film and music companies didn't charge so much for their products, piracy wouldn't be a problem.
4 Any professional sportsperson caught using illegal drugs should be banned from their sport for life.

6 Read the article *The Gameboy generation* about the effect computer games have on child development. Answer the questions.

1 Where were the two studies carried out?
2 What are the main conclusions of the two studies?
3 What do the two studies both agree on?

The Gameboy generation

Do computer and video games damage or develop our children? Two new scientific studies have reached opposing conclusions.

One study in Japan concludes that computer and video games are creating a generation of children who are far more likely to use violence than their parents' generation. But the <u>tendency to lose control</u> is not due to the violence and aggression in the games themselves, but to the fact that playing the games prevents the proper development of the brain.

Professor Ryuta Kawashima of Tohoku University measured the brain activity in hundreds of teenagers playing a computer game and compared it with the brain activity of other students doing a <u>simple arithmetical exercise</u>. Before starting his <u>investigation</u>, Professor Kawashima expected to find that playing computer and video games <u>stimulated brain activity</u>, and that this would encourage the manufacturers and <u>reassure</u> parents.

However, he was <u>startled</u> by what he discovered. He found that playing the computer game only stimulated the parts of the brain associated with vision and movement. The arithmetical exercise, on the other hand, stimulated brain activity in both the left and right hemispheres of the <u>frontal lobe</u>. The frontal lobe, which continues to develop in humans until the age of about 20, is the part of the brain that exercises self-control and stops <u>anti-social</u> and <u>violent behaviour</u>.

'This is a very important discovery,' Kawashima told reporters. 'The implications are very serious for an increasingly violent society. These students won't develop proper self-control and good behaviour if they continue playing games, instead of learning arithmetic. It's also important for children to play outside with other children, and <u>interact</u> and communicate with others.'

However, another study in Britain has concluded that children who become addicted to computer and video games could actually be more intelligent than average. In some cases, they could be more certain to go to university and get higher-ranking jobs. The research looked at game addicts five years on. Many of the children had become highly intelligent, motivated, and successful people.

The government researcher, Jessica Harris, said that there was no evidence to show that the 'Gameboy generation' had suffered any <u>lasting damage.</u> Although it is true that many of the games have high levels of aggression, this is also true for many sports, such as racing, karate, and wrestling, which all focus on the player's level of aggression. In fact, one part of the survey found that regular game use <u>had a calming effect</u> on the children because it provided 'an outlet for aggression and the open expression of competition'.

There is at least one thing that both sides agree on – more research is needed before any definite conclusions can be made about whether playing computer and video games is good or bad for children.

7 Explain the meaning of the underlined words and phrases in the text. Use a dictionary if necessary.

8 Work in groups.

1 Do you think playing computer games damages children or helps them develop?
2 Are there any toys or games that you would not allow your children or children you know to play?
3 What games and activities are best for the educational and social development of children?

Social responses. Common expressions. Saying goodbye

Social responses

1 🎧 **12.3** Listen to the telephone conversation between Rosa and María Ferrando. Answer the questions.

1 What good news does Rosa tell María?
2 When did the investors make their decision?

2 Match the offers and invitations made by people at NMP's party in A with the replies in B.

A

1 María, would you like another drink?
2 Do try one of these canapés. Eric made them. They're delicious.
3 We're having a barbecue on Thursday evening. Would you like to come?
4 We're going to see that new musical next week. How about coming with us?
5 Would you like me to give you a lift back to your hotel after the party?

B

a Yes, I'd love to see it. When are you going?
b That's very kind of you, if you're sure it's no trouble.
c Did he? Then I must try one.
d Oh, I'd love to but I'm afraid I'll be away on business then.
e Thanks, Piet. I'd love some more wine.

Pronunciation

1 🎧 **12.4** Listen to these dialogues. Mark each 1 (=quite enthusiastic), or 2 (=very enthusiastic).

Comment	Response	
a I got the job.	Really? Great.	2
b Do you like the new area manager?	Oh, yes. He seems very friendly and efficient.	
c I'd like you to go to the conference in Florida for us.	Of course. I'd love to go.	
d I see you've got your name in the newspaper.	I know. I didn't realize they were going to print it.	

2 Work in pairs.
Practise the dialogues. Try to continue them as long as possible, and be very enthusiastic.

3 🎧 **12.5** Listen to some more comments made by people at the party. Tick the most appropriate response.

1 a Never mind. ☐
  b It's Claire. Claire Hallan. ☐

2 a Thank you. Do give him mine. ☐
  b Does he? ☐

3 a It's OK. ☐
  b Not at all. ☐

4 a Thanks. I hope so too. ☐
  b Do you? ☐

5 a Black, one sugar, please. ☐
  b It doesn't matter. ☐

6 a Really? ☐
  b Oh, I'm sorry to hear that. ☐

7 a Never mind. ☐
  b Don't mention it. ☐

8 a Yes, I expect so. ☐
  b Thanks. The same to you. ☐

4 🎧 **12.6** Listen and check your answers.

Common expressions

1 Match the expressions in A with their uses in B.

A

1 Talking of (*weekends, why don't you come and stay with us soon?*).
2 As I was saying, (*their daughter has just started her own business*).
3 That reminds me, (*I must get in touch with him again*).
4 If you ask me, (*I think he's making a big mistake*).
5 As you say, (*the economic situation isn't getting any better*).

B

a to give an opinion, without being asked for one
b to repeat and agree with what someone has said
c to introduce a new topic by linking it to a present one
d to say something that the present topic has reminded you of
e to take the conversation back to an earlier topic

2 Complete the extracts from conversations with a suitable expression from **1**.

1 _____, Eric, I'd say good food is definitely one of life's pleasures. (= *that's what I think*)

2 _____, María, Señor Pérez sends you his regards. (= *I've just remembered*)

3 _____, Rosa, we've got a very busy year ahead. (= *you said it before and I agree*)

4 _____ good wines, Eric, what was the name of that wine you recommended? (= *a new topic that links to the last one*)

5 _____, Rosa, I think Jean Leblanc would be ideal as consultant for the programme on France. (= *I was talking about this topic earlier*)

3 🎧 **12.7** Listen and check your answers.

Saying goodbye

1 🎧 **12.8** Listen to people saying goodbye at NMP's party. Answer the questions.

1 What does María say to show she's leaving?
2 Do you think Piet wishes he had Rosa's job? Why/Why not?

2 Work in pairs. Decide what you would say in these situations.

a You're on a business trip and your host has taken you out to dinner. It's very late and you have to catch an early morning plane.
b Some colleagues invited you out to lunch for your birthday. You've got a meeting at work in ten minutes.
c You've just spent three days staying with some English friends. They're seeing you off at the airport. You'll see them again next summer.
d You've spent the day at a foreign branch of a company, learning how to use a new computer system. Everyone there has been very helpful.

3 🎧 **12.9** Listen to four people saying goodbye. Match situations a–d from **2** with speakers 1–4.

Situation	a	b	c	d
Speaker				

REVIEW UNIT C

▼ AGENDA
▶ Grammar ❶–❹
▶ Focus on functions ❺–❼
▶ Vocabulary ❽

This unit reviews all the main language points from Units 9–12. Complete the exercises. Use the Pocket Book for areas that you need to review again.

❶ Present Perfect Simple and Present Perfect Continuous, Time clauses, Time phrases

1 Complete the letter from Antonio Parisi, a candidate in the elections, to his constituents. Use the correct tense and form of the verb in brackets.

Dear voter,
Our party _____ ¹ (be) in government for the last five years. During that time, we _____ ² (work) hard to improve the standard of living in our cities. We _____ ³ (build) thousands of low-cost flats for our key workers, we _____ ⁴ (open) hundreds of new schools, and we _____ ⁵ (improve) the transport system. We _____ ⁶ (achieve) all this, but we _____ ⁷ (not raise) taxation. We _____ ⁸ (not finish) our work yet. At our regular public meetings we _____ ⁹ (listen) to what people say and want, and we _____ ¹⁰ (produce) an action plan on such concerns as housing and pollution. Although there is still a lot to do, we _____ ¹¹ (try) to solve the problem of pollution. Until we _____ ¹² (deal with) this problem, we _____ ¹³ (not be able) to attract significant numbers of tourists to our country. As soon as we _____ ¹⁴ (begin) our second term in office, we _____ ¹⁵ (start) work on the next stage of these plans.

Vote Democratic – Vote Parisi!

2 Complete the sentences from Antonio Parisi's manifesto with *before*, *after*, *for*, *since*, or *in*.

- We have built 10,000 low-cost flats _____ last year.
- We have opened 300 new schools _____ the last five years.
- The rate of inflation has been stable _____ several years.
- It will only be a short time _____ we see the full benefit of this period of economic stability.
- Pollution will be reduced _____ we introduce our new proposals on use of cars in cities.

❷ Expressing probability, 1st and 2nd Conditionals

Read the news headlines from the future. How likely or unlikely do you think the events are to happen? Describe the possible consequences by writing sentences like the ones in the example.

More young people go to university

Average working week now only 20 hours

More controls on use of drugs in sport

Computer games made illegal for under 16s

Leaders agree to form World government

Example   WORLD'S CITIES CONTINUE TO GROW
I think it's very likely that the world's cities will continue to grow.

If they continue to grow, governments will need to spend more on housing.

If everyone moved to the cities, there wouldn't be anybody to work on the farms.

❸ *should have (done)/shouldn't have (done)*, 3rd Conditional

What went wrong when Hi-Tec Systems used the A to Z Removal Company to relocate its offices? Write two sentences, using *should have (done)/shouldn't have (done)* and the 3rd Conditional.

Example   *removal company booked to start work at 6 a.m., arrived 10 a.m.*
The removal company should have arrived at 6 a.m.

If they had arrived on time, they would have had enough time to do the job.

1 used inexperienced staff who took much longer
2 didn't have enough packaging materials, so damaged some of the equipment
3 took lots of breaks, so lost time
4 used an old van which broke down
5 didn't read the address properly so went to the wrong destination
6 dropped a very valuable picture

4　Reporting spoken language

Report what was said on the day for each of the problems in ③ .

Example　*A to Z: 'We're a little late because the traffic is heavy.'*
　　　　　　A to Z said that they were a little late because the traffic was heavy.

1　A to Z: 'We've taken on a new member of staff and we're training him up.'
2　A to Z: 'You didn't tell us that you had so many computers. Do you want to wait while we get head office to send more packaging?'
3　A to Z: 'It's a very hot day, so we'll need to take one or two drinks breaks.'
4　Hi-Tec: 'Why have you turned up in such an old van?'
5　A to Z: 'I can't read the writing on the address document.'
6　Hi-Tec: 'Be careful with the picture. It's very valuable.'

5　Writing emails, Business correspondence

Write the following messages. Decide whether an email, a fax, or a letter is most appropriate.

1　to a friend describing a new flat you have just moved into
2　to a furniture company ordering some items for your new flat
3　from Hi-Tec Systems to the A to Z Removal Company complaining about the job they did
4　to your colleagues proposing some new strategies for motivating staff at work
5　to an international colleague describing the political system in your country

6　Describing a process, Interviewing techniques

Choose one of these topics:

• a recipe and instructions for making a typical dish from your country
• the procedures you go through when revising and preparing for an exam
• the process of recruiting and appointing new staff

1　What are the different stages involved in the topic you have chosen?
2　Work in pairs. Interview your partner about their topic for a radio programme.

7　Social responses, Common expressions, Saying goodbye

What would you say in these situations?

1　Invite a colleague for a drink after work.
2　You want to help a colleague rearrange his or her desk.
3　Your boss's car has broken down and you'd like to give him or her a lift, but you're worried your car is in a mess.
4　Say goodbye to a visitor who you are going to visit next month.
5　You've been invited out for a meal but you want to go home early to prepare for an important presentation you're giving tomorrow.
6　Say goodbye to your colleagues at your place of work or study, but you want to arrange to meet up again in the future.

Work in pairs. Role-play each situation with a partner. Try to continue the conversation for as long as possible. Include some of these expressions: *As I was saying …, That reminds me …, Talking of …, If you ask me …, As you say … .*

8　Vocabulary test

Work in two groups, A and B. Write a vocabulary test to give to the other group. Choose ten of the words below. Write a sentence or phrase to help the other group guess the word.

Example　Word *strike*
　　　　　　Clue　*when people refuse to go to work as a protest*

strike ✓	bureaucracy	downsizing	culture shock	economic sanctions
key workers	organigram	addicted	Cc	market economy
coalition	generation	appraisal	log on	privatization
come across	fulfilling	recover	electorate	spokesperson
summit	adjourn	back-up	scenario	keyboard skills

Listening scripts

Unit 1

1.1

P=Piet, E=Eric

P   … OK, then, yes, goodbye. That was Rosa. She's leaving the office now. She'll be a little late, I'm afraid.

E   No problem. So, you and Rosa started NMP together?

P   That's right. Rosa and I set up the company fifteen years ago. But we've known each other since we were at university. The company started as NVP – Network Video Productions. We've been NMP for two years. We decided to expand into other multimedia production work – web design, media presentations, management training, and e-learning.

E   Have you expanded the management as well, or is it still just you and Rosa?

P   We've recruited two more managers since we became NMP, but Rosa and I are still very active.

E   Do you and Rosa have separate roles?

P   Yes, although we always discuss everything together. Rosa's the creative person. She gets the ideas. She knows the market very well and understands what the customers want. Rosa manages the projects from start to finish. My job is mainly to develop the business. I negotiate with the people who buy the programmes. For the big projects that cost a lot, I look for financial partners who will share the costs – and the profits.

E   I see. And what about the two new managers?

P   Paul, our new Financial Manager, deals with the financial aspects of running the business. We also have a new Promotions Manager, Louise. You're meeting her this afternoon. She handles all the marketing and advertising. She's working on two big launches at the moment, so currently she's very busy.

E   Do you and Rosa travel much?

P   Yes, we both do. I usually go abroad at least four or five times a month. And Rosa is rarely in her office for more than two days at a time. At the moment she's working on two major projects, so she's travelling even more than usual. And Louise is very busy with the launches here.

1.2

L=Louise, E=Eric

L   Right, Eric. Thanks for coming along. As Piet probably explained, I need to get some information on you for our publicity department, for when we start to promote the project.

E   OK.

L   I'd like to ask you a few things about your background first. Where were you born?

E   I was born in Cornwall, in a small seaside town, but my parents moved to London when I was four.

L   Did you grow up in London?

E   Yes, I grew up in London and went to school there.

L   What did you do after school?

E   I went to college to study for a diploma in Cookery, Catering, and Hospitality Management. I'd been interested in cookery since I was fourteen. My mother went out to work then and I had to cook for my younger brother and sister.

L   What did you do when you finished the cookery course?

E   After the course I started working as a chef in London. I worked at two restaurants, the Hilton and the Buckingham, where I was Head Chef.

L   Where did you work after that?

E   After the Buckingham, I went to France and then Italy. Partly to learn more about cooking and partly to learn the languages.

L   What languages do you speak?

E   I speak English, French, and Italian. I really enjoy speaking other languages – although I'm not so good at writing.

L   How long have you had your restaurant?

E   I've had my own restaurant since 1999. It's hard work, but I love it.

L   What do you enjoy doing in your free time?

E   Apart from cookery, I enjoy playing tennis in the summer and skiing in the winter.

L   OK, and finally, do you have any plans for the future?

E   Yes, I do. My ambition is to open my own cookery school.

L   Great. Well, thanks Eric. I think we've got what we need. Good luck with the project.

E   Thanks.

1.3

P=Piet, E=Eric, C=Claire

P   Hello, Eric, how are you? Good to see you again.

E   I'm fine thanks, Piet. And you?

P   Yes, very well. Eric, I'd like to introduce you to Claire, our secretary. Claire, this is Eric Carlin. He's going to play a major role in our new project.

C   Yes, Rosa's told me all about it. Pleased to meet you, Mr Carlin.

E   Pleased to meet you too.

C   I recognize you from your television programmes of course. I really enjoy them …

P   Claire's another of your fans, Eric! Anyway, come into my office. I want to show you our plans for the project.

1.4

P= Piet, W=Mr Wyatt

P   So, did you have any problems finding us?

W   No, none at all. I walked here. My hotel is only a few minutes away.

P   Oh really? Which hotel are you staying in?

W   I'm staying at the Garrick. It's in King Street. Do you know it?

P   I know the name. What's it like?

W   Oh, it's very pleasant. I always stay there when I come to London.

P   How often do you come to London?

W   Four or five times a year. What about you? Do you travel abroad much?

P   Yes, I do quite a lot of travelling – mostly in Europe, but I go to Canada and the States as well – about two or three times a year.

W   Canada? That's interesting. Have you been to Toronto?

P   No, I've never been to Toronto, but I had a wonderful holiday on Vancouver Island not long ago.

1.5

1

P   How long are you staying here?

W   Just three days. I'm flying back the day after tomorrow.

2

P   How long have you been with your company?

W   I've been with Star TV for four years now.

3

W   Isn't this weather wonderful?

P   Yes, it is. We do get good weather in London sometimes.

4

P   Where did you spend your last holiday?

W   I went to New Zealand with my wife and our two daughters.

5

P   Do you do any sport?

W   Yes, I play ice-hockey in winter and I do some sailing in summer.

Unit 2

2.1

I=Interviewer, JP=Julie Pankhurst

I   Julie, when did you first get the idea for 'Friends Reunited'?

JP   Well, it really started in July 1999 when I was on maternity leave from work, and a lot of the time before the baby was born I didn't actually have much to do. I started to look back on my life. I thought about the friends I had at school, and I found myself wondering where they were now. Did they have families of their own? Did they still live in the same area? Were they married, divorced, still alive?

I   And you thought the Internet would be the ideal way to get in touch with old friends?

JP   Yes, that's right. I was a programmer at the time so I had the skills. And it fitted in with my husband Stephen's plans. He's a web designer and he and his partner Jason Porter wanted to start a new company. So, the three of us set up Friends Reunited dot com.

I   And how does it work? What do you have to do?

JP   It's a very simple idea, really. You have to be a member. For a small registration fee, members can put their details and messages on the site and then they can get in touch with former school friends. You just look up the school, look up the year, and away you go! We didn't want to make it difficult – we wanted people who didn't use the Internet very much to be interested as well.

I   What sort of things do people do when they're online?

JP   I think a lot of them just browse and find out what has happened to their old schoolmates. But often they exchange memories, discuss old teachers, funny things that happened, and so on. Lots of them arrange to meet and have real reunions.

I   The idea grew quite fast, didn't it?

JP   Very much so. After just three years, in 2002, we had seven million members and 45,000 schools and universities were registered.

I   I know Friends Reunited has been one of the most successful dot com companies. But what about future plans?

JP   Well, we started in the UK, but since 2002 we've launched international sites in Australia, South Africa, New Zealand, and many other countries in Europe and beyond. We've also added over 400,000 workplaces to the system so that people can locate old work friends. We just want to keep on expanding, but keep the idea simple.

I   Julie, thank you for talking to us. That was Julie Pankhurst, founder of …

2.2

I = Interviewer, ML = Martin Leach

I In this edition of 'Working lives' I'm pleased to welcome Martin Leach, CEO of the Italian sports car manufacturer, Maserati. Martin, can I start by asking you to tell us something about the company?

ML Sure. It was founded in 1914, and in the early years it was run by the Maserati brothers from their base in Bologna in Italy. The local origins and a reputation for craftsmanship are still an important part of the company's style. The quality sports car industry is an industry where tradition is important, but you also have to be modern.

I The company moved from Bologna, didn't it?

ML Yes, they moved the headquarters to Modena in 1940 and continued to produce cars for the international market as well as for racing. But I think the big change came in the 1990s; that's when Maserati really became a modern company.

I In what way?

ML Well, the Fiat Car Company bought 100% of the share capital in 1993 and in 1997 there was a takeover of Maserati by Ferrari.

I So Ferrari is the parent company and Maserati is a subsidiary?

ML Yes, although the two brands were kept separate. At the same time they closed the factory and installed an ultra-modern assembly line which opened for production in 1998 and increased output to two thousand cars a year. And in fact nowadays we produce about 25 a day. That's still not a lot compared to the big companies, but remember we're a specialist company. There were more changes in 2004, particularly with senior staff, including my own appointment as CEO in June 2004.

I What do you think are the key factors in the success of this Maserati 'relaunch' in recent years?

ML I think tradition and reputation is important, as I said before. The company pays a lot of attention to design, and to research and development. We also have good client loyalty, and we involve our owners and enthusiasts in new developments and designs. Above all, we're a local company with an international appeal. We have representatives in 45 countries, and we're always looking for new markets.

2.3

I I can't help noticing that you're British. Is it unusual to be in charge of an Italian company?

ML Perhaps. But my background is in cars, and sports cars in particular.

I When did you first become interested in cars?

ML When I was small, our family used to go to Italy for our holidays. I have a picture of me in the first ever Ferrari I went in – I was about seven and it was owned by the hotel owner's son. Then at the age of eleven I started racing go-karts – in fact I won the European Cup and came third in the World Championships.

I Your first job was with the Ford Car Company, I believe?

ML That's right, at the age of 17. They also sponsored me to study engineering in England. I think that over the years I've worked in every department at Ford: the engineering department, marketing, sales, forecasting, and so on.

I Did you work outside the UK before joining Maserati?

ML Yes. I worked in Japan for Mazda from 1996 to 1999, then moved to Germany to be vice-president of product development for Ford Europe. In 2002, I became CEO of Ford Europe – until 2003. Then I was a freelance consultant for a while and then joined Maserati as CEO in June 2004.

I Do you speak Italian?

ML I suppose I'm Intermediate, but I'm learning fast. At the moment we've agreed to hold all senior meetings in English. In fact we use a bit of both languages, and for me that's probably the best way to improve my Italian.

2.4

I So, can you describe a typical week for you?

ML I usually leave my house in Bologna at 7.15, and start work around 8 a.m. and finish around 7.30 in the evening. I'm responsible for the whole Maserati operation in Modena, and I like to start early. There's plenty of variety in my work. Last week for example, on Monday morning, after checking my emails of course, I started with a meeting with Claudio Berro, the head of the racing department. It's important to understand all aspects of our product, and racing is a very important part.

I And one that you have a particular interest in.

ML Yes, indeed. After lunch, I made my usual tour of the factory. It's my job to make sure everyone is working to the best of his or her ability. I think when you're the CEO, you need to be visible, and show people who you are and that you're interested in their work. My job involves a lot of contact with different people – which I like – from the directors, to the department heads, to the workforce themselves. On Tuesday morning, I had a meeting with the Product Marketing team to look at plans for a new model, and in the afternoon there was a long meeting with the directors in the boardroom. On Wednesday, there was *another* meeting – with the Honorary President of the Maserati Members Club. As you can see, I spend a lot of time in meetings! On Wednesday afternoon, I had to give a speech – in Italian – to around 3,000 Ferrari and Maserati suppliers. It was only fifteen minutes, but I was very nervous. The part of my job that I enjoy most is working with the cars, and on Thursday I spent a few hours on the test track evaluating a prototype of a new car. Then I flew to Rome for a ceremony with the Italian President on Friday morning. We presented him with a new car with special features, including extra security protection.

I And then you came back home?

ML Yes. After lunch with the head of Fiat, I got back to Bologna just in time for an ice cream with the children. I always try to have time with the family in the evening. You have to know how to balance work with relaxation – that's the most important skill to have. I think that was a fairly typical week.

2.5

R=Rosa, E=Eric's answerphone

R Er, let's see, where's Eric's number? Ah, here it is.

E Hello. I'm sorry I can't take your call at the moment. Please leave your name, number, and message, and I'll get back to you as soon as possible. Please speak after the tone. Thank you for calling.

R Hello Eric, it's Rosa Lanson. I'm calling to arrange a meeting. Could you manage next week? Monday or Tuesday would be best if you could make it then. Could you call me to arrange a time? Thanks. Goodbye.

2.6

C=Claire, E=Eric

C Good afternoon, Network Multimedia Productions. Can I help you?

E Good afternoon. Could I speak to Rosa Lanson?

C I'm afraid Ms Lanson isn't here today. Can I help you?

E Is that Claire?

C Yes, it is.

E Hello, Claire. This is Eric Carlin.

C Oh, hello Eric. How are you?

E I'm fine, thanks. Erm … I got a message from Rosa on my answerphone, asking me to contact her about a meeting.

C Ah, yes. Rosa told me about it. Could you make it on Monday or Tuesday?

E Unfortunately, I can't make it on Monday or Tuesday morning, but Tuesday afternoon would be OK.

C I see. Would two fifteen suit you?

E Yes, that would be fine.

C Good. Then let's make a provisional appointment for two fifteen. That's Tuesday the third, right? But I need to check the time with Piet and Rosa. Could I call you back to confirm?

E Yes, of course. Speak to you later. Goodbye Claire.

C Thanks Eric. Goodbye.

2.7

E=Eric, C=Claire

E Hello, Eric Carlin speaking.

C Hello, Eric. It's Claire again. I'm phoning about the meeting next weekend. I'm sorry, but Piet isn't available at the time we arranged, he's got another appointment. But he's free later on. Would four o'clock be possible for you?

E So that's four o'clock instead of two fifteen?

C Yes. Is that time convenient for you?

E Yes, that's fine.

C Good. So, we look forward to seeing you next Tuesday, then. Goodbye, Eric.

2.8

six	Tuesday	this	think
seventy	Wednesday	then	thirteen
Saturday	hours	there	thirty
weeks	miles	mother	Thursday

2.9

1 sick   2 thing   3 think   4 mouse
5 path   6 worse

2.10

Tuesday the third of March
Saturday the twelfth of August
Thursday the thirteenth of July
Monday the sixteenth of April
Wednesday the twenty-fourth of February
Sunday the twenty-sixth of September
Friday the thirtieth of December

Unit 3

3.1

I=Interviewer, AH=Andrea Harris

I If you want to be a better communicator in the international business world, you need languages. So, let's hear from someone who uses languages every day in her work. Andrea Harris, you arrange business trips for companies keen to promote themselves in Europe and Asia. Is that right?

AH Yes, it is. It's demanding but also really enjoyable. I often have to deal with clients who don't speak English. My two other languages are Spanish and Japanese, which are totally different to each other.

I Can you tell us a little bit about how you learnt these languages?

AH Sure. The first thing I realized is that learning a foreign language can be a lot harder than you think. As a child I studied French at school, as most people do in Britain, and learning a language when you're young is much quicker and easier than when you're older. I think your brain slows down over time. But a few years ago, I started learning Spanish. At first it was a little harder than I'd expected. For me, Spanish was slightly more difficult than French, and the other students in the class seemed to make much better progress than me. I nearly gave up. But after a while it got a little easier and I started to enjoy the lessons.

I How did you practise outside the lessons?

AH My husband, whose Spanish is excellent,

helped me. Now, five years later, my Spanish is pretty fluent. One day, I would like it to be as good as my English. I think to achieve this I would have to go and live where Spanish is spoken by everybody. I can now look back and say that learning Spanish was one of the most interesting and most useful things I've ever done.

I And what about your Japanese?

AH Of course, it's the least like the other languages I speak. My company paid for me to have lessons. My teacher, who was Japanese, was the best teacher I have ever had. He's from Osaka originally but he now lives in London, where we met. He's really one of the nicest and most patient teachers you could hope for! And he had to be – I was useless at first, much worse than I'd been at Spanish. But then, as I said, Japanese is much more difficult than Spanish for English speakers anyway – there aren't many words in Japanese that are similar in English, and then there are the written characters to learn.

I So, how good is your Japanese now?

AH Good question! I can actually communicate with Japanese clients now without too much difficulty. I'm not sure what my exact 'level' would be! Certainly, my Japanese is not as fluent as my Spanish, but one day it will be. I would also like to study Arabic, but it's a matter of finding the time. Anyway …

3.2
P=Presenter, RC=Ruth Chan

P And now to our technology update. We've all heard of the Rosetta Stone but how many of us know about the Rosetta Disk? Linguists and scientists are hoping it's going to be as important in recording information about the languages of the world today as its predecessor was over two thousand years ago. We sent Ruth Chan to find out more.

RC The aim of the new Rosetta Project is to create a permanent physical archive of one thousand of the world's languages. The new Rosetta 'Stone' will be a spherical container which will hold and protect a special micro-etched disk. The project organizers also plan to produce two other media: an online archive and a single-volume reference book. The project was the idea of linguists and scientists who work at the Long Now Foundation, which is based here in San Francisco. The disk will contain a description of each language, which will include its grammar and pronunciation system, a word list of two hundred core words, and a parallel text from the Bible – Genesis, chapters one to three. This text was chosen because biblical texts are the most widely and carefully translated texts on the planet. The new Rosetta Disk will be quite small. People will need a microscope to read it – with magnification of 1,000 times. The project organizers plan to produce lots of disks, which will be distributed throughout the world to help ensure their survival. Material on languages is collected through a website, www.rosettaproject.org, where scholars and native speakers contribute their research. There are currently 664 volunteers working on the project throughout the world. I asked one of the organizers to show me some of the fascinating information they've already collected …

3.3
R=Rosa, E=Eric, P=Piet

R Right. Shall we start? The aim of this meeting is to discuss our new project. As you know, we're planning to make ten programmes on the food and drink of other countries. The cost of the first three programmes will be financed by NMP, but to produce the other seven programmes we'll need investment from other companies. In this meeting we must decide first which countries we want to have in the pilot programme. So, what are your views? Eric, would you like to start?

E Well, in my opinion the first programmes should be about the most exotic countries – say Japan, Mexico, and Thailand. I'm sure the programmes about these countries will be the most exciting ones because everything there is so different.

P Yes, you could be right, Eric, but from a financial point of view, the cost of making programmes in those countries will be too high for NMP's budget, so I'm afraid I can't agree with that idea. We must have European countries in the first three programmes.

E OK. Then how do you feel about having Japan, Mexico, and Thailand in later programmes?

P Yes, I agree with that, on the condition that we can get the investment we need, of course—

R Yes, Piet's right, Eric. We must think of the cost. Personally, I think France, Italy, and Spain would be the best choices. I really do think it's better to start with high-profile countries because—

E Sorry, Rosa, I don't quite follow you. Could you explain what you mean by 'high-profile countries'?

R Well, I mean countries whose food and drink is well-known in other countries, well-known internationally.

E Maybe, but the French or Italian or Spanish food that other nationalities eat in their countries is often very different from the real thing!

R Yes, and if people don't know that already, they'll discover it from watching our programmes!

E Let's hope so.

R Right. Do we all agree then? France, Italy, and Spain for the first three programmes?

P Yes, definitely!

P Yes, I'd go along with that.

R Good. Then let's move on to the next topic – the pilot programme. We need to decide which country …

3.4

E So, the pilot programme is very important?

R Oh, yes, it's extremely important. Our pilot programme has to do two important things – first to make investors want to put their money into the project and second to make TV companies want to buy the programmes. Of the three countries—

P Just a minute, Rosa. Could I just ask something? When you and I discussed this before we agreed that the pilot programme would be one of the ten programmes, didn't we?

R Yes, we did. So, of the three countries I'm inclined to think that France would be the best choice. However, before we make a decision we need to find a consultant for each programme, someone who knows the country and its cuisine very well, so we can get the information we need before we plan the programme in detail.

P Yes, that's an important point. Do you think someone who's written a book about the country's cuisine would be the kind of person you need?

E Oh, before you go on, could I say something? I know a Spanish person who's written an excellent book on Spanish cuisine. She lives in London and her name's María Ferrando.

R Really? Do you think she'd be interested in being a consultant for the programme on Spain?

E I'm quite sure she would.

R That's great! Then let's contact her straightaway. If she says yes, do we all agree on Spain for the pilot programme?

P I agree completely.

E Yes, definitely.

P That's lucky, Eric. Maybe you know some experts on French and Italian food and drink as well?

E Yes, I'll think about it. Maybe I do …

R Well, I think that's everything. Is there anything else you want to discuss?

E No, I'm fine.

P No, I don't think so.

R So, to sum up, then. We've agreed that the first three programmes will be about France, Italy, and Spain, and that if we can get María Ferrando as a consultant, we'll have Spain in the pilot programme. Good, let's call it a day, then. Thanks Eric, Piet. Well, I don't know about you two, but I could do with a drink now.

3.5
1 Could you explain that again?
2 Could you explain that again? ✓

3.6
1 a Could you begin, James? ✓
  b Could you begin, James?
2 a Excuse me. Could I come in here?
  b Excuse me. Could I come in here? ✓
3 a Can we get back to the main point?
  b Can we get back to the main point? ✓
4 a Would you mind repeating that? ✓
  b Would you mind repeating that?
5 a Could you go over that again? ✓
  b Could you go over that again?

3.7
1 Could you begin, James?
2 Excuse me. Could I come in here?
3 Can we get back to the main point?
4 Would you mind repeating that?
5 Could you go over that again?

Unit 4
4.1
The graph shows the average number of hours that people watched television in the UK last year. During the winter, particularly in December and January, people always watch more television. In January last year, the average number of weekly viewing hours stood at 28.1. This figure went down steadily for the next two months, reaching 27.2 in February and 25.5 in March. The number of viewing hours then fluctuated a little: they increased slightly to 26.1 in April. They then fell dramatically to 23.3 in May. The figure then rose very slightly to 23.5 in June and then more or less levelled off for the summer, which is traditionally the time when people watch the least television. The figure decreased slightly back to 23.3 in July and reached its lowest point in August at 23.2. Average viewing hours went up sharply in September to 25.3 and then increased more gradually for the rest of the year to 26.1 in October, and 27.4 in November. The figure reached its highest point in December at 28.2 hours per week. So the overall seasonal trend last year was a gradual fall in the first part of the year, a levelling off in the summer, and then a steady rise in the last part of the year.

4.2
P=Presenter, JR=John Rivetts, NK=Naomi Kent

P Globalization is certainly a hot topic. As consumers, it seems that we are all increasingly using the same products, eating the same food, even watching the same TV programmes and films. Does this mean that the differences between our societies are disappearing, with more and more people buying fewer and fewer brands? If so, how does the average consumer feel? To try to answer these questions, I have with me John Rivetts, an economics journalist, and Professor Naomi Kent, a consumer affairs specialist. John, is globalization in consumer products really increasing that fast?

JR Yes, I think it is. People in the developing world want many of the things that they see coming from the developed world, and in the West we're constantly looking for new markets. We're very successful at persuading people to buy everything from fast food to cigarettes and designer clothes.

P And how does the average consumer feel about this?

JR Well, you have to ask 'Who is the average consumer?' You could argue globalization means some consumers can get the products they really want. However, other consumers see it as 'a bad thing'. Look at cigarettes, for example. Global production of cigarettes is increasing more slowly than before, as people in the developed world in particular become more worried about the health risks. But manufacturers have identified developing countries as potential growth markets. Between 1975 and 2000, annual deaths due to tobacco in developed countries rose steadily from 1.3 million to 2.1 million, but in developing countries they went up dramatically from 0.2 million to the same figure of 2.1 million. But it's not all bad – there are many positive and responsible forms of trade between the developed and the developing world.

P Naomi, do you share John's opinion?

NK Yes, but I think it's important to say that there's a growing trend in imports from the developing world. More and more people in the West and the developed world in general are buying products that are different and unusual, and they are asking questions about the origins of these products. Consumers won't accept that products have to be made by badly-paid workers in 'sweatshop' conditions. That's the idea behind the fair-trade movement, of course.

P What other issues worry this new kind of 'ethical consumer'?

NK Products that cause environmental damage, products tested on animals—

JR Yes, but the total market share of ethical goods and services in the UK remains at under 2%. Perhaps we need to think of the 'bigger picture'. Take the Hollywood film industry, for example. It dominates world cinema and stops film industries in other countries developing. It also advertises western consumer products and lifestyles.

NK I don't think it's as simple as that. Local consumers in developing countries don't just buy what the West tells them to buy – they make choices. You mentioned Hollywood. In India, the home-grown film industry is much more important, particularly in Mumbai, or Bombay, the home of the so-called 'Bollywood' movies. And the all-singing, all-dancing Bollywood films are in fact now becoming popular in the West.

JR Yes, I accept that it's a two-way process, but I worry that the 'traffic' is heavier in one direction. We certainly have to be careful about trends in international trade.

NK I agree, but I think more and more people in the West are becoming ethical consumers, thinking very carefully about what they buy – you know, reading the labels on products or supermarket shelves. This is making manufacturers think about these things as well. Put very simply, people enjoy their coffee more if they know it's been produced by workers who are not exploited.

4.3
R=Rosa, MF=María Ferrando, E=Eric

R First, María, I'd like to say how pleased we are to have you as a consultant for our programme on Spain.

MF I'm very happy you asked me. It sounds like a very interesting project.

R We hope so. As I explained in my letter we would like to focus on three regions with

quite different cuisines, to give some idea of the variety of Spanish cuisine. What would you suggest?

MF If you want three quite different regions, my advice would be to choose the Basque country, Catalonia, and Andalucía. Basque cooking has the reputation of being the best in Spain, and many of Spain's best chefs come from the Basque country. There are lots of interesting seafood specialities, and San Sebastián is famous for its men-only gastronomic clubs, where men get together to cook gourmet meals for themselves! It might be a good idea to include them in your programme as they're also a local speciality.

E Yes, that sounds like a good idea!

R Yes, I think we should do that. Good, so we'll definitely have the Basque country as one of the three regions … Now, María, what about you appearing in the programme on Spain, perhaps to talk about the different regions—

MF Oh, I'm afraid I'm not very keen on that idea. It's very nice of you to ask me, though.

R Well, we might persuade you to change your mind later … Now, how about some coffee, María? Eric?

4.4

MF Well, I'd suggest you include Catalonia as one of the three regions because it has a very interesting and varied cuisine. Its capital, Barcelona, is considered to be one of the best places to eat in Europe. I'd recommend you include some of Barcelona's tapas bars in your programme. I think you should also visit the Penedés region of Catalonia where Spain's well-known sparkling wine, *cava*, is produced.

R Yes, let's do that. Do you think we should explain the origin of typical Spanish foods like *paella* – describe where the idea came from and how these dishes vary in different regions?

MF Yes, that's an interesting idea. Then you could go to Valencia because that's where *paella* originated, although of course you find paella everywhere in Spain today.

R Right. Now, what would you advise us to do in Andalucía?

MF Well, if I were you, I'd go to Jerez de la Frontera, where sherry comes from. And you could go and see the bar in Seville where the custom of eating *tapas* probably originated. And another thing Andalucía is famous for is its confectionery – traditional Spanish sweets and cakes. There's a convent in Seville that's famous for the confectionery made by its nuns, so I'd suggest you go there too.

R Yes, that's something different. Well María, you've given us lots of helpful advice. What Eric and I need to do now is discuss all these ideas, and draw up a detailed plan for the programme on Spain. Then, how about meeting again in about a week's time, to finalize details of the programme?

MF Yes, I'll be happy to do that. In the meantime, good luck with the preparation.

4.5

1	sherry	cherry
2	shoes	choose
3	dish	ditch

4.6

1 Would you like a cherry?
2 Excuse me. This is my share.
3 I can't see any ships.
4 Did you say they were cheap?
5 Shall I watch it?
6 Do you want me to cash it?

4.7

1 a Would you like a sherry?
   b Would you like a cherry?
2 a Excuse me. This is my share.
   b Excuse me. This is my chair.

3 a I can't see any ships.
   b I can't see any chips.
4 a Did you say they were sheep?
   b Did you say they were cheap?
5 a Shall I wash it?
   b Shall I watch it?
6 a Do you want me to cash it?
   b Do you want me to catch it?

4.8

1	chess	5	merchant	8	shops
2	shelf	6	dish	9	chops
3	rich	7	ditch	10	Czech
4	shells				

Unit 5
5.1
DB=David Bowers, D1=Delegate 1, D2=Delegate 2, D3=Delegate 3

DB Well, good morning, ladies and gentlemen, and welcome to the Crowne Plaza business centre at Coogee Beach. I'm David Bowers, your host for the next two days, and I just want to give you some practical information. Another conference is being held at the hotel at the same time as this one. They are using the conference rooms on the first floor, so you may see some delegates you don't recognize – don't worry. They are being looked after by my colleague, Lidia Marchiori.
OK. coffee, tea, and cold drinks are served all day in the café which is located just inside the main entrance to the conference suite. Lunch is served between 12 and 2.30 in the private dining room next door to this room. This evening you are invited to join the management for drinks by the swimming pool. The General Manager usually makes a short welcome speech.
I'd like to apologize for the temperature. I'm afraid it's a little warmer than usual in here because the air-conditioning in the business centre is being repaired. However, the work will be completed before lunchtime.
Right. There are some changes to the conference programme. Unfortunately, one of the main speakers has cancelled her talk and so a couple of the sessions have been cancelled or rescheduled. Some of the rooms have also been changed. The updated programme is being printed at the moment. My colleague Anna is working on it and it will be available in the lobby, in good time for the first session.
One more thing: the business service centre is currently being extended, but there is a temporary business centre, which can be found in the reception area.
Now, before we go for breakfast, are there any questions?

D1 Are we expected to dress formally for dinner?

DB No, we ask everyone to be 'smart casual'. You're not permitted to wear shorts, but we try to be informal.

D2 Will we be shown round the fitness centre?

DB Yes, you'll be given an induction session this evening before dinner, if you're interested. The Fitness Centre Manager will come to the drinks party as well.

D3 Er, sorry but my newspaper wasn't delivered to my room this morning.

DB Oh. Did you request it at reception last night?

D3 Yes, I did.

DB OK, I'll look into it.

5.2

1 Abib Cury
I try to do some kind of exercise or sport most days. Sometimes, it's hard to find the time, because I have a full-time job and I'm also doing an MBA part-time. My gym opens at 5.30 a.m., so I try to fit in a 45-minute workout before I go to the office. There's a start-the-week class on Monday mornings and I rarely miss that. It helps me get in shape for the week. I lift weights once or

twice during the week too, but it depends how much energy I have. Swimming is another regular activity – my gym has a 20-metre pool, which is OK for a quick swim in the morning.

I think it's important to be healthy and fit. I probably don't eat as well as I should. I never have breakfast, just a strong black coffee. And I usually phone out for lunch and have a sandwich at my desk. I really enjoy eating out with friends in the evening. I do that at least three times a week and I don't always think about what's healthy. I never eat before 11 at night and usually not until after midnight. At weekends and in the summer, I like to spend time at the beach with friends. We play soccer on the beach and there's always lots of watersports going on. But these days I rarely go because I have coursework to catch up with at the weekend. The building where I live has a tennis court, so I usually play tennis on Sunday evenings. I also play soccer for my sports club team on Friday evenings. It means I have a good excuse to get out of the office at the end of the week.

2   Gao Da Cheng
I work most of the day and I don't have much time for recreational activities. On my day off on Sunday, I like to spend time with my family. I used to play basketball in school, but it's a long time since I did any real sport.
I think it is important to be healthy. In terms of health, I'm very lucky. I believe that good health comes from a good, regular diet and a happy and positive outlook on life. As far as exercise goes, I sometimes join my father early in the morning in the local park for t'ai chi, a very old Chinese martial art. It is very good for the mind as well as the body but my generation, and certainly people younger than me, tend to look at t'ai chi as a little old-fashioned. So, it isn't as popular as it was in the past, but I enjoy doing it – it certainly pleases my father!
I always eat at regular times, which is very, very important – breakfast at 6.30, lunch at midday, and dinner at 6 p.m. I think my body is better for this … and I must admit I don't feel right if I eat at unusual times!
I read a lot about the health of people in the West and all the exercise they do – running, working out in the gym, playing squash, and so on. I think they are trying to stay young for a long time! I don't worry too much about becoming older – it's a natural thing and, in Chinese culture, I think older people are respected much more than in the West.

5.3
1   Hi, you've reached Rosa and Colin. We're not here right now to take your call, but if you'd like to leave a message we'll get back to you as soon as possible.
2   This is Executive Travel Services. The office is closed at the moment. Our office hours are nine o'clock to six o'clock Monday to Friday, and nine o'clock to one o'clock on Saturday. Thank you for calling.
3   Hello, I'm sorry I can't take your call at the moment. Please leave your name, number, and a message, and I'll get back to you as soon as possible. Please speak after the tone. Thank you for calling.
4   The person you called is not available. Please leave a message after the tone. You can re-record your message by pressing 1 at any time.
5   Thank you for calling Compu-Help. All our operators are busy right now. If you want you can hold, or if you prefer you can leave your name, number, and a short description of the problem you are experiencing and an operator will phone you back in the next 30 minutes. Thank you.

5.4
1   This is a message for María Ferrando. This is Rosa Lanson. I just wanted to thank you for all the help and information you gave us. I'm going to research a few things and then we'll fix up another meeting. Thanks again.
2   Hello, this is Rosa Lanson on 020 84 double 8 3497. I'm having trouble connecting up to the Internet – my computer keeps crashing. Could you get back to me soon, please? It's just after four o'clock. Thanks.
3   Hi, Eric. It's Rosa. I've got some more information from the Internet about the places María suggested, so we ought to have another meeting. Could you manage later this week? Thursday or Friday would be best if you could make it then. Call me when you get a moment. Bye.
4   Hi, Rosa. It's Eric. I got your message. I'm afraid I can't make Thursday or Friday morning, but Friday afternoon's OK. How does that sound? Let me know – any time from two o'clock. Speak to you soon. Bye.

5.5
Hi Eric. It's Rosa. I've got some more information from the Internet about the places María suggested, so we ought to have another meeting. Could you manage later this week? Thursday or Friday would be best if you could make it then. Call me when you get a moment. Bye.

5.6
1   Sorry, I can't hear you.
2   You're breaking up.
3   It's a bit difficult to talk at the moment.
4   I'll be quick, the battery's r …
5   I'm in a meeting. Can I call you back?
6   I'm afraid I lost you just then.
7   Sorry, can you repeat that?
8   What was that?

Unit 6
6.1
I=Interviewer, CM=César Murillo
I   Where do you come from, César?
CM I come from Huelva, a city in the southern Spanish region of Andalucía.
I   When did you come to England?
CM I came to London in 1998. I was studying English Literature at a university in the south of Spain when I had the chance to come to the UK. I wanted to make a new start and London seemed like the ideal place.
I   You got a job as a teacher?
CM Yes. Before I went back to university, in Spain, I'd taught for five years in a Catholic school. So, I had some experience. But the teaching was very different.
I   How was it different?
CM At the beginning it was difficult. It was completely different from what I'd known before. The pupils came from so many different backgrounds and cultures, and a lot of them were from very poor families. There were also problems of discipline and classroom behaviour. I was teaching one day when a pupil stood up and shouted, 'This is boring', and walked out. That type of thing had never happened in Spain. But I saw this as a challenge. What at the beginning I thought was rudeness in my pupils was, in most cases, a different way of understanding life and learning.
I   What do you like about London?
CM I like the variety of London. It has every food and culture. Before I came to London, I had never seen anyone from India, for example. I also like the village atmosphere, the sense of different Londons within London, the way you can be in three different worlds in one day.
I   Do you still enjoy what you do?
CM Oh yes, even after all this time. There are more than seven million stories in London and I'm lucky to hear some of them as I work in a school with 1,200 students.

6.2
I=Interviewer, CS=Chris Stewart
I   Tell us a little bit about your background. You were a musician to start with, I believe?
CS Well, sort of. When I was at school some friends were putting together a band. I'd learnt the guitar, but I also played drums and they needed a drummer, so I was invited to join. We played a few gigs, made a record or two, and became 'Genesis' – you may have heard of them. The others left school to continue the band, but I stayed on to do my exams. I don't regret it. I did a lot of different exciting things.
I   Such as?
CS I worked as a shepherd. I learnt languages. I travelled a lot.
I   You wrote travel guides, didn't you? How did that happen?
CS I met these people at a party and got talking to them about travelling and my desire to go to China. They didn't say anything, but a week later, I was sitting at home when the phone rang. It was Mark and he told me he was the editor of a series of travel guides and asked if I wanted to go to China, expenses paid, to write 'The Rough Guide to China'.
I   When did you decide to move to Andalucía?
CS I suppose it started in 1973, when I was working in France. I was picking grapes on the *vendange* when I met an American woman. She told me how wonderful Seville was, especially as a place to study the guitar. When the grape-picking finished, I immediately hitched to Seville, and fell in love with the place – the architecture, the music, dances and songs, the poetry, and the whole romance of southern Spain. I went back whenever I could.
I   But you didn't move there until much later?
CS That's right – in 1988. I'd met Ana and got married by then. One day we were feeling miserable and talking about how dull and unexciting our lives had become. 'If only we lived in Spain', we said to each other – and so we did. We moved soon after and bought *El Valero*, this wonderful old farm, with no access road, no running water, no electricity.
I   So, you suddenly became a farmer and had to take care of pigs and goats as well as crops like olives and lemons. Was it difficult?
CS Ana and I had already farmed in England for many years when we came here, so we knew about sheep and farming. I'd learnt to shear sheep at the age of 21, for example. But there was, and still is, an awful lot to learn. They were very hard but happy days.
I   And now? Is it still exciting?
CS Oh, yes. There's always something to do. Right now the sky looks very dark over to the west. That means heavy rain, which means we'll probably lose the bridge again. So, more bridge-building for me. And then there's plenty more olives and oranges …

6.3
I=Interviewer, DD=Dean Douglas
I   Dean, could you tell me why you decided to take a gap year?
DD I was working as an investment banker. It was a well-paid job, but it was a stressful environment. I thought a lot about it, and then three years ago, after I'd collected my bonus, I handed in my notice. I was 34. I had no definite plans, but a few days later I was walking past a travel agency and I saw an advert for a round-the-world trip. I just went in and bought it!
I   So, where did you go?
DD Cuba first, then Mexico, then Australia, New Zealand, and south-east Asia.
I   What was the best bit?
DD The complete freedom. Every day I woke up and thought 'Shall I stay here, go somewhere else, or even go home?' I fell in love with New Zealand.
I   And the worst?

DD In Cuba I was very sick. I checked into a smart hotel and was treated by a local doctor. I lost about a third of my body weight, and nearly came home.

I What do you do now?

DD When I first got back, I joined an Internet company, but when that wasn't going very well, I changed direction and set up a gardening business. It's not as well paid as banking, but I'm very happy. And I'm planning to go back to New Zealand some time soon.

I=Interviewer, AR=Alicia Rubio

I Alicia, you took a gap year a few years ago when you were 21 years old. Why did you do it then?

AR I was a medical student in Madrid, and I was studying very hard and coming to the end of the first part of my studies. I was enjoying it a lot and could see my future working as a doctor in Spain, and everything. I liked the idea but I also knew that I wanted to get some wider experience and see what medicine was like in other countries, outside Europe. We had a chance in our course to take an elective programme – a year's work experience, so I said 'Yeah, I'd like to do it in Africa'.

I Where exactly did you go?

AR I went to Ghana and worked in a hospital in Accra, the capital. Mainly just doing basic nursing duties, but it was fascinating.

I What did you like most about it?

AR I suppose the fact that it was just so different. And also that I got to have more responsibility. I was working mainly in the maternity department, and one day, quite early on actually, I had to deliver a baby all by myself because I was the only one on duty! I was so frightened, but everything went well. That was definitely the best bit.

I And the worst?

AR Not understanding the local language properly at the start. It can make you feel really lonely and a bit useless. My Spanish wasn't much use, but I had good English and French, and I soon picked up what I needed. But at the start it was difficult.

I So what do you do now? Has the experience helped you?

AR Definitely. I'm working in a big hospital, in the maternity department, and I think every day I use a technique or something that I learnt in Ghana.

I = Interviewer, HR=Hortense Robert

I Hortense, you were a teacher before you took your gap year, weren't you?

HR Yes, I'd worked as a teacher for nearly 30 years, teaching science. And I took early retirement.

I Did you know what you wanted to do?

HR I wanted to travel, but I also wanted to do something with conservation and use my knowledge of science. I had one or two options, but in the end I chose a placement in Malaysia, northern Borneo to be precise, working on a marine project to help conserve the coral reef.

I Why did you choose that?

HR In my youth I'd been a very keen diver and I was in fact a qualified scuba instructor. The project involved a lot of diving and I knew I probably wouldn't be able to do it for long, but they also needed instructors to train and supervise the younger volunteers, as well as work with the local people – giving basic teaching and raising conservation awareness. I just knew it was for me.

I So, you went out to Malaysia for a full year?

HR A year and a half in the end.

I Is that because you enjoyed it so much?

HR That's right. The best thing was my first proper dive out on the reef. I hadn't dived for about ten years, and it was just so spectacular. There are some of the best dive sites in the world out there, and you see everything – fish of all sorts, not to mention

the corals, lobsters, and crabs. I realized a year wasn't going to be enough.

I Was it all good, or did you have any bad experiences?

HR It was virtually all good, but I had one bad experience at the end, when I got into trouble on a dive and lost consciousness. Luckily I was with others, but it was the worst experience I'd had, very scary. I thought to myself: 'I'm in my early 50s, I'd better slow down a bit'. That's when I made the decision to come back.

I I gather you still do work for marine conservation.

HR Yes, I give lectures and talks, and try to recruit people for some of the projects going on round the world.

6.4

R=Rosa, C=Claire

R Hi, Claire. I know you're very busy, but could you do something for me?

C Yes, of course.

R Would you mind phoning Executive Travel Services to get some information?

C Not at all. Is it for your research trip to Spain?

R That's right. Eric and I need to visit quite a few places. Do you think you could find out about flights?

C Yes, that's no problem. Could you give me the details?

R Right. We want to go to San Sebastián first. Er ... I think the nearest airport is Bilbao, but do you mind checking that with them?

C No, of course not. If it is, would you like me to ask about flights to Bilbao?

R Yes, if you could, for Sunday the second.

C So, London to Bilbao on Sunday the second.

R Then we'd like to fly from Bilbao to Seville on Tuesday the fourth, and possibly from Seville to Valencia on Friday the seventh.

C Just a minute ... Bilbao to Seville on Tuesday the fourth, and Seville to Valencia on Friday the seventh. Right, I've got that.

R After that we want to go to Barcelona. Erm ... I'm not sure which day yet. Can you get flight times for Saturday and Sunday – that's the eighth and ninth.

C Yes, I'll do that.

R And then we'll fly back to London on the Tuesday.

C Shall I get flight times from Barcelona?

R Thanks, Claire, but you needn't bother. There are plenty of flights between Barcelona and London. Good, that's everything.

C Well, that's quite a trip!

R Yes, I just hope that at the end of it we'll be able to remember who we met and where we met them!

6.5

J=Jan, C=Claire

J Good afternoon, Executive Travel Services. Jan speaking. How can I help you?

C Oh, hello, Jan. It's Claire from NMP. I'd like some information on flights, er, quite a lot of information, actually.

J Right, where to?

C To Spain. First, do you happen to know if Bilbao is the nearest airport to San Sebastián?

J Yes, it is.

C Good, then could you tell me what flights there are from London to Bilbao on Sunday the second?

J That's the second of this month, is it?

C Yes, that's right.

J Right, let's see ... OK. There's a daily flight to Bilbao in the morning, departing at 11.15 and arriving at 13.05.

C So, departing 11.15, arriving 13.05.

J And there's another one in the afternoon too, leaving at 18.15, arriving at 20.15.

C Sorry, did you say twenty fifteen or twenty fifty?

J Twenty fifteen.

C OK, I've got that. Now I'd like some information about domestic flights in Spain.

First, can you tell me if there are flights between Bilbao and Seville on a Tuesday?

J Bilbao to Seville on Tuesday ... I'm just looking for that. Yes, there's one at 8 in the morning. That arrives at 9.10.

C Right, thanks. Next, I'd like to know if there's a flight from Seville to Valencia on a Friday.

J Valencia ... Yes, there's a daily flight, departing Seville at 12.25 and arriving in Valencia at 14.25.

C So, departing 12.25, arriving 14.25.

J No, sorry I've made a mistake. It arrives at 13.25, not 14.25.

C OK, arriving 13.25. Just one more question, Jan. Is there an evening flight from Valencia to Barcelona, on a Saturday and a Sunday?

J Let me check ... Yes, there's one at 19.10, that's the last flight of the day, arriving at 19.50.

C So, departing 19.10, arriving 19.50. Right. That's everything, Jan. Thanks a lot. I'll get back to you as soon as possible to book the flights. Bye.

6.6

1 No, not the 7th, the 17th.
2 No, not Málaga, Madrid.
3 No, not 10.35, 10.25.

6.7

1 No, not the 14th, the 4th.
2 No, not the 30th, the 13th.
3 No, not Zürich, Geneva.
4 No, not Berlin, Frankfurt.
5 No, not 12.45, 12.30.
6 No, not 07.20, 07.30.

6.8

a So, travelling on the 7th—
  No, not the 7th, the 5th.
b So, departing at 11.45—
  No, not 11.45, 11.35.

6.9

1 So, travelling on the 13th of June—
  No, not the 13th, the 30th.
2 So, departing on the 9th of September—
  No, not the 9th, the 19th.
3 So, staying in Milan—
  No, not Milan, Rome.
4 So, travelling to Chicago—
  No, not Chicago, Toronto.
5 So, arriving at 13.30—
  No, not 13.30, 13.45.
6 So, arriving at 15.15—
  No, not 15.15, 15.50.

Unit 7

7.1

WC=Wu Chao, MM=Mike Millard

WC It's my first trip to the US, of course. I know I must be prepared for things to be very different.

MM As you say, you mustn't expect the way of doing business to be the same. For me, the biggest difference for people from Asian countries is the speed of negotiation – Americans are fast and direct. They're not always very patient and sometimes they can be insensitive to other cultural differences. You have to remember that American business culture is largely individualistic – they stress the importance of individual initiative and achievement, and they can be very competitive in work and leisure. You need to think clearly and quickly when you're doing business.

WC Yes, that's what worries me.

MM Oh, you needn't worry. In American business culture, they stick to the rules. They'll give you time to make decisions – but make your point as quickly as you can. Americans tend to dislike periods of silence in meetings. They may continue to speak simply to avoid the silence. You don't need to spend a long time on social formalities. Things like status, protocol, and honour are not so important to Americans. It's all about doing business.

7.2

WC And do I need to know about American popular culture – sports, TV, that sort of thing?

MM It helps, but it's mainly for small talk.

WC It says in my notes that in conversation you mustn't talk about religion, politics, or other controversial subjects. I suppose that's fairly obvious, but what topics is it advisable to talk about – for example, when starting a conversation?

MM You could ask about a person's job in general terms, sports they play, leisure interests, and so on. You mustn't ask questions that are too personal. For example, you shouldn't ask a person how old they are, and it's not a good idea to ask a woman if she's married. But if she tells you, you may ask a few questions about her husband and children.

WC What else must I be careful about?

MM You may find you don't understand everything people are saying. But the important thing to remember is that you can stop the person you're talking to and ask for clarification. It's perfectly acceptable. You mustn't interrupt them in an angry or rude way of course, but you needn't be shy either. And also, going back to the sports thing, if you're there for a longer period of time, you might be invited for a round of golf. Some Americans do a lot of business on the golf course. You should practise your golf before you go!

WC Hm. I'm leaving tomorrow! Oh, one last thing – timekeeping. It says in my notes that you always have to be punctual. Is that true? Do I have to be on time for everything?

MM Yes, you have to be on time for meetings and business appointments. But for parties and social occasions you don't have to arrive exactly on time – you can be a few minutes late.

WC Great – that's all really helpful advice. Thanks a lot, Mike. And now, I must go and pack. My flight is at seven in the morning.

MM Good luck! And send me a postcard!

7.3

1 I don't have to go to the talk.
2 You really mustn't be late.
3 You needn't worry about me.
4 You don't need to take an umbrella.
5 We mustn't forget to ask him.
6 Do you have to leave early tomorrow?
7 He has to work very hard.
8 What do you think I should do?

7.4

Welcome to the San Francisco convention and visitors' bureau information line. We hope you will enjoy all that San Francisco has to offer, from its unsurpassed beauty to its world famous attractions and activities. We offer suggestions to ensure that your stay here is enjoyable and safe. Please select from the following options:
Press 1 for advice and information on sightseeing.
Press 2 for advice and information on shopping.
Press 3 for advice and information on personal security.
Press 4 for advice and information on vehicle safety and parking.
Thank you for selecting vehicle safety and parking. The best advice to those visiting San Francisco by automobile is: 'Park it!' Rely on your feet and public transport. If you must drive, remember cable cars and pedestrians always have the right of way. A full international driving license and auto insurance are required for all drivers. The wearing of seatbelts is obligatory, and it is forbidden to drive under the influence of drugs or alcohol. When parking on San Francisco's 'roller coaster' hills you must curb your wheels – turn the tires towards the street when facing uphill, and towards the curb when facing downhill. It is forbidden to stop or park at red curbs at any time. Only commercial vehicles are permitted to load at yellow curbs.

All vehicles are allowed to stop at green curbs for a maximum of ten minutes. The following tips are recommended for tourists driving in the Bay Area: Do not advertise that you are a visitor. Place maps, travel brochures, and valuables out of sight in the glove compartment or trunk. If your car is bumped, do not stop. You should drive to the nearest public area and call 415-553-0123 to report the incident to the police. Always lock your vehicle and take the keys. Check the interior of your vehicle before getting in. Park in well-lit busy areas.
Thank you … and happy driving! To return to the main menu, please press zero.

7.5

M=Mark, P=Paula, J=John

M What do you think about the increase in international outsourcing – is it a good thing or a bad thing?

P Well, it's certainly a growing business – most western companies are doing it at the moment. So, I suppose it must be a good thing for them. I think they do it mainly for cost reasons. It's cheaper to base your call centre in a country like India because all your costs – labour, rent, equipment, and so on – are cheaper.

J I think the companies often get a better standard of operative as well. A lot of the call centre staff are university graduates, for example. The job has higher status than it sometimes does in the West.

M But are there any disadvantages for companies?

P Obviously there's the lack of control – they have to trust other companies to do the training and the monitoring of staff. But the main problem I think is cultural differences. Someone phoning a call centre for information or for advice, or even to complain, likes to feel that they're talking to someone who understands their situation and comes from the same background as them.

J I agree that cultural difference can be a disadvantage, but I also think it can be exaggerated. After all, the main point is that the call centre operative is friendly and efficient, not that they can chat about the weather and the latest sports news.

M What about for the countries where these companies that outsource are based, mainly western and developed countries – is it a good thing for them?

J If it keeps costs down and gives the customer a cheaper service with no loss of quality, then yes. But there is also a danger that you are taking away jobs from the home country. In times of rising unemployment that could be a definite disadvantage – and it could also make the companies that do it unpopular.

M And for the countries where the call centres are based?

P On the whole, I think it's a good thing. It brings income into the country and helps the economy. It also helps to develop their telecommunications and IT industries. On the other hand, there is the danger of exploitation – the workers might be paid lower wages for example, and there could be the feeling that the western companies are dominating and keeping the wealth for themselves.

J There is increasing evidence that a lot of call centre operatives are under stress – working long hours, often late at night because of the time difference …

7.6

CH=Carol Hunt

CH Good morning everyone, and welcome to our seminar. This morning, I'm going to give you guidelines for preparing and delivering talks and presentations. I'm going to start by looking at preparation. This stage is extremely important and there are six key areas you need to think about when

preparing your presentation or talk. The first one is objectives. You need to think carefully about the aim of your talk, and what you want to achieve. Second, the audience. Think about who they are, and what they need to know. The third area is content. Concentrate on giving the important information and make sure it's interesting. The fourth area is organization. Your presentation needs to have a clear and logical organization. You must make certain that you are using what we call 'signposting language' so that the audience can follow each stage of your presentation. The fifth area is visual information. Presenting information visually, for example through a computer, or on an overhead projector or a flipchart, adds interest to a presentation and makes it easier to follow, but make sure you know how to use the equipment and that you're not showing too much information on the screen or slide at one time. The last key area is practice. When you've finished preparing your talk, practise giving it. This way you'll discover if there are any problems and be able to check the timing. It should also make you feel more confident. Now, before I move on to the second part of my presentation, are there any questions?

7.7

CH Now we come to the last part, delivery. You need to consider five key areas here. The first one is nerves. Most of us feel nervous when we speak in public, especially if we're speaking a foreign language. It can help if you breathe deeply. Breathing deeply calms you down and stops you speaking too quickly, which usually happens when you're nervous. The second area is voice. Obviously it's important to speak clearly and not too quickly, but it's also important to sound interesting. If your voice sounds monotonous your audience will fall asleep! Next, body language. Try to give the impression that you're relaxed and confident even if you're not, and try to avoid nervous gestures or movements. An important element of body language is eye contact, and keeping eye contact with the audience is important to keep them interested in what you're saying. For this reason you shouldn't read your talk or presentation. Instead, list key points on a flipchart or transparency, and refer to notes as well, if you need to. Stand rather than sit, but make sure you don't stand in front of visual information. And visual information is the fourth key area on our list. I mentioned earlier the importance of not presenting too much information at a time, and you saw in the handout phrases for focusing the audience's attention on what you want them to look at. Remember, too, to give them enough time to take in the information you're showing them. The fifth and final area is questions. The best policy is to answer questions in a polite, diplomatic way. The phrases in the handout should give you some help here. So, to sum up, the five areas you need to think about when delivering your talk or presentation are nerves, voice, body language, visual information, and questions. Well, this brings me to the end of my presentation. Thank you for your attention, and now if you have any questions I'll be happy to answer them. Yes, you have a question there … ?

Unit 8

8.1

WA=WaterAid representative, D1=Delegate 1, D2=Delegate 2, D3=Delegate 3

WA Right, everyone. Thanks for coming along today. The idea of this meeting is to go through some details of the itinerary for the Ethiopia trip. So any last-minute ideas, thoughts, or suggestions that you have will be very welcome.

D1 Can I just ask – is everything finalized in terms of the programme? I'm thinking particularly of the dates.

WA The main points are, yes. For example, the flight leaves on the 4th of March and returns to London on the 14th at 8 p.m., and the internal itinerary once we're in Ethiopia is fixed – because we had to arrange the transport and accommodation. Let's start with the itinerary. You've got the outline in front of you. I'm going to send all the travel documents on to you, but are there any questions at this stage?

D2 Sorry, what time does the flight get into Addis Ababa?

WA Erm. It arrives at 15.00 on the 4th, then we're transferring to the hotel, checking in, and getting ready for the reception at the Government offices. You can see that it's going to be a tiring day. We're not doing anything on the 5th, so there's time to rest before the main itinerary.

D3 Who's coming to the reception? Any important government leaders?

WA Unfortunately, the President of Ethiopia isn't available so he isn't coming, but a number of senior ministers are coming, and also representatives of most of the ten regional governments.

D3 Isn't it important to meet some local people and local leaders?

WA Definitely, so, after a day in Addis Ababa, on the 6th you're travelling out to the east of the country to a rural village. This is where some of the worst water problems exist.

D3 And who are we going to meet there?

WA You're meeting local community leaders at the village on the 7th. Then the day after, on the 8th, you're also meeting *woreda* and *kebele* leaders, as well as a women's group. We see the role of women as particularly important in getting the message of hygiene and sanitation across.

8.2

D1 What about the language? Are we going to take any professional interpreters? My Human Resources department has a good contact if we need to take an interpreter.

WA No, we're not going to take interpreters – I'm afraid it's too expensive. We're providing local interpreters from our volunteers already working out there. I think you'll find them good enough.

D1 That's fine. I won't contact our HR people.

D2 I'm interested in the rainwater harvesting schemes. When are we visiting one of the projects?

WA On the 9th of March – we're going to a project in the Rift Valley. Rainwater harvesting is one of our key projects – we're starting five more rainwater harvesting projects next year. As you can see, on the 10th and 11th we're also visiting a sanitation scheme and a factory where they build sewage disposal systems. Back in Addis Ababa on the 12th we're seeing a redevelopment project in slum areas.

D2 It looks great, you've clearly arranged things so that we're seeing a full range of activities. Can I just ask about publicity – are we going to take a photographer?

WA We're going to take a small TV crew and our own photographer for publicity and press coverage.

D2 I don't know if you're interested, but I'm coming with my wife who's a professional photographer. She's interested in doing the publicity shots if you want.

WA Fantastic! In that case, we'll leave our photographer behind. Are you sure it's OK?

D2 I'll check with her, but yeah I'm sure.

D3 Could we see any photos or articles on previous trips like this? Have you got any here?

WA That's a good idea. I'm sure we could find something. I'll just call through to the press department. We could have a break while we're waiting?

D1/D2/D3 Yes, good idea. Why not?

8.3

1

D2 Sorry, what time does the flight get into Addis Ababa?

WA Erm, it arrives at 15.00 on the 4th, then we're transferring to the hotel, checking in, and getting ready for the reception at the Government offices. You can see that it's going to be a tiring day. We're not doing anything on the 5th, so there's time to rest before the main itinerary.

2

D1 Are we going to take any professional interpreters? My Human Resources department has a good contact if we need to take an interpreter.

WA No, we're not going to take interpreters – I'm afraid it's too expensive. We're providing local interpreters from our volunteers already working out there. I think you'll find them good enough.

D1 That's fine. I won't contact our HR people.

3

D2 Can I just ask about publicity – are we going to take a photographer, for example?

WA We're going to take a small TV crew and our own photographer for publicity and press coverage.

D2 I don't know if you're interested, but I'm coming with my wife who's a professional photographer. She's interested in doing the publicity shots if you want.

WA Fantastic! In that case, we'll leave our photographer behind. Are you sure it's OK?

D2 I'll check with her, but yeah I'm sure.

8.4

R=Representative, J1=Journalist 1, J2=Journalist 2, J3=Journalist 3

J1 … so what makes London so suitable?

R Well, with a major event like this you've obviously got to look at the infrastructure of the city – airports, transport, accommodation, stadiums – as well as the running costs of the event itself. Now, London is in a good situation here. The basics are there – good airports, good roads, good transport, and plenty of accommodation.

J1 But won't they need to be improved and expanded? What's the expenditure?

R Yes, but this is already going to happen under existing plans, separate from the Olympics. However, we have allocated some money for infrastructure development in the 403 million pounds for the building of new facilities.

J2 403 million pounds sounds a lot of money, but what does that actually buy?

R That will mainly be for a new 80,000-seat stadium. The next item is the buying of land in east London on which to build the new stadium and facilities, which we estimate will cost another 325 million pounds. We've included three other main items of expenditure. The first is for the cost of actually staging the event, which we estimate will be 679 million pounds. Then there's approximately 50 million for the cost of security.

J2 A major concern these days, no doubt.

R Indeed. We've also allocated 127 million pounds towards improving the British team's chances of winning some medals, and finally 106 million pounds on what we call 'risk money' to cover any unforeseen problems. So, the total expenditure would be 1.69 billion pounds. On the income side we're looking at a total figure much bigger than that.

J3 Can you give us some details of your income estimates?

R Of course. We calculate there will be at least 1.3 billion pounds in direct revenue. That's 864 million from ticket sales and 436 million from other sources. Then there'll be a contribution from the IOC – we don't quite know how much, but it could be about 100 million pounds. As well as that there's all the sponsorship and advertising deals, which we estimate will be approximately half a billion pounds. Then after the event the resale of surplus land used for the Games will bring in at least 430 million pounds. And, of course, tourism generated by Olympic visitors and the tax from the 9,000 jobs created will bring in another 810 million pounds.

J3 So, your final estimated profit figure is?

R Just under one and a half billion pounds, but we think it could be much higher in practice. Also there are the business opportunities that the Games will bring – job creation, investment in poor areas leading to economic revival, housing, food and catering, advertising. It's all good for business and these are all long term benefits that will generate income for years to come, and add to the profit side of the balance sheet. Are there any further questions?

8.5

P=Piet, R=Rosa

P … so, have you finished planning your trip to Spain yet?

R Just about. Would you like me to give you the details?

P Sure.

R Right. Well, I haven't finalized all the details yet but we've decided which places we're going to visit and we've booked some of the flights and hotels. We're still waiting for one of the hotels to fax through confirmation. We also had a problem with one of the flights.

P Yes, I saw your memo to Claire.

R Yes, there was a change to one of the flight times and I wanted her to check all the others, just in case.

P Did you decide to follow María Ferrando's advice?

R Yes. María's been very helpful in arranging visits and meetings for us.

P Hmm, good. So, tell me your plans.

R Well, we're leaving in two weeks, on the 2nd of May. We're going to San Sebastián first, so we're taking a flight to Bilbao on the 2nd. In San Sebastián we're planning to interview the chef of one of Spain's top restaurants. He's very famous but quite old-fashioned and doesn't usually give interviews. But with María's help I've written him a letter explaining the project.

P And he's agreed?

R Yes, apparently he phoned María the other day and said he'd be delighted. Then on the 4th, we're flying to Seville and staying until the 7th. We're going to the bar where the custom of *tapas* began and we're going to visit a convent where traditional Spanish confectionery is made. If we have enough time, we'll go to Jerez de la Frontera to find out all about sherry production. From Seville, either we'll fly straight to Barcelona or we'll go to Valencia. If we go to Valencia, it'll be to see *paella valenciana* being prepared, and to eat it of course!

P It sounds as if you're going to spend most of your time on this trip eating and drinking!

R Some of it, yes, but that's an essential part of researching these programmes! On the 8th, that's a Saturday evening, a friend of María's who lives in Barcelona is going to take us on a tour of all the best *tapas* bars. And on the 9th, we're hoping to spend the day visiting vineyards in the Penedés area of Catalonia, talking to *cava* producers. Then we're flying back on Tuesday. I'm going to write a full report on all the visits for the editorial and production team – I'll copy you in of course.

P Hmm, it all sounds very enjoyable. Now I understand why you wanted to make these programmes on the food and drink of different countries! You knew what fun it would be!

R Well, maybe that was one of the reasons, but of course not the main one!

P OK. Shall we go out for lunch later on? I've invited Eric – I've left a message on his answerphone. Would María be able to join us as well?

R I think she said she's out of the office all morning. I know, I'll text her and tell her where we're going to be.

P Great, see you later.

8.6

1 He won't have time to come to the meeting.
2 Are you coming on the excursion with us on Saturday?

8.7

1 Are you planning to work abroad next year?
2 I'll meet you at the cinema after the film.
3 Is it true that you're going to change your job again?
4 We're going to Canada for our holiday next summer.

Unit 9

9.1

I=Interviewer, P=Peter, J=Jola, Y=Yves

I Peter, Jola, and Yves, thanks for coming in to talk to us. We're here to find out about your opinion on lifestyles in the future – particularly the balance between working life and family life. Let's start with the family. Do you think the family will disappear as the main social unit? Peter?

P I'm sure that won't happen. The family is far too important. I suppose it's possible that it will become a little less important – that may happen – but it won't disappear.

I Yves?

Y I'm not so sure. I think it's very likely that the family as we know it will disappear – eventually. People will live more with people their own age, or with people they work with. I think that will be true even when people have children – they'll want to live in groups with people like them, not the traditional extended family. For example, after I finish my studies, I'll live with friends – it's better to be with people your own age. If I was a young child again, I'd like to be brought up in a group environment, not just my family.

I Jola, what do you think? Will young people move away from the parental home earlier and earlier?

J I doubt if that'll happen. I live with my parents and it suits me. If I left home, I wouldn't know how to look after myself. I need my family. When I'm ready to start my own family, I'll move out. But I'll certainly have to learn how to cook before I leave home!

I Peter, you wanted to say something?

P Yes, I agree with Jola. There definitely won't be a move away from the family for young working people – for financial reasons as much as anything. I'd like to have my own place, but I'll need to save a lot of money first, so I have to live with my parents – and most of the time it's OK. I won't leave the family house until I can afford a comfortable place.

I So, part of the problem for young working people is to find accommodation they can afford? Will there be cheaper independent accommodation for young people in the future?

Y That'll definitely happen. Society needs young people to work in the centres of cities, for example in businesses, in hospitals, in schools, and so on. I'm sure there'll be cheaper accommodation for young working people, and key workers in

general – maybe smaller and less comfortable, but affordable.

I Jola?

J I expect it'll probably happen, because, as Yves says, society needs it. But it's unlikely to mean the end of the family. If generations don't live together, maybe they'll be closer in other ways.

I OK, we must leave it there. Opinions are divided, but what do our listeners think? You can email us on …

9.2

1
P I'm sure that won't happen. The family is far too important. I suppose it's possible that it will become a little less important – that may happen – but it won't disappear.

2
Y I'm not so sure. I think it's very likely that the family as we know it will disappear – eventually.

3
J I doubt if that'll happen.

4
P Yes, I agree with Jola. There definitely won't be a move away from the family for young working people – for financial reasons as much as anything.

5
Y That'll definitely happen. Society needs young people to work in the centres of cities, for example in businesses, in hospitals, in schools, and so on. I'm sure there'll be cheaper accommodation for young working people, and key workers in general – maybe smaller and less comfortable, but affordable.

6
J I expect it'll probably happen, because, as Yves says, society needs it. But it's unlikely to mean the end of the family.

9.3

a My car has broken down.
b We've put the meeting off.

9.4

1 What time do you usually get up?
2 Did you turn on the TV?
3 Shall I turn it off?
4 Could you fill in this form?
5 They've managed to put the fire out.
6 Has the plane taken off?
7 I've just sorted out the problem.
8 What time did they set off?

Unit 10

10.1

I=Interviewer, LD=Lennart Dahlgren

I Mr Dahlgren, IKEA has been investing in Russia for several years, and you arrived at the start. How long have you been living in Russia?

LD I've been living here since 1998. That's when IKEA started operations in Russia.

I When did you open the first store?

LD We opened our first store near Moscow in 2000.

I I know that you've expanded since then. How many stores have you established?

LD We've opened five stores so far, and we've also built several large shopping malls in the last few years. These create a variety of smaller retail outlets. In our first year, sales were more than $100m. This doubled to more than $200m in the following year. In fact, sales have been increasing every year – and we think this will continue.

I It does seem a remarkable growth. Why do you think it's been successful?

LD Russia offers a huge market. Consumer demand has been growing steadily since we opened the first store – dramatically even – and if this continues the market will be unlimited for companies like IKEA, and for most Western companies who are able to come here.

I Russia is not just important as a consumer market – I believe it's also an important supply source?

LD Yes, it is. Russia offers good natural resources, such as wood, oil for plastics, and metals. It has 25% of the world's hardwood reserves, for example. It also has many factories able to produce in huge volumes. We've been increasing the percentage of our global supply that comes from Russia for a number of years. We've opened several factories throughout Russia – near St Petersburg, Moscow, and Karelia.

10.2

I The business has obviously been successful, but have there been any major problems?

LD Yes, I would say there have been two main difficulties for us. Firstly, the bureaucracy can sometimes be frustrating. When we started there was a lot of paperwork – licences and so on. But bureaucratic problems have been getting fewer recently. For example, the Government has reduced the number of licences that are needed for a new company to set up.

I And the second difficulty?

LD I suppose the attitude of some of the older industrial leaders has also been a bit old-fashioned. However, we've been doing a number of things in the time we've been here. We've set up management training programmes to help new Russian entrepreneurs. We've tried to show how a modern company has to work to survive in the international market. The younger generation understand this, and it's no surprise that the richest and most successful business people in Russia are all relatively young. There's a lot of ambition in this country.

10.3

a performance   b encouragement
c satisfaction

10.4

1 appearance   6 expectation
2 definition   7 explanation
3 development   8 improvement
4 dismissal   9 promotion
5 establishment   10 resistance

10.5

I=Interviewer, R=Rob Yeung

I Rob, you've been working as a management consultant for a number of years and you've written on the psychology of job interviews. What general changes have you noticed in the way interviews are conducted?

RY I think in general job interviewers are becoming more professional in their approach, asking much more wide-ranging questions. They're particularly interested in putting candidates to the test. For example, they might ask questions to throw the candidate off-balance. If you stay cool, then they know that this person can cope under pressure. You occasionally hear questions like 'Could you tell me what sort of animal you'd like to be?', or 'Do you know how many cars there are in Australia?', or 'Would you mind if I recorded this interview?' The first question is probably a bit silly, but the interviewer is just interested to see how you react. But the second one is more revealing. The idea is not to make a wild guess, but to give a reasoned explanation about how you would calculate it. The candidate who manages to get a fairly accurate answer by estimating population, ratio of people to cars and the number per household, is showing a willingness to think a problem through – this person is good at thinking logically.

I And the question about recording the interview?

RY The question about recording the interview is

partly because it can be useful for the interviewer to analyse things afterwards, but it's also to see if the candidate doesn't mind being put under pressure. The answer of course is: 'Go ahead. I don't mind being recorded.'

10.6

I   But interviews these days are not just question-and-answer, are they?

RY   No, indeed not. Many companies are keen on giving assessment tests and tasks. These might be in-tray exercises, role-play or simulation, and presentations. They're usually timed. For the in-tray exercise, the candidate is given a tray full of documents and the interviewer or assessor wants to see how you deal with it, and how good your organizational skills are. The best thing is usually to divide the contents into three piles: urgent information that needs immediate action, important information that needs action but only when the most urgent items have been sorted out, and the non-urgent information that can wait until later. Sometimes, there may be regular interruptions as you are given more material to test how you perform under pressure.

I   Are there any other typical tasks that interviewers give?

RY   Obvious things really. Like if you're going for a job using a computer, you'll probably be given a short keyboard exercise to see if you really do know how to use it. If you're applying to be a waiter, they'll want to see that you're good at working with people and you're able to remember orders. They might give you a memory test, so be ready for it – you might be asked something like: 'Do you remember the name of the receptionist who showed you in?', 'What items do you remember from the menu board you saw at the front?' That sort of thing.

I   Is there any particular advice you would give?

RY   I'd say the main weakness of most candidates is poor preparation. Too often in the interview they rely on giving stock responses rather than talking about the relevance their skills have to that particular job. If I only give one piece of advice, it's this: study the job ad, research the company, understand what the company is looking for, and tailor your approach accordingly. If you succeed in doing those things, you're halfway there – and you can look forward to starting the job of your dreams.

I   Rob Yeung, thanks very much.

10.7

E=Eric, JP=Javier Pérez

E   Well, first, Señor Pérez, thank you for welcoming us here today to your *bodega* to talk about the production of sherry. Could I start by asking you about the area of production? Is sherry produced only in this area of Spain?

JP   Yes, that's right. It's produced in the area formed by the three sherry towns – that's Jerez de la Frontera, where we are now, and the two coastal towns, El Puerto de Santa María and Sanlúcar de Barrameda.

E   So, all sherry comes from this area?

JP   Yes. Since a European Union law of 1966, only wine from this area, which is called 'the classified sherry zone', can be called sherry. Wines from other areas, or other countries can't be called 'sherry' because it's a protected name, like *champagne* in France.

E   Yes, I understand. Now, I imagine a lot of the sherry that's produced is exported – Is that the case?

JP   Oh, yes, certainly. Today about 70% of total production is exported. And in fact exports of sherry represent a quarter of all Spanish DO wine exports.

E   Er … By 'DO wine' do you mean the wine produced in classified areas?

JP   Yes, in Spanish it's *Denominación de Origen*, it's like *appellation contrôlée* in French, so yes, wine from an area where quality is controlled.

E   I see. Thank you. And which countries are your main export markets?

JP   Historically, Britain has always been our most important export market but today Holland is our number one export market, with Britain next, and Germany third. They're our three big markets. Then come the USA, other European countries, and Canada.

E   So, if 70% of sherry is exported, then only 30% is actually drunk in Spain?

JP   Yes, that's right. And Spanish tastes are different. In Spain we prefer the dry, lighter sherries, whereas the export markets prefer the medium and sweet sherries, although tastes are beginning to change.

E   You say tastes are beginning to change. Could you explain in what way?

JP   Well, a lot of changes have taken place in the sherry industry in the last decade or so. Most of the big sherry companies are now part of multinational drinks groups, although there are still some Spanish-owned sherry producers. The traditional markets for sherry are in decline so we want to give sherry a more youthful image that will attract the younger market. We're promoting the dry, lighter sherries for this market, and it's showing definite signs of growth.

10.8

E   Could we talk about the final stage of production now? Earlier, on our tour of the *bodega*, you referred to the *solera* system and said it was the system used for maturing the sherry and for maintaining a consistent quality. Could you describe how the *solera* system works?

JP   Yes, by all means. A *solera* is several rows of barrels, usually four or five rows, one on top of the other. In a *solera*, the oldest wine is in the barrels at the bottom and the youngest wine is in the barrels at the top. When wine is needed for bottling, it's taken from the barrels on the bottom row, and these barrels are filled with an equal amount of wine from the next row up. Then the barrels on that row are topped up with wine from the row above and that process continues until the top row is reached. Finally, at the end of the process, new wine is added to the barrels on the top row. In this way, the characteristics of the older wine are taken on by the younger wine and the quality of the wine is kept consistent.

E   And how long does it take for the wine on the top row to progress through the *solera* system?

JP   The minimum period is three years. For a good sherry it will be longer – five to six years, and for a premium sherry it's likely to be eight years or longer.

E   Well, thank you very much, Señor Pérez. It's been most interesting.

JP   It was my pleasure. Now you must come and try some of our sherries …

Unit 11

11.1

a   The boss is still the boss, even outside work. The Australian employee should have been a little more formal, and he should have waited to be introduced to the Director's family. Also, he shouldn't have shown that he knew more than his boss about cars, especially in front of his family. If he'd waited for the Director to speak to him, he might have asked for his opinion. That way, he would have made a good impression. An easy mistake to make perhaps. In general, Australian culture is more direct and friendly than German culture.

b   She shouldn't have criticized the worker in public. It would have been better if she'd just found out the facts, expressed her concern, and then let them deal with it themselves. The Japanese production team would have supported the worker responsible, and made sure he didn't make mistakes in the future. The American boss should have realized that the Japanese culture of the subsidiary company was different to the US parent company. In Asian culture, it's fair to say there's more emphasis on the group rather than the individual.

c   They should have taken more time to get to know the company. They shouldn't have rushed so quickly to the business side of things. Also, perhaps they were over-confident. If they'd built up a good personal relationship with their potential clients, the British sales team would have won the contract. The 'social' side of business is important in Argentina, and in South America generally. The Swedish sales team obviously understood this.

11.2

a   He should have waited to be introduced.
b   They shouldn't have rushed so quickly.

11.3

If they'd built up a good relationship, they would have won the contract.

11.4

I=Interviewer, LP=Leah Pattison

I   I'm joined by Leah Pattison, who was 'Woman of the Year' a couple of years back, and is co-founder of the charity START, which works with Indian women who have leprosy. Leah, the idea of lepers, ever since Biblical times, is of people at the bottom of the heap: untouchable, terrifying, disfigured, incurable. Actually, that's years out of date, but there is still a terror associated with the word 'leprosy'.

LP   Yes, there is. In India it's known as *maharugi*, which means 'big disease'. It's 100% curable, but the tragedy is that despite that, women particularly are hiding their condition, and not coming forward for early treatment.

I   Why not?

LP   I think it's because they're ashamed. Modern India now puts a lot of pressure on women to be educated, beautiful, and so on. So, if you have a disease like leprosy, it really does spoil that, and these women can become outcasts, rejected by society.

I   You were a university graduate in Fine Arts, so what first took you into a leper colony nine years ago?

LP   To be perfectly honest, when I look back, perhaps naivety, just a sense of wonder about the world and wanting to go out and explore it. It was as simple as that for me. Initially, I'd gone there to teach. It was a working holiday, with an element of wanting to see rural India. Yet when I got into the colony I was faced with young girls, young women of my age, who really made me look at who I was, and ask questions about myself.

I   Did you find it hard at first?

LP   Well, I was shocked by the appearance of some of the patients in the colony who were very deformed, but what happened over the course of six months was that these leprosy patients became people, became individuals. Suddenly the deformities were secondary. I didn't notice them. That made me think about the whole importance of being an individual, and having rights as an individual rather than being grouped together as a mass. The women need support and treatment of course, but above all they need to understand they are individuals with rights and with a future.

11.5

I   Were you afraid of catching leprosy yourself?

LP   No, not at all. Maybe I should have been,

because I did catch it. I have to stress that leprosy, despite the fact that I caught it, is a very difficult disease to catch. One day I had patches on my left hand and wrist, but I didn't think they were important. Luckily, there was a specialist in the colony at the time who noticed them and said, 'I'll see you in the clinic tomorrow'.

I   You could have returned to the UK and had specialist treatment, but you didn't. That was a tough choice and brave decision, wasn't it?

LP I don't think so. I suppose it would have been easier to recover if I had returned to the UK, but it wouldn't have been right. I wanted to be with the women I was working with. My friend, Usha Patil, had had leprosy as a child and I took courage from that. For me there was no decision to make. I stayed in India, had the treatment, and recovered.

I   You mentioned your friend Usha Patil. You and Usha founded the charity START to help Indian women with leprosy. How do the women respond? Do you find them easy to get through to at first?

LP No. It's quite a tough job in that these are women who have been isolated. They've been abused – physically and verbally – for many, many years. They've lost social skills. They don't know how to interact with people. Usha and I spend our days trying to break through that barrier and find the personality behind the patient. A lot of these women consider themselves to be nothing other than leprosy patients, but they're not – they're individuals. They had a disease, and that's it. No big deal.

I   Well, Leah. Thank you very much for sharing your story. I'm not sure I would have made the same choice as you if I had contracted leprosy – it seems a very courageous one to me. And now, let's turn to …

Unit 12

12.1

You are looking down at the main chamber. The parliament is made up of 129 elected members, or MPs, using a proportional representation system. The MPs sit in a U-shaped arrangement with the Government members on the left as you look, and the Opposition on the right. MPs for other parties, such as the Greens and the Liberals, sit between the Government and the Opposition. One MP is elected to be the Presiding Officer or Speaker. He or she sits in the chair at the centre of the chamber. The front benches of the Government side are where the Prime Minister and the Cabinet sit. As you know, the Cabinet is the group of senior ministers in government. The public gallery, where you are standing, is divided into two sections. At the front there are seats for members of the electorate, the voters in other words, who have arranged with their MPs to visit Parliament. At the back there are seats for the general public. Opposite you on the left is the press gallery for reporters and journalists, and on the right is a gallery for the official reporters and VIPs. Push button 8 to continue the tour.

12.2

1

Research published yesterday claims that children who become addicted to computer games may actually be more intelligent than average, and even be more likely to go to university and get higher-ranking jobs. The study looked at kids who had been hooked on games for at least five years. Although many of the games were aggressive and violent, it didn't find any evidence that the children became aggressive and violent adults. In fact, a follow-up study of the same children five years later discovered they had generally done well at school, gone to college, and then into top jobs.

2

Are celebrities being treated differently by the courts? The question has been asked again after the recent case of pop-star Cool T, who was given a six-month driving ban and a fine for a drink-driving incident in which a pedestrian was badly injured. In the same week, in a separate incident, a minicab driver was given a prison sentence of one year for a similar offence. Outside the court, the family of the minicab driver said there seemed to be one law for the rich and famous, and another for ordinary members of the public.

3

New figures published by the Motion Picture Association, which represents the world's largest film studios and TV production companies, show that DVD and video piracy is on the increase. This is especially true in Asia, which the MPA believes now accounts for a quarter of the three billion dollars lost to film piracy each year. China, Malaysia, and Taiwan were identified as leading centres for mass copying, with new blockbuster movies becoming available in pirate versions way before official release. An MPA spokesman warned that what had already happened to CDs, was now happening to DVDs. He called for tougher laws to stop the problem getting worse.

4

As another top level professional footballer is banned from the sport for twelve months, fears are growing that drug abuse in football is more widespread than previously thought. And it could even be getting out of control. Drug abuse has long been recognized as a problem in sports like athletics, cycling, and baseball, but recently it's emerged in sports such as tennis and football. A spokesperson for the International Sports Council said she feared drug abuse was spreading in many sports. 'At the same time,' she said, 'it's getting more difficult to tell the difference between illegal performance-enhancing substances and ordinary medicines and food supplements that sports men and women are allowed to take.'

12.3

R=Rosa, MF=María Ferrando

MF Hello, María Ferrando speaking.

R   Hello, Maria. It's Rosa. I'm phoning to tell you the good news – we've got the money to complete the *Food and drink* project!

MF Really? Oh, that's wonderful, Rosa! Congratulations! When did you hear?

R   Well, yesterday Piet and I presented the project to two investors. We told them our ideas for the ten programmes and showed them the programme on Spain. They were really impressed with the programme, María, so we've got a lot to thank you for. Well, we didn't expect them to make a decision for some time but at the end of the meeting they said they thought the project would be a great success and agreed to the investment.

MF That's marvellous. Is Eric pleased about it?

R   Pleased? He's absolutely delighted! Anyway, on Saturday we're having a party to celebrate, so you and your husband must come. I hope you're not doing anything then?

MF No, we're not. Thanks, Rosa, we'd love to come.

R   Great! It's at Piet's flat, starting around eight o'clock. And Eric's preparing a big buffet, so don't eat before you come.

MF Mmm, sounds good. So, look forward to seeing you all on Saturday, then.

R   Yes, bye for now, María.

MF Bye, Rosa.

12.4

[1]=quite enthusiastic, [2] = very enthusiastic

1 I got the job.
    Really? Great! [2]

2 Do you like the new area manager?
    Oh, yes. He seems very friendly and efficient. [1]

3 I'd like you to go to the conference in Florida for us.
    Of course. I'd love to go. [1]

4 I see you've got your name in the newspaper.
    I know. I didn't realize they were going to print it! [2]

12.5

1 I'm afraid I didn't catch your name.

2 Eric, do you remember Antonio? He sends his regards.

3 Do you mind if I open this window?

4 I hope the next programme goes well.

5 How do you like your coffee?

6 I'm afraid Sara couldn't come. She hurt her back yesterday.

7 Oh, dear. I've just spilt some wine.

8 I hope you have a good weekend.

12.6

1 I'm afraid I didn't catch your name.
    It's Claire. Claire Hallan.

2 Eric, do you remember Antonio? He sends his regards.
    Thank you. Do give him mine.

3 Do you mind if I open this window?
    Not at all.

4 I hope the next programme goes well.
    Thanks. I hope so too.

5 How do you like your coffee?
    Black, one sugar, please.

6 I'm afraid Sara couldn't come. She hurt her back yesterday.
    Oh, I'm sorry to hear that.

7 Oh, dear. I've just spilt some wine.
    Never mind.

8 I hope you have a good weekend.
    Thanks. The same to you.

12.7

P=Piet, R=Rosa, E=Eric, MF=María Ferrando,

1 P If you ask me, Eric, I'd say good food is definitely one of life's pleasures.

2 R That reminds me, María, Señor Pérez sends you his regards.

3 E As you say, Rosa, we've got a very busy year ahead.

4 P Talking of good wines, Eric, what was the name of that wine you recommended?

5 MF As I was saying, Rosa, I think Jean Leblanc would be ideal as consultant for the programme on France.

12.8

MF=María Ferrando, P=Piet, R=Rosa, E=Eric

MF Piet, Rosa, we really must be going. Thanks for a really enjoyable evening.

P   We're very pleased you could both come.

MF And Eric, the food was wonderful.

R   Yes, everyone's said how good it was, Eric.

E   Thank you. Well, I must say after all that excitement I'm ready for a good night's sleep!

R   Yes, me too. It's wonderful to know we've got the money to go ahead with the programmes, but now we've got to make all of them!

P   Oh, Rosa, you and Eric are going to enjoy every minute of it, I mean, touring the world, eating the best food, meeting all sorts of interesting people—

R   You make it sound like a holiday, Piet. It's going to be lots of hard work!

P   Oh, I know, I know, Rosa. But I'm sure you'll manage to enjoy it, too? Just a little?

R   Yes, of course!

12.9

1 I really must be getting back to the office. Thanks very much for inviting me out to lunch. I've really enjoyed it.

2 I think I understand the system now. Thank you very much for all your help. I really appreciate it.

3 I think I should get back to my hotel now as I'm leaving very early tomorrow morning. Thank you for a superb meal.

4 I must go now or I'll miss my plane. Thank you so much for all your hospitality. I've had a wonderful time and I'm really looking forward to seeing you again.

Answer key

Unit 1
Language focus p.6
❶ 1 An independent multimedia production company specializing in the travel and cultural sector.
2 Video and television programmes, web design, consultancy and management, media presentations, management training videos and e-learning products.
3 The International food and drink project.
4 The presenter and interviewer of the International food and drink project.
❷ 1 Fifteen years ago.
2 Since they were at university.
3 Rosa is the creative person and Project Manager. Piet is the Business Manager, deals with negotiations, looks for financial partners.
4 Paul is the Financial Manager, deals with the financial aspects of running the business. Louise is the Promotions Manager, handles marketing and advertising.
5 Yes.
❸ 1 past a   present d, e, f   time from the past to the present b, c
2 Present Simple d, e   Present Continuous f   Past Simple a   Present Perfect Simple b, c

> **Present Simple and Present Continuous**
> 1 b   2 a   3 d   4 f   5 c   6 e
>
> **Action and state verbs**
> • Verbs which express an action or activity, e.g. *bring*, *arrive*, *manage*, *travel*, *work*, are used in both simple and continuous tenses. They are called **action verbs**.
> • Verbs which express a state, e.g. *understand*, *believe*, *know*, *want*, *be*, *like*, are not normally used in continuous tenses. They are called **state verbs**.
> • Some verbs, e.g. *have*, *see*, *look*, *taste*, *think*, are used in both simple and continuous tenses. They express either an action or a state.

Practice p.8
❶ 1 am/'m travelling
2 comes
3 look, are
4 tastes
5 am/'m seeing
6 don't understand
7 is/'s thinking, is/'s not
8 are you tasting
9 has
10 see
11 Are you looking, think
12 travel
13 are/'re having
14 Do you bring
❸
2 Did you grow up in London?
3 What did you do after school?
4 What did you do when you finished the cookery course?
5 Where did you work after that?
6 What languages do you speak?
7 How long have you had your restaurant?
8 What do you enjoy doing in your free time?
9 Do you have any plans for the future?

Wordpower p.10
Organizing vocabulary
❶ (Possible answers)

Home/location	Education	Work	Leisure interests
centre	subject	full-time*	surfing
flat	degree	colleagues	exercise
suburbs	course	salary	holiday
garden	college	commute	evening class*

* could also go in Education
❸ (Possible answers) to make an arrangement/an appointment/a decision/a phone call
financial/promotions/bank/hotel manager
course/hard work
work force/room/shop/station
❹ employ   employment   employable   employee/employer
negotiate   negotiation   negotiable   negotiator
operate   operation   operational   operator
tour   tour/tourism   touristy   tourist
❺ (Possible answers)
home cooking   college friends/programme/year
working hours   TV programme

dress code   gap year
health club/programme   family pet/friends

Recording vocabulary
❷ 1, 2, 3 (stress only), 4, 5, 7

Asking for help with vocabulary
❶ 1 d   2 a   3 b   4 e   5 f   6 c
❷ (Possible answers)
1 What's the meaning of … ?
2 Sorry, can you say that again?
3 How do you say … in English?
4 Can you spell it for me?
5 Could you lend me your dictionary?
6 Could you say that more slowly?

Skills focus p.12
❷ (Possible answers)
Brazil – fun-loving, carnival, football
Germany – practical, rational, engineering
Italy – stylish, fashion-conscious
Ireland – traditional, fun-loving, Guinness
Jamaica – relaxed, reggae music
Japan – high-tech, technology
New Zealand – adventurous, the outdoor life
Scotland – traditional, authentic, heritage
Singapore – high-tech, technology
Switzerland – efficiency, precision
❹ 1 It can become trapped by its image, and it is difficult for people to accept 'non-typical' brands.
2 New Zealand, Ireland, Spain, Scotland
3 The economic development agency created a special project ('Scotland the Brand'), defined a positive image, held marketing events and promotions, and recruited companies to promote the brand.

Focus on functions p.14
Introductions and greetings
❶ 1 Hello, Eric, how are you? Good to see you again.
2 Eric, I'd like to introduce you to Claire, our secretary.
3 Pleased to meet you (too).
❸ a 3   b 4   c 1   d 2   e 5
❹ a N/F   b N/F   c N   d N/F   e I
❺ 1 b   2 e   3 a   4 g   5 h   6 c   7 f   8 d
❻ a 3, 6, 8   b 1, 2, 4, 5, 7

Welcoming a visitor
❸
1 Which hotel are you staying in?   4 Do you travel abroad much?
2 What's it like?   5 Have you been to Toronto?
3 How often do you come to London?
❺
1 How long are you staying here?
2 How long have you been with your company?
3 Isn't this weather wonderful?
4 Where did you spend your last holiday?
5 Do you do any sport?
❻ 1 Both the host and the visitor.
2 No.
3 By asking more questions relating to what the speaker has just said.

Unit 2
Language focus p.16
❷ (Possible answer)
It does all its business either online (70%) or over the phone (30%). It offers very big discounts on flights (up to 65%) and a complete range of other travel products.
❸ 1 package holidays   3 potential   5 contracts
2 discounts   4 negotiate   6 staff
❺ 1 T   2 F   3 F   4 T   5 F   6 T
❻ 1 b Past Simple   2 d Present Perfect Simple   3 a Past Simple
4 c Present Perfect Simple

Practice p.18

❶ 2 Julie Pankhurst was.
3 Stephen is.
4 Stephen and Jason did.
5 Members do.
6 Seven million (were).
7 International sites (have).
8 Over 400,000 (have).

❸ (Possible answers)
1 What does ebookers.com specialize in?
2 Who set up ebookers.com?
3 What helped Dinesh when the internet revolution arrived?
4 When did Dinesh open an online department of his travel agency business?
5 How much discount was Dinesh able to negotiate?
6 Where does ebookers operate?
7 How many staff does ebookers employ?
8 What is the largest internet consumer sector in Europe?

Wordpower p.20

❶ somebody   something
singular   plural
uncountable noun   countable noun
American English   British English

❷ **Company**   **Employ**   **Work**
1 co.   un-, -er, -ee, -ment   *work* is more general and is uncountable; *job* describes the particular work that you do to earn money, and is countable
2 both   an employment agency   out of work
3 ● ●●   ● ●●   ●● ●●
4 a good b keep   a as b on   a for b on

❹ customer, client, buyer; establish, set up, found; lay off, fire, make redundant; income, salary, earnings

❻ a sack b perks

❼ (Possible answers) company car, private health insurance, free lunch, reduced gym membership

❽ overtime, overtake/take over, overheads, all over/overall

❾ 1 dishonest inflexible unmotivated impatient
indecisive uninteresting irresponsible impractical
2 *re-* to do again   *co-* to do together

❿ note (money)   holiday
catalogue   social security
mobile phone   place in an office where a person works
rubber   – especially with a desk and computer
work experience

Skills focus p.22

2 1 d   2 e   3 b   4 a   5 c

❸ 1 1914
2 headquarters
3 1940
4 1993
5 takeover
6 subsidiary
7 assembly line
8 2,000
9 25
10 June 2004
11 reputation
12 design
13 development
14 client

❹ Nationality: **British**
Began racing go-karts at the age of **eleven**. Won European Cup and came **third** in World Championships.
Started work for Ford Car Company at the age of **17**.
Studied **engineering** in England.
Worked in various departments at Ford: engineering, **marketing**, sales, forecasting.
1996–1999 worked in **Japan** for Mazda.
1999–2002 Vice-President of **Product** Development for Ford **Europe**
2002–2003 CEO of Ford **Europe**
2003–2004 Freelance consultant
Joined Maserati as CEO in **June** 2004.
Languages: English (native speaker) and Italian (**intermediate**)

❺ 1 8 a.m.–7.30 p.m.
2 check emails, meeting with the head of the racing department, tour the factory, meeting with the Product Marketing team, meeting with the directors, meeting with the Honorary President of the Maserati Members Club, give a speech to suppliers, evaluate a prototype of a new car on the test track, fly to Rome for a ceremony with the Italian President, lunch with the head of Fiat
3 working with the cars
4 how to balance work with relaxation

❻ 1 the whole Maserati operation
2 understand all aspects
3 make sure everyone is working
4 be visible
5 contact with different people
6 in meetings
7 working with the cars
8 balance work, important skill

Focus on functions p.24

❶ (Possible answers)
1 This is Claire Hallan.
2 Could I speak to Ms Lanson, please?
3 I'm sorry, her line is busy.
4 Can I take a message?
5 Could you spell that, please?
6 The reason I'm calling is to …
7 What time would be convenient for you?
8 Would next Tuesday be convenient?
9 I'm afraid I'm busy then.
10 Yes, that would be fine.

❷ To be polite.

❸ 1 To leave their name, number, and message
2 To arrange a meeting

❹ 1 to arrange a meeting
2 you manage
3 could make it
4 you call me

❺ 1 On Monday or Tuesday morning.
2 Because she needs to check the time with Piet and Rosa.

❻ 1 Could you make it
2 I can't make it
3 would be OK
4 Would two fifteen suit you
5 that would be fine

❽
1 speaking
2 phoning
3 available
4 appointment
5 free
6 possible
7 instead
8 convenient
9 fine

❾ 1 busy
2 call me back early
3 connect you
4 disconnected
5 repeat that
6 Do you want to wait?
7 There's some noise on the line, I'll finish this call
8 difficult to hear, speak more loudly
9 Could you wait and be patient
10 postpone, happened unexpectedly

> **Pronunciation p.25**
> 2 1 sick   2 thing   3 think   4 mouse   5 path   6 worse

Unit 3

Language focus p.26

❶ 1 Cantonese 2 French 3 Catalan 4 Basque 5 French 6 Romansch
❸ 1 Three 2 French 3 a as an adult b learning Spanish c Japanese
❹ 1 a lot harder
2 quicker, easier than, older
3 slightly more difficult
4 a little easier
5 most, most, things
6 nicest, most patient
7 much more
8 as fluent as
❺ 1 b   2 g   3 a   4 c   5 h   6 d   7 f   8 e

Practice p.28

❶ 1 which/that D   4 who   ND   7 who   D
2 which   ND   5 where   D   8 whose   ND
3 where   D   6 which/that D   9 which/that D

❷ (Possible answers)
1 The population of China is 1.3 billion, which is the highest in the world.
2 Beijing, which is the capital of China, has a population of 13 million.
3 The political leader of China, whose title is President, lives in Beijing.
4 Badaling is a popular tourist location where you can see part of the Great Wall.
5 China manufactures electrical goods, textiles, and clothing which are sold throughout the world.
6 Most Chinese people are descended from the Han people, who came from North East China.

❹ 1 easiest
2 slightly/a little more
3 a lot/much more difficult
4 most difficult
5 slightly/a little less
6 less difficult
7 as
8 as

Wordpower p.30

❷ interested, bored, thoughtful, aggressive, neutral, suspicious, hostile, open-minded, distracted, rude, attentive, supportive, encouraging, intrusive, decisive

❸ 1 attentive – distracted, bored – interested
2 inattentive, indecisive, unfriendly, uninterested, unsupportive
3 discouraging, biased, polite

❹ 1 friendly   4 encouraging, supportive   7 decisive
2 distracted   5 indecisive   8 rude
3 intrusive   6 rude/unfriendly

❺ 1 responsible   5 confident   8 analytical
2 punctual   6 diplomatic   9 thorough
3 motivated   7 flexible   10 enthusiastic
4 innovative

Skills focus p.32

❷ (Possible answers)
1 They were being used in Egypt at the time.
2 Over 2,000 years ago.
3 French soldiers.
4 The town in Egypt where it was discovered.
5 Jean-Francois Champollion.
6 It was used to check the meaning of early written languages.
7 To preserve basic knowledge of the world's languages for future generations.

❸ 1 one thousand   2 Long Now Foundation, San Francisco   3 664

❹ 1 one thousand   5 book   9 one to three
2 disk   6 grammar   10 microscope
3 container   7 pronunciation 11 world
4 online   8 two hundred 12 rosettaproject.org

Focus on functions p.34

❶ 1 Three
2 Japan, Mexico, and Thailand
3 The cost of making programmes in those countries will be too high for NMP's budget.
4 France, Italy, and Spain

❷/❹

Asking for opinions	Agreeing
How do you feel about …?	I agree completely.
Do you think …?	Yes, that's an important point.
Do we all agree?	Yes, definitely.
Giving opinions	Yes, Piet's right.
I'm sure…	Yes, I'd go along with that.
Personally I think …	Yes, I agree with that.
I really do think …	**Expressing doubts and reservations**
I'm inclined to think …	Maybe, but …
I'm quite sure.	**Disagreeing**
	I'm afraid I can't agree with that idea.

❸ 1 Investors and TV companies.
2 They need someone who knows the country and cuisine well.
3 Maria Ferrando agreeing to be their consultant on Spain.

❺ 1 a I'm sure … , I'm quite sure … , I really do think …
   b I'm inclined to think …
2 Yes, definitely. I agree completely.

❻ (Possible answers) Sorry, but I don't agree.
I'm afraid I can't agree with that idea.

❻

Opening	Checking agreement
Shall we start?	Do we all agree then?
Interrupting	**Moving on**
Before you go on, could I say something?	Let's move on to the next topic.
Asking for clarification	**Summarizing**
Sorry, I don't quite follow you.	So, to sum up, we've agreed that …
Could you explain what you mean by … ?	

Pronunciation p.35
1 1 b
2 1 a   2 b   3 b   4 a   5 a

Unit 4

Language focus p.36

❷ 1 g   2 h   3 a   4 f   5 c   6 b 7 e   8 d

❸ (Possible answers)
1 more shopping at night-time; more spending on communications technology; earning and spending more money; living longer so spending more
2 more night-time opening; eating less traditional food and more western-style food, drinking less sake and whisky, more red wine and beer; more working women; doubled between 1980 and 2000; increased dramatically

❹ (Possible answers) Growth in sales of communications technology, increase in sale and use of mobile phones, increase in telephone bills, increase in divorce rate, more single-person households, fall in birth rate, increase in life expectancy, more elderly people. Past Simple. Retail outlets expanding opening hours, people consuming less traditional food and more western-style meals, business people in their 50s spending more on communications technology, more women working and earning more. Present Continuous.

❺ 1 33%   3 33%   5 over 100%   7 17.7%
2 10%   4 over 60%   6 5.7%   8 26.8%

❼ 1 c   2 a   3 d   4 b

> • We use *of* after a noun and before the amount.
> • We use *in* after a noun and before the topic.
> • We use *by* after a verb.
> • We use *from* and *to* after a verb and before two amounts.

Practice p.38

❶ b People are watching more television and video./More people are watching television and video.
c People are going to the theatre less./Fewer people are going to the theatre.
d People are going to bars and cafés a lot more./A lot more people are going to bars and cafés.
e People are reading books a lot less./A lot fewer people are reading books.

❸

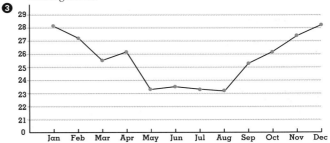

❹/❺ 1 went down   5 rose   9 went up
2 fluctuated   6 levelled off 10 increased
3 increased   7 decreased   11 reached
4 fell   8 reached

❻ They are adverbs because they end in *-ly*. Add *-ly* to the end of the adjective. For adjectives ending in *-y*, change the *-y* to *-i* and add *-ly*.

❼ 1 dramatic, c   2 sharp, e   3 steady, d   4 gradual, a   5 slight, b

Wordpower p.41

❶ 1 c   2 d   3 a   4 b

❷ 1 chicken, bacon, sirloin steak
2 shellfish, sushi, oysters, octopus, salmon
3 mushrooms, salad, olives, tomatoes, grape, potatoes, apples, bananas, grapefruit
4 wine, champagne, sake, coffee, orange juice, beer
5 cheese, yoghurt
6 pastries, cakes, antipasti, spaghetti, mushroom sauce, soup, cereals

❹ 1 c   2 j   3 f   4 e   5 h   6 i   7 b   8 a   9 g   10 d

❺ (Possible answers)

1	2
chilled – melon	roasted – meat
deep-fried – chips (BrE)/fries (AmE)	barbecued – sausages
grilled – fish	grated – cheese
ground – spices	sliced – cucumber
marinated – meat	crushed – garlic
poached – eggs	
sautéed – potatoes	
smoked – fish	
stuffed – peppers	

Skills focus p.42

❷ 1 d   2 g   3 l   4 i   5 j   6 b   7 h   8 k   9 c   10 e   11 a   12 f

❸ 1 T   2 T   3 F   4 F   5 F   6 T   7 F   8 F

❹ (Possible answers)
1 Global production is increasing more slowly.
2 They rose steadily from 1.3 million to 2.1 million.
3 They went up dramatically from 0.2 million to 2.1 million.
4 It dominates world cinema and stops film industries in other countries developing.
5 It is becoming more popular in the West.

❻ 1 c   2 a   3 d   4 b

❼ 1 Amount spent on organic food products (by 2002).
2 Amount spent on 'green' household products (by 2002).
3 Amount spent on cosmetics not tested on animals (by 2002).

4 Amount spent on responsible tourism (by 2002).
5 Amount invested in funds with ethical criteria (in 2003).
6 Rate of growth per annum in investment in funds with ethical criteria.

Focus on functions p.44

❷ 1 The Basque country, Catalonia, and Andalucía.
2 Basque cooking has the reputation of being the best in Spain.
3 Its men-only gastronomic clubs.

❸/❻

Asking for advice and suggestions	Accepting ideas
Do you think we should … ?	Yes, I think we should do
What would you suggest?	that.
What would you advise us to do … ?	Yes, let's do that.
Giving advice and suggestions	Yes, I'll be happy to do that.
It might be a good idea to … T	Yes, that's an interesting idea.
I'd suggest you …	**Rejecting ideas**
I'd recommend you …	I'm afraid I'm not very keen
You should …	on that idea.
If I were you I'd …	
You could … T	
How about …	

❹ I'm sorry but that's out of the question.
That's very interesting, but …
❺ 1 It's very interesting and varied.
2 *Cava* is produced there.
3 *Paella* originated there.
❼ 1 b 2 d 3 a 4 f 5 g 6 c 7 e

> ### Pronunciation p.45
> **❷** 1 b 2 a 3 a 4 b 5 b 6 a

Review Unit A

❶
1 is working	6 has worked	11 has built up
2 comes	7 married	12 doesn't like
3 moved	8 owns	13 researched
4 studied	9 is opening	14 is looking
5 has lived	10 knows	15 wants

❷ (Possible answers)
1 Where is Vanessa working now?
2 When did she move to the United States?
3 Who did she marry?
4 How many restaurants does Claude Blanc own?
5 What does Vanessa not like doing?
6 What did she research last year?

❸
Argentina	Brazil	Peru	Venezuela
Spanish	Portuguese	Spanish	Spanish
Buenos Aires	Brasília	Lima	Caracas

❹ (Possible answers)
2
2 The smoking of cigarettes fell/dropped/declined sharply in the 1990s.
There was a sharp fall/drop/decline in the smoking of cigarettes from 1990 to 2000.
3 The consumption of alcohol fell/dropped/declined steadily in the 1990s.
There was a steady fall/drop/decline in the consumption of alcohol from 1990 to 2000.
4 The consumption of fruit and vegetables rose/increased/grew gradually in the 1990s.
There was a gradual rise/increase/growth in the consumption of fruit and vegetables from 1990 to 2000.

❽ (Possible answers)
1 Hello. (Eric) speaking.
2 Good morning. (NMP). Can I help you?
3 Could I speak to (Rosa Lanson)?
4 Just a minute. I'll put you through.
5 Why don't we meet next Tuesday?/Could you make it next Tuesday?
6 When would be convenient for you?
7 I'm afraid I'm not available then.
8 Thank you. We look forward to seeing you next Tuesday. Goodbye.

Unit 5

Language focus p.48

❸ a Crowne Plaza Coogee Beach: conference facilities, air-conditioning, satellite TV, high-speed Internet access, swimming pool, fitness centre.
b Desert Resort Mandawa: moonlight camel rides, private entrance to each guest room, swimming pool.
c Misión del Sol: year-round sunshine, health treatments.
❹ 1 Another conference is being held at the same time.

2 It's served all day in the café.
3 It's served between 12 and 2.30 in the private dining room.
4 Guests are invited to join the management by the swimming pool.
5 The air-conditioning in the business centre is being repaired.
6 There are some changes to the programme.
7 It can be found in the reception area.
8 They are going to have breakfast after questions.
❺
1 is being held	4 is being repaired, will be completed
2 are served, is located	5 have also been changed
3 are invited	6 is currently being extended, can be found

> 1 Present Simple: a, b   Present Continuous: e, f
> Present Perfect Simple: c, d   Past Simple: i, j   *Will* Future: g, h
> 2 Passive: a, d, e, g, i   Active: b, c, f, h, j
> 3 When the person or thing that did the action is not known or isn't important.
> 5 For questions, invert the verb *be* and the subject; for negatives, use the negative form of the verb *be* in the appropriate tense.

Practice p.50

❶
1 hope	9 hasn't/has not been cleaned
2 are asked	10 were woken up
3 takes	11 was built
4 is being decorated	12 opened
5 are installing	13 'll/will be asked
6 is being served	14 'll/will be given
7 have been fitted	15 won't/will not disturb
8 have cancelled	

❷ 1 Where is the hotel located?
2 What will be opened next year?
3 What are guests requested to wear?
4 How are the bedrooms furnished?
5 What entertainment has been arranged?
6 What is currently being extended?
7 What has recently been opened?
8 How was one delegate treated?
❹
1 was started	5 are also planned
2 is still continuing	/being planned
3 's/is finished	6 will be opened
4 will be provided	7 will host

Wordpower p.53

❷/❸
go for	+ an action	a run, a walk
go to	+ a place	the spa, the driving range
join	+ a club	a reading group
play	+ a game	rugby, tennis, netball
play for	+ a team	a local softball team
take	+ a course	a computer course, pottery classes
take part in	+ a play or competition	an athletics competition
take up	+ a hobby or interest	a new hobby, t'ai chi

Skills focus p.54

❹ 1 gather 3 aromatherapy 5 flexible
2 initiative 4 conventional 6 alert
❼ (Possible answers)

	Abib Cury	Gao Da Cheung
morning	workout at gym before work, start-the-week class on Mondays, lift weights, swimming	sometimes joins father for t'ai chi
breakfast	strong black coffee, nothing to eat	regular at 6.30 a.m.
lunch	sandwich at desk	regular at midday
dinner	eats out with friends at least three times a week – usually eats after midnight	regular at 6 p.m.
weekends	soccer on beach and watersports (but rarely), tennis on Sunday evening, soccer on Friday evening	spends Sunday with family

Focus on functions p.56
Leaving recorded messages
❶ a 3 b 1 c 4 d 2 e 5
❷ 1 first 2 second 3 second 4 second 5 first
❸ 1 c 2 e 3 a 4 b
❹
1 a message for b just wanted to c fix up
2 a 020 848 3497 b get back to c four o'clock
3 a some more b manage c get a moment
4 got your message b Let me know c Speak to you soon

Using mobile phones

❶ (Possible answers)
   1 Advantages: can be used anywhere/at any time, can be taken on trips or abroad. Disadvantages: line not always good, lack of network coverage, possible lack of privacy, possible nuisance factor in public places
   2 sending/receiving text messages, taking/sending/receiving digital photographs, accessing the Internet, diary or calendar, alarm call, phonebook, playing games
❸ 1 Sorry, I can't hear   5 I'm in a meeting. Can I
   2 breaking up   6 lost you
   3 It's a bit difficult   7 Sorry, can you
   4 I'll be quick, the   8 What

Unit 6

Language focus p.58

❸ 1 1998
   2 He studied English Literature at a university in the south of Spain.
   3 The pupils are from different backgrounds and cultures.
   4 Problems of discipline and classroom behaviour.
   5 The variety of London (e.g. food and culture), the village atmosphere.
   6 Yes.
❹ 1 T   2 F   3 F   4 T   5 F   6 T
❺ 1 a came   b was studying   c had   d wanted
   2 a was   b 'd known   c was teaching   d stood up
      e had never happened
   3 a started   b was working   c was picking   d met   e finished
   4 a had already farmed   c came   d 'd learnt

Past Simple, Past Continuous
1 stood up, shouted, walked out, rang
2 was teaching, was sitting
3 teach, sit
4 *was/were* + present participle (*-ing* form)

Past Simple, Past Perfect
1 teaching, farming   2 teach, farm   3 had + past participle

---

Practice p.60

❶ 1 was teaching, decided   5 arrived, were going through
   2 was studying, met   6 was, enjoying, rang
   3 saw, was waiting   7 started, was living
   4 was living, had   8 was reading, saw
❷ (Possible answers)
   She had worked on a farm in Australia by the time she started Glasgow University.
   When she married her boyfriend, she had already taken her Master's degree.
   She had started work for a Canadian engineering company by the time her son was born.
   By the time her son was born, she had been married for three years.
   She had been back at work for a year when she was promoted to a senior management position.
   Her daughter had been born by the time she visited Scotland for a 3-month vacation.
❹ 1 came   9 was shining   17 was writing
   2 was walking   10 got up   18 heard
   3 had visited   11 had had   19 saw
   4 was working   12 had fed   20 had escaped
   5 made   13 had finished   21 was enjoying
   6 had taught   14 came   22 had lost
   7 was showing   15 had prepared
   8 thought   16 was sitting

Wordpower p.62

❶ 1 put a 'destruction date' on every document before filing it
❷

Verb + gerund	Verb + preposition + gerund	Verb + gerund or infinitive
need improving	be used to keeping	stop worrying
recommend following	be interested in	remember being told/
avoid filing	finding out	to turn
finish working	look forward to living	love to help
enjoy throwing		like to be/thinking
suggest doing		
(not) mind answering		

---

❷ 1 creative analogies to suit individuals
   2 see table
   3 *prefer/hate* + gerund or infinitive, *would prefer/would hate* + infinitive
❸ 1 infinitive   3 infinitive   5 gerund
   2 gerund   4 gerund   6 infinitive
❹ 1 seeing   2 to write   3 to have   4 playing

Skills focus p.64

❷ (Possible answers)
   1 A traditional gap year was usually taken by students before going to university, but a gap year for adults is for adults of any age.
   2 Because employees with a 'portfolio career' involving a range of interesting activities are often more employable.
❸ Dean Douglas: b   investment banker   34
   Alicia Rubio: c   medical student   21
   Hortense Robert: a   teacher   early 50s

❹

Dean Douglas	Alicia Rubio	Hortense Robert
break from stressful job	get wider experience, see medicine in other countries	travel and work with conservation
Cuba, Mexico, Australia, New Zealand, SE Asia	Accra (Ghana)	northern Borneo (Malaysia)
complete freedom	so different, having more responsibility, delivering a baby	my first dive
being sick in Cuba	not understanding the local language	got into trouble on a dive, lost consciousness
gardening business	working in maternity department of big hospital	give lectures and talks, recruit people

❺ adventurous – unadventurous   hard-working – lazy
   ambitious – unambitious   optimistic – pessimistic
   cautious – reckless   relaxed – uptight

Focus on functions p.66

❷ London – Bilbao   Sunday 2nd
   Bilbao – Seville   Tuesday 4th
   Seville – Valencia   Friday 7th
   Valencia – Barcelona   Saturday 8th/Sunday 9th
❸ **Requesting**   **Offering**
   Would you mind … ?   Shall I … ?
   Do you think you could … ? **Accepting**
   Do you mind … ?   –
   Can you … ?   **Declining**
   Agreeing   –
   Not at all.
   Yes, that's no problem.
   No, of course not.
   Yes, I'll do that.
❹ (Possible answers)
   I'm sorry but that's not possible.   I think that will be very difficult.
   I'm afraid not.   Sorry, but …
❼ Dep   Arr
   11.15   13.05
   18.15   20.15
   08.00   09.10
   12.25   13.25
   19.10   19.50
❽ **Asking**   **Confirming**
   Do you happen to know if … ?   Yes it is.
   Could you tell me …   OK. I've got that.
   Can you tell me …
   I'd like to know …
   Checking   **Showing understanding**
   Sorry, did you say … ?   Right.
   Correcting
   Sorry, I've made a mistake.

---

❾ 1 What time will the 10.30 flight from Paris arrive?
   2 Are there any cancellations on the 8 a.m. flight to Moscow?
   3 Where can I get some foreign currency?
   4 Where did you buy your tax-free goods?
❿ 1 In indirect questions there is no inversion or auxiliary form, as in direct questions.

2 Indirect questions
3 Indirect questions
⑪ (Possible answers)
1 Could you tell me if there are any seats available on that flight?
2 Can you tell me if the plane from London has arrived yet?
3 I'd like to know if there's a connecting flight to Manchester.
4 Do you know which terminal I should go to?

Unit 7
Language focus p.68
❷ getting to the venue, registration time and date, what to bring

❸/❹
negotiations are faster in US, Americans can be insensitive to cultural differences, individual initiative and achievement very important, making decisions – think quickly and clearly, periods of silence in meetings are not liked, social formalities not that important, but punctuality is.

❺ 1 must   2 mustn't   3 have to
4 need to   5 needn't   6 don't need to

❻ 1 You could ask about a person's job in general terms, sports they play, leisure interests.
2 You mustn't ask personal questions (how old they are, if a woman is married).
3 You can stop the person and ask for clarification.
4 You have to be on time for meetings and appointments, but you can be a few minutes late for parties and social occasions.

❼ 1 could 2 shouldn't 3 may 4 may 5 can 6 might 7 should

❽ 1 must, have to   4 may   7 shouldn't
2 needn't, don't need to   5 may, can
3 mustn't   6 should

1 To make questions, we invert the subject and verb, *Must I ... ?*
2 To make questions, we invert the subject and the verb, as for *must*, e.g. *Should I ... ? Can you ... ?* To make negatives, we add *-n't*, or *not*, e.g. *may not, cannot/can't*
3 We use the auxiliary verb *do*, e.g. *Do you have to ... ? Do you need to ... ?*
4 had to
• *needn't* is used to express no necessity or obligation to do something.
• *mustn't* is used to express a necessity or obligation not to do something.
• *must* usually expresses the personal opinion of the speaker about what is necessary or obligatory.
• *have to* usually expresses a general obligation outside the control of the speaker, or an obligation based on a rule or a law.
• *need to* is used in both contexts to express necessity.

Practice p.70
❶ 1 have to   4 needn't   7 must
2 must   5 mustn't   8 mustn't
3 don't need to   6 don't have to   9 mustn't

Pronunciation p.70
1 1 8 2 5 3 5 4 7 5 6 6 7 7 6 8 7
2 1 don't have to 3 needn't worry 5 mustn't forget 7 has to work
2 really mustn't 4 don't need to 6 you have to leave 8 do you think

❷ 1 a required   b obligatory   c forbidden   d forbidden
e permitted   f allowed   g recommended
2 permission = e, f   advice = g   obligation = a, b
obligation not to do something = c, d
3 a You have to have a full international driving license and auto insurance.
b You have to wear a seat-belt.
c You mustn't drive under the influence of drugs or alcohol.
d You mustn't stop or park at red curbs at any time.
e Commercial vehicles may/can load at yellow curbs.
f All vehicles may/can stop at green curbs for a maximum of ten minutes.
g Tourists driving in the Bay Area should listen to the following tips.

Wordpower p.72
❸ foggy – climate   peaceful – parks
cosmopolitan – city   lively – city
hot – climate   extensive – range of retail outlets
cold – climate   interesting – architecture
dramatic – hills   exciting – ethnic neighborhoods
accessible – city   quick – getting around (public transport)
safe – city   clean – city
stunning – beaches   chilly – climate
famous – tourist   cheap – getting around (public transport)
 attractions   soaring – skyscrapers
fascinating – city

❹ dirty – clean   dull – lively/interesting/exciting/fascinating
noisy – quiet   limited – extensive
dangerous – safe   boring – lively/interesting/exciting/fascinating
warm – cold/chilly   expensive – cheap
❺ 1 a AmE/BrE   c BrE/AmE   e AmE/BrE   g AmE/BrE
b AmE/BrE   d BrE/AmE   f BrE/AmE   h AmE/BrE
2 theaters, neighborhoods

Skills focus p.74
❶ (Possible answers)
1 When a company uses a different company in another country to manage some of their business tasks.
2 A telephone help and information line.
3 It's cheaper.
❷ 1 India, Philippines, Sri Lanka, Mexico, Poland, Russia, Romania.
2 Because of advances in technology, falling costs of international phone calls, and cheaper labour costs.
3 Polite, friendly, helpful, able to give information clearly and respond to customer questions. Also sympathize with callers and understand their problems.
4 Given Western pseudonyms, watch films from UK and US, attend courses in British culture, set clocks to the time of the country that is calling, receive weather reports, make small talk.
❸ 1 elocution   4 sympathize   7 pseudonym
2 accent   5 go to great lengths   8 crash course
3 advances   6 challenges   9 puddings
❹

		Advantages	Disadvantages
1	companies	cheap, better educated operative	lack of control, cultural differences
2	home countries	customer gets cheaper service	takes away jobs
3	countries where call centres are located	brings income, helps economy, develops IT and telecommunications	exploiting workers stress, wealth goes to western companies

Focus on functions p.76
❷ 1 Giving talks and presentations.
2 Statements that indicate what the speaker is going to talk about next.
❹ Objectives 2, 6   Organization 3, 9
Audience 1, 11   Visual information 8, 10
Content 5, 12   Practice 4, 7
❺ 1 Introducing the topic   6 Checking understanding
2 Referring to questions   7 Referring to visual information
3 Introducing each section   8 Referring to common knowledge
4 Summarizing a section   9 Concluding
5 Referring to common   10 Dealing with questions
understanding
❻ 2 voice 3 body language 4 visual information 5 questions

Unit 8
Language focus p.78
❷ 1 b 2 c 3 f 4 e 5 a 6 d
❸ (Possible answers)
1 To help create a world where everyone has access to safe water and effective sanitation.
2 The world's poorest people, local organizations.
3 Individuals, businesses, appeals, and special events.
❹ 1 Arrive 4th March 15.00, Return 14th March 8 p.m.
2 a 7th b 4th c 8th d 5th e 6th
❺ 1 a rainwater b sanitation c factory d slum
❻ 1 does, arrives, we're transferring, going to be, not doing
2 going to take, not going to take, 're providing, you'll find, won't
3 going to take, going to take, I'm coming, we'll leave, I'll check
❼ 1 a Present Simple   4 b Present Continuous
2 c *be going to* + infinitive   5 d *will* + infinitive
3 f *will* + infinitive   6 e *be going to* + infinitive

• We use *be going to* + infinitive for a future intention when the decision has been made in the past.
• We use the Present Continuous for a definite arrangement (one that is written in a diary for example).
• We use *will* + infinitive for a spontaneous decision about a future action.
• The contracted form of *will* is *'ll* (e.g. *I'll, she'll, we'll*).
• The negative (contracted) form of *will* is *won't*.
• To form questions for the Present Continuous and *be going to* forms we invert the subject and the auxiliary of *be*.

Practice p.81
❶ 1 leaves, are you leaving, going to book
2 I'll book
3 I'm not going to have, I'll try
4 does, land, Are you going to meet

❷ 1 I'm travelling
2 are you flying, am/'m attending, gets in
3 going to have, am/'m meeting
4 is going to be, he's staying, won't go

Wordpower p.82

❸ 2 (no preposition)   3 for   4 back   5 off
❹ 1 to   2 from   3 back   4 out, off/back   5 for, by   6 on
7 into   8 in
❺ 1 refund   5 withdraw   9 transactions
2 deposit   6 PIN   10 overdraft
3 direct debit   7 statement   11 branch
4 fraud   8 balance   12 standing order
❻ 1 All the time.   2 It's free.
3 All details are confidential and there are high levels of security.
❼ **access:** bank account, statement   **set up:** bank account, overdraft,
check: bank account, balance,   standing order
statement, standing order   **cancel:** standing order
transfer: money between accounts **download:** statement
pay: bills   **print:** statement
pay off: overdraft, loan   **amend:** standing order
apply for: overdraft, loan   **open:** bank account
order: foreign currency, travellers' cheques

Skills focus p.84

❸ (Possible answers)
Student A
a 40,000 people gathered in Montjuïc stadium in **2002** to celebrate the tenth anniversary of the Games.
b As a result of the Games, Barcelona continued to grow despite a **recession** that lasted until the mid-1990s.
c The number of passengers handled by **Barcelona's airport** has risen from 2.9 million in 1991 to over 21 million.
d Tourism is now worth **12.5%** of Barcelona's GDP.
e The increase in hotel beds as a result of the Games has produced **12,500 new jobs.**
f **In eight years** Barcelona had built infrastructure that would usually take fifty years.
g Barcelona invested **$8bn** in a ring road, a new airport, a telecommunications system, and an improved sewage system.
h The harbour and port area were transformed by a **$2.4bn** waterfront development.
Student B
a The number of visitors to Sydney rose **11%** in 2000.
b **The major beneficiaries,** other than tourism, were the convention and construction industries, and the eco-industry.
c **Homebush Bay** was the disused industrial estate where the Olympic Park was built.
d The government spent **137m Australian dollars** cleaning up chemical waste before they could begin construction.
e **The athletes' village** was the world's largest solar-powered suburb and became ordinary homes after the event.
f The construction programme included environmental initiatives, such as the preservation of **the green and golden bell frog.**
g **Stadium Australia** uses 30% less energy than conventional designs.
h **Recycled water** is used and cuts drinking water consumption by 50%.
❺ 1 Because the basic infrastructure is already there, and there are existing plans to improve things.
2 80,000 seats.
3 1.69 billion pounds.
4 Just under one and a half billion pounds.
5 Business opportunities, job creation, economic revival of poor areas, housing, food and catering, advertising.

❻

Expenditure		Income	
Building of new facilities	£403m	Ticket sales	£864m
Buying of land	£325m	Other direct revenue	£436m
Staging the event	£679m	Contribution from IOC	£100m
Security	£50m	Sponsorship and advertising	£500m
Improving the team	£127m	Resale of land	£430m
Unforeseen risks	£106m	Tourism and tax from jobs	£810m

Focus on functions p.86

❷ San Sebastián Interview the chef of one of Spain's top restaurants.
Seville   Go to the bar where the custom of *tapas* began, visit a convent where traditional Spanish confectionery is made, go to Jerez de la Frontera to find out about sherry production.
Valencia   See *paella valenciana* being prepared.
Barcelona   Go on a tour of all the best *tapas* bars, spend a day in Penedés visiting *cava* producers.
❸ 1 fax, memo, letter, phone, report to be sent by email, answerphone message, text message
2 face-to-face, e.g. for Rosa checking flight times with Claire

❹ 1 a we're leaving b We're going c we're taking d we're planning
2 a we're flying b staying c We're going d we're going to visit
e we'll go f we'll fly g we'll go
3 a we're hoping b we're flying back c I'm going to write
d I'll copy
4 a I'll text b we're going to be

Pronunciation p.87
2 The following words are stressed:
1 planning, work, abroad, year   3 true, change, job, again
2 meet, cinema, film   4 Canada, holiday, summer

Texting
❷ (Possible answers)
a Would you like to come to lunch with Piet and Eric? We're meeting at 1.30 at Bar Lorca.
b OK. I'll see you there.
❸ 1 as soon as possible 4 Great!   7 tonight
2 before   5 Are you coming? 8 I'm happy/Good news
3 See you later   6 tomorrow   9 I'm sad/Bad news
❹ (Possible answers)
1 Coffee? Grand Café 11?   3 r u coming 2 seminar 2nite?
2 Can u bring yr laptop tmrw?   4 Call me asap. Urgent!

Review Unit B

❶ 1 was introduced   7 played for   12 won't be picked
2 was appointed   8 are being   13 I'll support
3 has been done   encouraged   14 have learnt/am/
4 has developed   9 are taken   'm learning
5 organized   10 is provided   15 are not treated/
6 have been arranged 11 are given   being treated
❷ 1 left   3 wrote   5 took over
2 chose   4 began   6 wanted
❸ 1 must, have to   4 should, shouldn't
2 needn't, don't have to   5 could, might
3 mustn't   6 can, may
❹ 1 am/'m flying   4 will/'ll have to
2 leaves   5 am/'m giving, am/'m not doing
3 am/'m going to ask   6 're taking, won't take

Unit 9

Language focus p.90

❷ (Possible answers)
2 Scenario 1: Terrorist attack on a pipeline, loss of power, transport problems, army control.
Scenario 2: Higher number of retired people than working people, tax increase, demonstrations and riots, national strike, collapse of transport and financial systems.
Scenario 3: Nearly all senior positions taken by women, leading female politicians will help to end wars, the world more peaceful and co-operative, families dominated by women, men marginalized but decide to fight back for their rights, gender battle, men's groups.

Time clauses
1 Present Simple
2 future time
3 *Will* Future

1st Conditional
1 future
2 Present Simple
3 *Will* Future
4 yes
6 Negative: *If* + subject + Present Simple, subject + *won't* + infinitive
Question: *If* + subject + Present Simple, *will* + subject + infinitive

2nd Conditional
1 *there would*
2 Past Simple
3 *would* + infinitive
4 b
5 Negative: *If* + subject + Past Simple, subject + *wouldn't* + infinitive
Question: *If* + subject + Past Simple, *would* + subject + infinitive

Practice p.92

❹ 1 Peter – definitely not, Yves – likely
2 Jola – unlikely, Peter – definitely not
3 Yves – definite, Jola – likely
❺ 1 sure that won't happen, suppose it's possible, that may happen
2 think it's very likely
3 doubt if that'll happen
4 definitely won't be
5 That'll definitely happen, sure there'll be
6 expect it'll probably happen, it's unlikely

6

Definite:	That'll definitely happen.	I'm sure there'll be …
Likely:	I think it's very likely.	I expect it'll probably happen.
Possible:	I suppose it's possible.	That may happen.
Unlikely:	I doubt if that'll happen.	It's unlikely.
Definitely not:	I'm sure that won't happen.	There definitely won't be …

Wordpower p.94

2/3
1 work out*   4 plug in*   7 set up*   10 find out*
2 come up   5 print off*   8 write up*   11 break down
3 sort out*   6 look up*   9 turn on*   12 log on
* = can take an object

4 1 get on with   4 the verb is separable
2 take off   5 She was taken on as a trainee.
3 e.g. He took off his coat./The plane took off.

> In the dictionary examples here, the object word (*sb/sth*) is placed before the particle if the parts are separable and after the particle if they are not separable. Also, if the verb is separable, the symbol ↔ is used.

5 1 a   2 e   3 d   4 c   5 f   6 b
7 1 turn to   3 broken in   5 turned up   7 turned off
2 break up   4 turned, down   6 broke off   8 broke up with

> ### Pronunciation p.95
> **2** The adverbs/prepositions are stressed in sentences 1, 3, 5, 6, 8.
> • The adverb/preposition of a phrasal verb which doesn't take an object is stressed.
> • The adverb/preposition of a phrasal verb which takes an object is stressed when it is separated from the verb, and unstressed when it is not separated.

Skills focus p.96

3 (Possible answers)
1 bedroom with double bed, bathroom with toilet and shower, kitchen area with cooker, living/dining area, small balcony
2 a person who is single, doesn't have many belongings, goes out a lot
4 1 Selfridges' shop window, Oxford Street, London.
2 Young professionals and key workers (teachers and nurses).
3 a bed, a shower, high ceilings, a balcony, natural light, well-insulated walls, modern style of furniture, polished wooden floors, space to entertain friends
5 (Possible answers)

1 24-year-old bank clerk living in the 'microflat' as an experiment	He likes it and he's looking forward to living there.
2 Works for the architects who designed the 'microflat'.	It's a solution to the accommodation problems of young professionals.
3 Young woman who will replace Warren Bevis after a week.	No opinion – but probably likes the fact that it will be cheap.
4 14-year-old onlooker.	Loves it. Thinks it's 'cool'.
5 Student	Not convinced – too public.

Focus on functions p.98

2

Dear Rosa	email, letter	N	start
Hi Eric	email, phone	I	start
See you later	phone	I	start
Yours sincerely	letter, email	F	end
OK, I'll see you soon.	phone	I	end
Is that you Claire?	phone	N	start
cc Marketing Manager	letter, email	N	end, start
Get back to me asap.	email	N	end
It was good to talk to you the other day.	letter, email	N	start
I can't talk to you right now.	phone	I	start
Bye.	phone	I	end
Kind regards.	letter, email	F	end
Dear Mr van Els	letter, email	F	start
I look forward to hearing from you.	letter, email	F	end
I'm looking forward to seeing you at the weekend.	letter, email	N	end

3 1 To give details of the itinerary for the Spain trip and ask for any last-minute suggestions.
2 Eric Carlin.
3 The contact details of Maria's friend in Barcelona, and ideas for a present for her.

Unit 10

Language focus p.100

1 (Possible answers)
1 The Soviet Union or USSR ceased to exist, communism collapsed, and Mikhail Gorbachev was replaced by Boris Yeltsin as president of the 'new' Russia.

2 The former states of Estonia, Latvia, Lithuania, and Ukraine have become countries in their own right. Russia itself has embraced a 'western-style' market economy.

2 1 b   2 h   3 d   4 e   5 g   6 f   7 c   8 a
3 1 1991   5 McDonald's, Rolls Royce,
2 Before 1991   Ferrari, IKEA
3 State oil and mining   6 Roman Abramovich
  companies were sold off.   7 (own opinion)
4 It helped to promote a mini-boom.
4 2 2000   3 five   4 more than $100 million   5 oil, metals
5 1 a has been investing b have you been living c 've been living here
  d started
2 a have you established b 've opened c 've also built
3 a has been growing b opened
4 a 've been increasing b 've opened
6 1 bureaucracy, old-fashioned attitudes
2 new Russian entrepreneurs
7 1 have been getting, has reduced
2 've been doing, 've been, 've set up, 've tried
8 1 a, b   2 c, d, e   3 We have opened, it has been   4 Past Simple: a,
  b Present Perfect Simple: d, e Present Perfect Continuous: c

> ### Present Perfect Simple and Present Perfect Continuous
> 1 b, e, f, h
> 2 a, c, d, g
> 3 Present Perfect Simple: b, e, f, h
>   Present Perfect Continuous: a, c, d, g
>
> **Time phrases**
> 1 since   2 for   3 in

Practice p.103

1 1 been working   7 finished
2 have/'ve been working   8 have/'ve written
3 has/'s been investing   9 has/'s been studying
4 have opened, have not/   10 has not/hasn't learnt
  haven't moved   11 crashed
5 been doing   12 has/'s been doing
6 have/'ve been writing

2 1 went   6 have/'ve been   11 have not/haven't
2 have decided   working   regretted
3 travelled   7 arrived   12 have/'ve been working
4 have/'ve seen   8 have made   13 have/'ve had
5 have/'ve   9 has changed   14 moved
  lived   10 came back   15 won

Wordpower p.104

2 (Possible answers)
encourage a feeling of satisfaction for a job well done and recognition by peers, make your expectations clear, agree goals and targets with employees, give a clear reward for goals achieved (e.g. public praise, promotion, pay bonus, regular feedback – formal appraisal, informal comment), avoid criticism, don't let one person get away with poor performance, bonus schemes, pay fair salaries

4

-ment	-tion	-ance	-al
agreement	contribution	appearance	appraisal
commitment	definition	assistance	dismissal
development	expectation	disappearance	
encouragement	explanation	performance	
establishment	promotion	resistance	
improvement	satisfaction		
payment			

> ### Pronunciation p.105
> **2** 1 appearance   ●●●   6 expectation   ●●●●
>   2 definition   ●●●●   7 explanation   ●●●●
>   3 development   ●●●●   8 improvement   ●●●
>   4 dismissal   ●●●   9 promotion   ●●●
>   5 establishment   ●●●●   10 resistance   ●●●
> **4** The syllable before -*tion* is stressed.
> **5** The syllable before -*ance* is usually stressed.
>   The second syllable before -*ment* is usually stressed.

5 1 satisfaction   2 promotion   3 encouragement   4 appraisal
6 adventurous   dangerous   profitable   rewarding   valuable
challenging   healthy   resourceful   successful   wealthy
7 competition   competitive
fulfilment   fulfilling
motivation   motivated/motivating
recognition   recognizable
8 full-time employment, annual salary, careers advice, flexible hours, job satisfaction, keyboard skills, motivated workforce, profit-related pay, formal appraisal, work experience

Skills focus p.106

❶ 1 Clare is the marketing manager for a big international company. Albert is a chef who owns his own restaurant.
   2 Clare likes travelling, meeting people from other cultures, and winning new clients. Albert likes cooking.
❺ (Possible answers)
   1 do something worth spending time, money, or effort on
   2 look carefully at the way you live
   3 know your product very thoroughly
   4 start dealing with your weaknesses straightaway
   5 look at things in a general way
   6 take the chance
   7 adapt your CV to a particular job
   8 most importantly
❽ (Possible answers)
   1 They're becoming more professional and ask wider-ranging questions.
   2 a To see how you react.
     b To see if you can give a reasoned explanation about how you would calculate it.
     c So the interviewer can analyse things after, and to see if the candidate minds being put under pressure.
❾ 1 in-tray exercises, role-play or simulation, presentations
   2 organizational skills
   3 urgent information that needs immediate action, important information that needs action but only when the most urgent items have been sorted out, non-urgent information
   4 a computer-user   b waiter
   5 Do you remember the name of the receptionist who showed you in? What items do you remember from the menu board you saw at the front?
   6 Be prepared: study the job ad, research the company, understand what they are looking for, tailor your approach

Focus on functions p.108

Describing a process
❶ 1 F 2 T 3 F 4 F 5 T
❷ 1 In the bottom row   2 Eight years or longer
❸ 1 is needed   3 are filled   5 is reached   7 are taken on
   2 is taken   4 are topped   6 is added   8 is kept
❺ 1 d 2 b 3 c 4 a 5 f 6 e 7 g

Interviewing techniques
❶

Introducing a topic
I'd like to ask you about …
Could you tell me about … ?
What exactly do you mean by … ?
Could we begin with … ?
Checking understanding
If I understand you correctly …
So, are you saying … ?
So, are you saying … ?
Asking for more information
Could you tell me more about … ?
What do you think was the reason for … ?

Asking for clarification
Could you explain what you mean by … ?
Showing understanding
Yes, I follow you.
Yes, I see what you mean.
Thanking
Thank you very much for finding time for this interview

Unit 11

Language focus p.110
❷ a 3 b 1 c 2
❹ a 2 b 3 c 1
❺ 1 a should have been b should have waited c shouldn't have shown d he'd waited e he might have asked f would have made
   2 a shouldn't have criticized b would have been better c 'd just found out d would have supported
   3 a should have taken b shouldn't have rushed c 'd built up d would have won

---

3rd Conditional
1 past   2 Past Perfect   3 past participle
4 *would have* = definite result, *might have* = possible result

should have (done)/shouldn't have (done)
1 no   2 no
1 yes   2 no
● We use *should have* and the past participle form of the verb when something was the best thing to do, but the subject didn't do it.
● We use *shouldn't have* and the past participle of the verb when the subject did the wrong thing.

Practice p.112
❶ (Possible answers)
   2 He should have taken his shoes off when he went into the temple./He shouldn't have gone into the temple wearing shoes. It is the custom to take off your shoes before entering a temple in India.
   3 She shouldn't have yawned loudly./She should have put her hand over her mouth. It is considered rude to open your mouth wide

---

without covering it with your hand.
   4 He should have made the dinner appointment much later./He shouldn't have made the appointment so early. Spanish people don't eat dinner early in the evening.
   5 He shouldn't have kept sniffing during the meeting./He should have stopped sniffing. Sniffing continually, instead of blowing your nose, is considered rude and annoying in some Western countries.
   6 She shouldn't have sat down next to the Buddhist monk./She should have found another seat. Buddhist monks are forbidden to touch or be touched by females.
   7 He shouldn't have worn any clothes./He should have gone into the sauna naked. It is considered unhygienic in Finland to wear anything in a sauna.
   8 He shouldn't have left his chopsticks sticking up out of the bowl of rice./He should have placed the chopsticks at the side of his bowl. Chopsticks are only left sticking up out of bowls of rice as a symbol of death at funerals.
❸ (Possible answers) Comptek didn't have a proper firewall to protect their own servers.
   They should have protected their own servers, and installed some of the basic anti-virus software they stocked themselves.
   They had a relaxed attitude to staff sending personal emails, etc.
   They shouldn't have had such a relaxed attitude to staff sending personal emails, etc.
❹ (Possible answers) If they had had a proper firewall, they would have protected their own servers.
   If they had installed some of the basic anti-virus software, they might have protected their system.
   If they had had a less relaxed attitude to staff sending personal emails, etc., they would have avoided operational problems, and saved time and orders.
   If the employee had been more careful about opening the attachment, the whole system might have been saved.
   If Comptek's clients had behaved like Comptek, they would have suffered the damaging effects of the 'worm' virus too.

Wordpower p.114
Culture file
❷ 1 cultural   2 cultured   3 culture   4 multicultural
   5 culture shock
Confusing words
❶ 1 agenda   3 appointment   5 forecast
   2 adjourned   4 intervene   6 revise
❸ 1 retired/resigned   5 accused/blamed
   2 hardly/hard   6 loosing/losing
   3 sensible/sensitive   7 raise/rise
   4 controlled/checked   8 opportunity/chance or possibility

Skills focus p.116
❸ 1 START
   2 Yes
   3 Because they're ashamed.
   4 Fine Arts
   5 To teach
   6 She was shocked, but then she didn't notice the deformities, and saw the patients as people.
❺ 1 F 2 T 3 F 4 F 5 F 6 T 7 T 8 T

Focus on functions p.117
❶ 1 Three. Name of company, address, and contact details
   2 Yours faithfully
   3 Yours sincerely
   4 When you don't want to indicate marital status.
   5 a enclosures b number c public limited company d signed on behalf of   e Road   f Street
   6 I look forward to -ing …
❷

Making reference
Thank you for your letter of …
Further to our telephone enquiry …
Apologizing
I apologize for not replying sooner.
Requesting
Would you kindly …
Would you please …
Agreeing to requests
I would be delighted to …
I will be very pleased to …

Explaining reasons
… owing to …
Giving bad news
I am afraid …
Unfortunately, …
Enclosing documents
I enclose …
Please find enclosed …
Closing remarks
Please let me know if you require …
Please give our kind regards to …
Referring to future contact
I look forward to meeting you …

Unit 12
Language focus p.120
2 a apathy, fraud, local election, turnout
b bacteria, dumping of waste, environmental disaster, pollution
c clinical depression, downsizing, lay-offs, sick leave

3 a the ILO
b a computer science expert
c a spokesperson for the Employers' Association
d a scientist
e a computer science expert

4 1 The tense changes.
2 tell is followed by an object. Other reporting verbs are: *add*, *explain*, *announce*, *warn*, *confirm*.
3 Direct statements:
50 years ago these problems didn't exist but today there is much less security in work. Companies are making more demands on their staff.
Many companies have made improvements in recent years. Employees can expect to see more help and support schemes in future.
The exceptionally hot weather in August has caused the bacteria to spread. A similar problem occurred at the same time last year.
We will introduce a special aid programme to help the 4,000 fishermen affected.
E-voting gives an opportunity for fraud. I can't believe that anyone is even considering using the Internet for national elections.
It will be at least ten years before systems are safe enough. We have decided to wait for further reports before introducing e-voting.

a Past Continuous
b Past Perfect
c Past Perfect
d *would*
e *could*
1 They change into the 3rd person.
2 They become *the year before, the day before, that day, the next day, the following year.*

Practice p.122
1 1 ... that they had looked at the problems of stress and mental illness at work in five countries.
2 ... that they were planning to employ a professional counsellor to help their staff.
3 ... that he didn't know if he would be able to survive until the following year.
4 ... that it couldn't be oil pollution because they had very strict controls.
5 ... that their party had lost the previous election because the turnout had been low.

2 2 Is the problem just as bad in other countries?
3 When can we expect more financial aid?
4 What are you doing to prevent another environmental disaster?
5 Do you think e-voting will be introduced in your lifetime?
6 Have there ever been any cases of fraud in electronic voting?

3 1 The verb form in reported questions is 'one step back' from the verb form in the direct question.
2 Reported questions do not have the same word as direct questions and the auxiliary is no longer necessary.
3 *If* is used in the reported question when there is no *Wh-* question in the direct question.

5 1 The professor asked the reporter to speak up a bit.
2 The Government warned representatives of the oil industry not to dump waste in the sea.
3 The speaker asked the reporter if he could finish his point.
4 The presenter told the companies not to make too many demands of their staff.
5 She asked the speaker to email her a copy of the report.
6 The official told them to re-count all the votes.

Wordpower p.124
1 1 budget 3 Minister 5 recession 7 taxation
2 stock market 4 parliament 6 inflation 8 interest rates

2 1 new constitution 5 foreign embassies
2 fresh elections 6 international aid
3 economic sanctions 7 public spending
4 diplomatic relations

3 1 f 2 i 3 e 4 h 5 d 6 j 7 g 8 c 9 a 10 b

5 a MPs, 129 g Government members
b proportional representation h MPs for other parties
c Press i Opposition
d VIPs j electorate/voters
e Presiding Officer/Speaker k public
f Prime Minister and the Cabinet

7 boom – recession government – opposition
privatization – nationalization left-wing – right-wing
majority – minority democracy – dictatorship

8 politics politician political
economics economist economic
diplomacy diplomat diplomatic
democracy democrat democratic

Skills focus p.126
2 1 c 2 h 3 g 4 f 5 a 6 b 7 e 8 d

3 1 Children and computer and video games
2 Celebrities and drink-driving
3 DVD and video piracy
4 Drug abuse in sport

4 1 T 2 F 3 F 4 T 5 F 6 F 7 T 8 T

6 (Possible answers)
1 Japan and Britain
2 Japan: computer and video games make children violent. Britain: children who become addicted could be more intelligent than average.
3 More research is needed.

Focus on functions p.128
Social responses
1 1 NMP have got the money to complete the *Food and drink* project.
2 Yesterday, at the end of a meeting.

2 1 e 2 c 3 d 4 a 5 b

Pronunciation p.128
1 b1 c1 d2

3 1 b 2 a 3 b 4 a 5 a 6 b 7 a 8 b

Common expressions
1 1 c 2 e 3 d 4 a 5 b

2 1 If you ask me
2 That reminds me
3 As you say
4 Talking of
5 As I was saying

Saying goodbye
1 1 We really must be going.
2 (Own answers)

3 a 3 b 1 c 4 d 2

Review Unit C
2 1

1 has been 6 have achieved 11 have been trying
2 have been working 7 have not raised 12 deal with
3 have built 8 have not finished 13 won't be able
4 have opened 9 have been listening 14 begin
5 have improved 10 have produced 15 will start

2 since, in, for, before, after

3 (Possible answers)
1 The removal company shouldn't have used inexperienced staff. If they hadn't used inexperienced staff, it wouldn't have taken so long.
2 They should have had more computer packaging materials. If they'd had more computer packaging materials, they wouldn't have damaged some of the equipment.
3 They shouldn't have taken lots of breaks. If they hadn't taken lots of breaks, they wouldn't have lost time.
4 They shouldn't have used an old van. If they hadn't used an old van, it wouldn't have broken down.
5 They should have read the address properly. If they had read the address properly, they wouldn't have gone to the wrong address.
6 They shouldn't have dropped a very valuable picture. If they had been more careful, they wouldn't have dropped a very valuable picture.

4 (Possible answers)
1 A to Z said that they had taken on a new member of staff who they were training up.
2 A to Z said that Hi-Tec hadn't told them that they had so many computers. They asked Hi-Tec if they wanted to wait while they got head office to send more packaging.
3 A to Z said that it was a very hot day, so they would need to take one or two drinks breaks.
4 Hi-Tec asked why they had turned up in such an old van.
5 A to Z said they couldn't read the writing on the address document.
6 Hi-Tec warned/told them to be careful with the picture because it was very valuable.